Two-week loan
Benthyciad pythefnos

ESSENTIALS
OF
BUSINESS ETHICS

ESSENTIALS
OF
BUSINESS ETHICS

George Chryssides
John Kaler

McGraw-Hill Book Company
London · New York · St Louis · San Francisco · Auckland
Bogotá · Caracas · Lisbon · Madrid · Mexico
Milan · Montreal · New Delhi · Panama · Paris · San Juan
São Paulo · Singapore · Sydney · Tokyo · Toronto

Published by
McGraw-Hill Book Company Europe
Shoppenhangers Road, Maidenhead, Berkshire, SL6 2QL, England
Telephone 01628 23432
Facsimile 01628 770224

British Library Cataloguing in Publication Data
Chryssides, George
   Essentials of business ethics
   1. Business ethics 2. Professional ethics
   I. Title II. Kaler, John H.
   174.4

   ISBN 0–07–707856–X

Library of Congress Cataloging-in-Publication Data
Chryssides, George D.
   Essentials of business ethics / George Chryssides and John Kaler.
     p. cm.
   ISBN 0–07–707856–X (pbk. : alk paper)
   1. Business ethics. I. Kaler, John H. II. Title
   HF5387.C488 1996
   174'.4—dc20
                                 95–50989
                                     CIP

McGraw-Hill

A Division of The McGraw-Hill Companies

345 CL 99

Typeset by Nick Allen Editorial Services, Oxford
Printed and bound in Great Britain at the University Press, Cambridge
Printed on permanent paper in compliance with ISO Standard 9706

Contents

Preface

Business ethics is a growth area, both in business circles and in colleges and universities, and with that growth has come a plethora of books on the subject. Why, then, yet another book on business ethics?

The earlier books on business ethics emanate from the United States, where laws are different and where the examples used are not so familiar. Other books consist solely of case studies, and some are anthologies of readings. Some of the current literature is by specialists in business, who are well able to identify issues of ethical concern, though may not be quite so familiar with the more abstract theoretical underpinning which is needed if such issues are to be resolved. At the other end of the spectrum there are philosophers who have studied ethics, but feel more at home with traditional abstract discussions of justice, democracy, human welfare and so on, and for whom the business dimension is something of an 'add on'. Then there are the campaigning books produced by ethical consumer organizations, or by interest groups such as environmentalists, feminists, vegetarians and champions of the rights of developing countries.

All these books have their place. However, the present authors have the advantage of having completed degrees in philosophy, taught ethics to a variety of students and worked in a business school for many years. This background enables us to offer the best of both worlds: a knowledge of what actually happens in reality in the worlds of business and finance, and an understanding of the more abstract theoretical issues which must first be resolved if meaningful debate on ethical issues is to proceed.

Our aim in writing is to enable readers to have a grasp of the basic issues in business ethics. The book is essentially 'non-campaigning': our aim is not to persuade students and companies to 'behave better', nor is it our intention to promote specific causes, however much we may sympathize with many of them. No author can achieve strictly neutrality, however, and in any case a book in which the author's colours never showed would probably turn out to be dull and clinical. Where readers disagree, at least we hope that we have provided some of the 'tools of the trade'—underlying theories, methods of argument, factual issues—by which to do so.

We have endeavoured to span a wide range of issues in business ethics. However, the book is not intended as a survey which merely summarizes what others have already written. While we have drawn on certain key writers and commented on some the most important areas of debate, our fundamental aim has been to link the various ethical theories which may be used to justify different stances in business ethics, and to show how different parties to various debates can justify their respective stances. We leave readers to decide where the truth lies.

Acknowledgements

As we have mentioned in the text, business ethics spans a wide variety of areas in business studies, at times stretching the authors' versatility to its limits! We have therefore greatly appreciated the help, suggestions and—usually constructive—criticism offered by colleagues and business people.

We should like to thank the following for sending material and answering correspondence: the Ethical Consumer Research Association, the New Economics Foundation, Greenpeace, Friends of the Earth, the Green Party and Baby Milk Action. Both McDonald's and the McLibel Support Campaign were more than willing to send detailed literature, putting the case for the respective sides of the 'fast food' controversy. Buckingham Palace kindly supplied us with a complimentary copy of *An Interfaith Declaration* drawn up by HRH Prince Philip and HRH Crown Prince El Hassan Bin Talal of Jordan, and which is discussed in Chapter 10.

Particular thanks are due to Liz Fleming of Fleming Associates (Financial Advisers), who patiently explained numerous technical points about ethical investment, and to John Chryssides, who gave pertinent advice on areas where our discussion impinged on economics.

Finally, we should like to thank Brendan Lambon, Senior Editor at McGraw-Hill, for his encouragement and patience while the book was being assembled.

1 *What Is Business Ethics?*

You, the reader, have already made decisions that involve business ethics. Perhaps you have tried to sell your old car or a second-hand fridge: do you point out to the vendor that the clutch is wearing or that the wiring is faulty, or do you wait until you are asked? If you are undercharged in a shop, do you own up, or do you accept this as a stroke of good fortune? Have you refused to buy a country's produce because you objected to its politics?

Whichever alternative you choose involves an ethical decision. Although we may label one alternative 'ethical' and another 'unethical', the truth of the matter is that ethical decisions are involved either way. We may decide that the onus is on the purchaser to discover any defects in what we are selling—in which case we support the age-old principle of *caveat emptor* ('May the buyer beware')—or else we abide by the principle of 'full disclosure'. (There is a third possibility: we may accept the principle of full disclosure, but through malice or weak will decide not to act by it.) We may decide that shopkeepers should look after their own interests, or we may take the view that we have a duty to abide by the agreed price. In the case of the proposed boycott, we can refuse to buy (say) Chinese goods on account of China's poor human rights record (a moral decision), or we can decide to keep politics out of shopping, thus adopting an ethical position that what we buy is largely a matter of ethical indifference. We may not have explicitly formulated the ethical principles which underlie our behaviour, but we cannot avoid presupposing at least some of them.

SOME MORAL DILEMMAS

Let us commence our discussion by considering some concrete situations. You are working as a researcher for a perfume company. You are developing a new perfume, but you need to be sure that it will not cause adverse reactions to people's skins. One way of testing this is to experiment on animals. Should you do this? Or should you risk harming human life? Or should you be developing a new product at all in this area, knowing that there are already ample numbers of brands already on the market?

Let us imagine another scenario. You are working for a company which persistently ignores safety precautions. You have drawn the management's attention to the problem repeatedly, but nothing has been done. Since the problem cannot be settled within the firm, perhaps it could be settled by going outside. Should you 'blow the whistle' by going to the press, or should you do nothing, taking the view that it is the management's responsibility to attend to matters of health and safety?

You are a (male) personnel officer for a large company. A close friend of yours meets you at a dinner party and informs you that his son badly needs a job, and reminds you that you and he have been friends ever since you were at the same public school. Do you do your friend a favour and give his son preferential treatment, or should you consider his application on the same terms as everyone else's and risk losing a long-established friendship?

Finally, you have inherited a fairly generous legacy. Your financial adviser suggests that you purchase Avarice Unit Trusts, since Avarice offers a secure investment with good returns. However, you have heard vague rumours that Avarice's portfolio includes companies who support oppressive political regimes, armaments firms and other business conglomerates with poor records in environmental matters. To invest or not to invest? Do you turn a blind eye, assuring yourself that unit trusts are all 'much of a muchness' ethically and that you need the money anyway, or do you try to find an ethically sound investment with a poorer finanical return? Or should you keep any of the legacy at all, when two-thirds of the world is in poverty?

These are all examples of ethical dilemmas relating to business. There are not always clear answers to these questions. Whether or not a perfume will irritate the human skin admits of a definite conclusion: a researcher can conduct controlled experiments to determine whether or not it does, usually (although not always) with definite results. The question of how fires start and spread can be determined by empirical investigation: a fire officer can examine the scene of a fire, and often reach a definite conclusion. A personnel officer can administer tests on candidates to determine what personality types they are, or which ones have leadership potential.

Whether all issues in business can be settled as straightforwardly and scientifically as this, of course, may be doubted. Some aspects of personality testing, for example, are as controversial scientifically as they are ethically. However, in these examples the investigators will look for evidence, and endeavour to reach a conclusion that is compatible with it.

In ethical matters it is not so clear how ethical conclusions relate to the 'evidence'. Sometimes campaigners in business ethics will attempt to use empirical evidence to persuade their opponents; for example, the British Union for the

Abolition of Vivisection (BUAV) has contended that animal experiments are seriously flawed and have never been instrumental in achieving an understanding of human reactions and behaviour. However, suppose a supporter of animal testing could (somehow) persuade the BUAV supporter that some animal experiments did indeed lead to valid conclusions about humans, the supporter could still maintain that, even if this were the case, animal testing is still morally wrong, since the wellbeing of animals should not be sacrificed to gain improvements in human comfort. The disagreement now is not about 'evidence', but about principles: it is about how the respective parties evaluate animal welfare, and the degree to which it makes sense to talk about 'animal rights'.

THE NATURE OF BUSINESS ETHICS

Business ethics, then, has two aspects. One involves the specific *situations* in which ethical controversy arise; the other concerns the *principles* of behaviour by which it is appropriate to abide. For this reason, we have chosen to apportion sections of this book respectively to *topics* (such as advertising, accounting, employee relations and environmental issues) and to *ethical theory*. If the former seems more concrete and more exciting than the latter, it should be remembered that we cannot judge what we ought to do unless we first know the moral principles which we should bring to bear.

Business ethics has been a growth area in the business world in recent times, particularly in the United States, where recent interest began. However, in other periods of history (such as eighteenth- and nineteenth-century Britain), business transactions have largely been conducted on the principle of *caveat emptor*. The onus was on the purchasers of goods and services to assure themselves that the products they intended purchasing were of the quality for which they would hope, and the vendor's duty was simply to fulfil a very few legal obligations.

Much has changed in recent times. The law is the most obvious source for ensuring that consumers receive a fair deal from retailers and manufacturers. The various health and safety laws have ensured substantial improvements in working conditions for employees. Contract law entails that employers no longer have complete freedom to make contracts, which in the past have often depended on the relative bargaining power of employer and employee, usually favouring the former. The Sale of Goods Act (1894) has been largely successful in ensuring that goods are of 'merchantable quality' and fit for the purpose for which they are intended. The Trades Descriptions Act (1968) has caused manufacturers and advertisers to ensure that no publicity or packing contains false or misleading information about goods and services. The Sex Discrimination Act (1975) and the Race Relations Act (1975) make it illegal in Britain to discriminate against anyone on the grounds of sex or colour. All these are, in one way or another, impositions of moral considerations on business.

This does not mean that business can leave the law to resolve its moral dilemmas. Much remains untouched by legislation. Until recently it was still permissible to refuse to employ someone because he or she is disabled, or because the applicant belongs to a religious community or political group which an employer dislikes. Factories continue to discharge chemical waste, causing environmental damage; firms who are otherwise more socially responsible often exaggerate the 'environmental friendliness' of their goods or production methods.

There may be a case for further legislation on such matters. However, there are grey areas where there is no obvious public agreement, and in which the law might seem an undue intrusion on individual conscience. For example, is animal testing defensible, particularly for seemingly unnecessary products such as new cosmetics? Should the sale of furs continue to be legal, when it appears to cause animal suffering and put the survival of species at risk? Is it defensible to invest in armaments manufacturers, or in companies who have interests in oppressive regimes? Should an employer dismiss one of the workforce for 'contraction of work' (a legally valid reason), knowing that the employee will have difficulty in securing alternative employment, and when it is still financially possible to maintain him or her?

Moreover, implementing the law will itself raise ethical problems. Do we exploit 'legal loopholes' to gain unfair advantage over customers, suppliers and employees? Do we demand our legal 'pound of flesh' in every transaction? Do we, for example, withhold payment to a supplier to the very last legal minute, regardless of the effect on that supplier's perhaps perilous finances? Do we set lawyers the task of seeking how to pay the minimum compensation to an injured employee, regardless of his or her hardship and our own ability to pay?

QUESTIONS WITHOUT ANSWERS?

The previous two paragraphs deliberately contain many questions, but no answers. Many students of business studies find this particularly hard to cope with. In most other subjects one follows the curriculum, getting an increasing amount of knowledge and—at least some of the time—clear answers to the questions one asks. How do you work a spreadsheet? How do you do double-entry bookkeeping? What is a SWOT analysis? What procedures must be followed if you are exporting goods? And so on. In business ethics it can sometimes seem as if the opposite occurs. Where there appeared to be answers before, one finds questions: indeed it may seem as if one is all the time learning less rather than more! However, unless we perceive that these questions are controversial and admit of a variety of possible answers, we have not properly understood what ethics is about. One cannot arrive at one's own answers without first being puzzled about the questions. Indeed, being puzzled is often the sign that we are making good progress! In this book we have aimed to create awareness of the issues: students must supply their own conclusions. The authors are not 'ethical consultants'!

WHY BE ETHICAL?

It may well be asked why business men and women should currently appear to take such an interest in business ethics. Cynics might suggest that their aim is to lull the public into a false sense of security in the belief that business people are responsible and fulfil their obligations to competitors, the public and the environment. Their concern for business ethics, they might argue, is a means of merely making business activity credible. Appearing to be ethical, it may be suggested, is simply good business: consumers are, arguably, more likely to buy from a company which can be seen to be acting ethically. Graduates are more likely to be attracted to companies which treat their employees fairly and give customers a fair deal. Others may contend that concern for business ethics is a means of forestalling legislation: business people do not want external restrictions or new possibilities for prosecution and litigation. Those who are less disenchanted with human nature will welcome this interest in responsible business behaviour as evidence that there is a genuine concern within the business world that consumers get a fair deal, that environmental pollution is brought under control, that men and women work in acceptable working conditions, and so on.

There is, how
ethically. To ask for
something more fun
seek the explanation
explained by 'Becaus
business degree?' ca
this line of 'Why?'
something like the
prosperity–happines
do sometimes) there
rejoinder is, 'Don't y
be happy?' there is
happiness is desirab
rather curious perso
nothing more.

Asking 'Wh
suggesting that bei
theory—see below).
important to achiev
ulterior motives for
as good reasons, and
ethical behaviour. If
asked why they are
questions is that suc

ethics is to treat it as a normative enquiry in the
meantime, it is important to state that in th
actions right is something we shall pursu
The question of the common
ethically justified, and, if so, what is
common factor which is shared
'full disclosure' when you a
returns or expenses claim
hold, and to try to mak
'weak' sense is to e
companies' track
we were under
that the clu
the mora
we ha
rea

because we fear detection, or because we have more interesting things to do, then we cannot pride ourselves in our standards of ethics at all: in fact, we would be admitting that we would if we could, or if we wanted.

Similarly, those business men and women who contend that they should be ethical because it is good for business, or because it forestalls legislation, may be revealing their own personal motives for acting ethically; but they are also revealing that they believe that profits and freedom from state intervention are more important than morals. They are also suggesting that they would not act in such a way if these incentives were not there.

A 'NORMATIVE' ENQUIRY

We draw the conclusion, then, that the importance of acting ethically has no other reason than that it is wrong not to do so. To say this may sound as if the authors are reformers or prophets who are urging those in the business world to clean up their act, and to act morally. It is important to emphasize that this is not the case, and to explain why.

It is often said that ethics is a 'normative' enquiry. By this it is meant that ethics is about 'norms' or standards. However, we can distinguish between two senses of the word 'normative'—a 'strong' sense and a weak sense. The 'strong' sense of 'normative' is a *prescriptive* one: if we are prescribing norms, then we are urging moral or ethical improvements and seeking to persuade readers to repent and to mend their ways, or perhaps to change their views. The 'weak' sense of 'normative' is the *descriptive* one: students of business ethics already have opinions about what is right and wrong, and—on this view—it is not the task of the ethical theorist to change this. Every reader is familiar with ethical dilemmas: even if some ders have not yet worked in business and do not recognize the earlier secenarios ve cited, there must have been situations where we were in two minds about lity of an action. (Should we have sold that old car without pointing out tch was slipping? Should we have pointed out to the shopkeeper that charged? Should we have invested the money without looking at the record on ethics?) To study ethics as a normative enquiry in the able you, the reader, to observe the ethical views which you e sense of them. *Why* do you think it is wrong to fiddle tax (if that it what you believe)? *Why* is there no need for re selling goods (if you think that)? Is there some y all the examples of actions which we believe are that factor (or set of factors)? actor, and what fundamentally makes right e much further in the next chapter. In the book the approach we have taken to 'weak' sense. That means that it is not our task to change the views of the readers, or to 'preach' to them about how unethical many business dealings are. That is the task of the social reformer, the pressure group (such as the Ethical Consumer Research Association or Friends of the Earth and the like), the campaigner or even the vicar. Our aim is to analyse, to clarify and to systematize.

FIVE VIEWS OF BUSINESS ETHICS

As part of this clarification process, we believe that it is possible to identify five different stances in all which might be taken by a business manager or by a student of business ethics.

BUSINESS IS BUSINESS

The first view of business ethics is often expressed in the maxim, 'Business is business'. Those who hold this view contend that a firm's aims are purely commercial (the maximization of profits, sales or market share), rather than ethical. The responsibility rests with the customer to inspect the offered goods and services, or for employees to assure themselves that they will be happy with the firm in which they decide to work.

When presented with this view, most students of business ethics are inclined to reject it immediately. After all, it seems to suggest that 'anything goes' and that the world of business is amoral. However, the maxim that 'business is business' need not entail moral licentiousness. The expression encapsulates the sentiment that businesses should relentlessly strive to achieve the goals which they have set themselves (usually the maximization of profits, or else ensuring the highest possible market share or sales turnover). This may entail some ruthless practices: sacking superfluous staff, engaging in industrial espionage, selling shoddy goods. However, one's business objectives are not normally achieved by acts of sexual harassment or nepotistic promotion policies. At least some business ethics remain, although perhaps not enough.

ACT CONSISTENTLY WITH THE LAW

Others would contend that legislation provides a baseline, below which business should not stoop. 'Business is business' suggests that anything goes: selling faulty or dangerous goods, sexual harassment in the workplace, deceptive advertising, industrial espionage. At least a firm should fulfil its *legal* obligations.

We may think that we are entitled to expect more of a business than mere conformity to law. When CFCs (used in aerosols and refrigerants) were found to be harmful, should not firms have stopped selling them at once, rather than wait for legislation? However, although one might hope that managers can be touched by moral as well as legal considerations, one big disincentive to go beyond the minimum legal requirements is that one's competitors may be morally nearer the bone and hence gaining a competitive advantage. It is for this reason that firms sometimes welcome the introduction of legislation: if something is made law, there is more reason to suppose that one's competitors will be accepting the same responsibilities and paying for doing so.

GOOD ETHICS MEANS GOOD BUSINESS

The third view is that 'good ethics' is simply good business. This view can be called the *coincidence theory*: virtue and prosperity fortuitously coincide. It may be argued that if we sell defective goods, customers will not return; if we discriminate against applicants on the basis of sex or race, or make appointments via the old boys' network, we deprive ourselves of the best person for the job; an ethically 'clean' company runs less risk of litigation. And so on.

There is much hard evidence to support the view that good ethics means good business. It has been shown that graduates are much more likely to be attracted to firms with a good track record on ethical matters: the ethical firm is therefore more likely to have first pick of the best recruits. The Battersea Park roller coaster disaster in 1974, in which 16 people were killed as a result of abysmally poor maintenance of the cars, led to the almost immediate closure of the fairground and prison sentences for the owners. (Poor ethics could not have been worse for business.) Litigation and adverse publicity have followed all the major disasters in the business world: the Zeebrugge ferry disaster, the Piper Alpha explosion and the Exxon oil spillage.

Yet while it is true that good business ethics is often good business, we must ask whether this is invariably true in all cases. It certainly seems a remarkable coincidence. What about a situation where the manager has to choose between maintaining existing staffing levels or introducing new and more profitable technology? Or what about the sales person who persuades a customer to use credit facilities when there is reason to suppose that this may cause financial hardship?

The coincidence theory is at best unproven. However, even supposing it were true, it would still not offer a good explanation as to why those who engage in business should act ethically. To have one's eye on profits rather than integrity, sincerity or human wellbeing is simply to act selfishly—hardly an ethical motive. Business people who assume that there is a coincidence between 'good business' and 'good ethics' may get the right answer, where such coincidence occurs, but they do so for the wrong reason.

CONVENTIONAL MORALITY

A fourth possible position is that business people should act in accordance with conventional standards of morality. We call this view *conventionalism*. Conventionalism means acting in accordance with the prevailing standards accepted by the public, or those standards which are typically accepted within comparable fields of business practice; for example, although some people may deplore the advertising industry's stereotyping of women, which sometimes implies that their pinnacle of achievement is to bake sponge cakes or to wash clothes whiter than white, the conventionalist can argue that in contemporary society women still perform the roles of cooking and washing, and that activities such as advertising should reflect ordinary social conventions rather than try to change or reform them.

But can we really trust conventional wisdom in these matters? If we did, businesses would still be employing child labour and adulterating food products as they did in Victorian times. What happened in the Victorian era was certainly not acceptable just because it was 'conventional'.

UNIVERSAL MORALITY

Finally, there is the view that people in the business world should maintain the same standards of ethical behaviour in business as they would in their private lives. This view can be labelled the *'no difference' theory*. Just as our next door neighbours would not expect us to dispose of our rubbish on to their gardens, so—it might be argued—we have a right to expect business companies not to pollute the environment with discharged waste, smoke or noise.

This fifth position may have an appeal. But it may be argued that, although it expresses a fine ideal, the nature of business activity necessitates what may appear to be a double standard. It would be all very well for a firm to be moral if it could be assured that its competitors would follow suit, but unfortunately (unless one accepts the 'coincidence theory') those firms which do not do so can gain a competitive advantage. It might be argued that business is like war (indeed we have come across managers who have used this analogy): although most private individuals would not inflict harm on their fellow human beings or damage to their property, in a state of war killing and destruction are often deemed to be morally acceptable.

We may agree that circumstances alter cases. However, even in a war one's basic ethical principles remain (or at least should remain) the same. If someone believes, for example, that one should promote the greatest happiness of the greatest number, then that person will fight in a war if he or she believes that the greatest happiness of the greatest number will in the end be achieved by such means.

Similarly, in business, circumstances alter cases too. A researcher who tests products on animals may indeed be very kind to animals in his or her personal life, but in a laboratory—it may be argued—the suffering inflicted on animals is more than offset by the human benefits that are gained. The fact that a war zone or a business environment can be different from that of one's personal life may cause us to change our overt behaviour to some degree, but there is no reason to suppose that such transitions demand that we assume different moral principles. Indeed the philosopher Immanuel Kant (1724–1804) pointed out that one important characteristic of the moral law was its universality: if something is right, it is right for all people, at all times and in all places. Where different situations occur, a moral principle will dictate different outcomes, but the basic principle remains the same universally.

WHO MAKES ETHICAL JUDGEMENTS ABOUT BUSINESS?

It is important to realize that no one can escape decisions about business values. To take the view that 'business is business' is itself a decision which reflects one's values (in this case—probably—the value that one should maximize one's own personal gain). To test products on animals entails the value judgement that such research is ethically justifiable (unless, of course, managers have taken the view that it is unacceptable, but that they will continue to do it none the less). To do nothing about business ethics can be construed as an ethical decision: when we receive the legacy we may choose not to inform ourselves about the track record of various shares. (After all, deciding to stay indoors and do nothing is as much a decision as deciding to go out.) Even the decision to study business is itself an ethical decision: the student of business has already made the decision that the world of business is worth entering into, and is not too tarnished to put itself beyond the pale. If such a value judgement seems too obvious to be worth mentioning, it is worth reflecting that by no means everyone believes in the worthwhileness of business activity: it is possible to choose to live as, say, a Buddhist monk—who is not permitted to handle money—rather than a business student. And indeed some people do decide to separate themselves from the world in this way, holding that there are goals which are infinitely superior to the acquisition of material wealth.

WHY STUDY BUSINESS ETHICS?

We have now dealt with the question, 'Why be ethical?' But there is another very obvious preliminary question which may present itself to the student of business: why study business ethics?

There are a number of objections which one sometimes hears from those who are sceptical about the kind of study on which we are embarking. One common objection is, 'I already know right from wrong. I already make ethical decisions, and they seem perfectly all right to me, even though I have never read a book on the subject or gone to a lecture or seminar.'

It is important to deal with this objection. Of course it is possible to make ethical judgements before formally studying ethics: we do this almost every day of our lives. However, there are many things that we are able to do in life without formal study, but which nevertheless benefit from serious enquiry. Many students of business have been able to sell things before embarking on a course (e.g. in temporary employment or part-time entrepreneurial activities), but this does not mean they cannot benefit from a course in marketing. Learning about SWOT and PEST analysis,[1] for example, enables the student to unravel the basic features of a business and to itemize the various factors which impinge on its operation. In a somewhat similar way business ethics examines what fundamental presuppositions lie behind our moral reasoning, and attempts to elucidate the meaning of ethical concepts. By asking about meanings and presuppositions, we are better equipped to be more consistent in making ethical judgements, and in a better position to determine what the crucial issues are when we are faced with an ethical dilemma or controversy.

There is another possible objection to studying business ethics. Someone might suggest that our ethics simply depends on where we happened to be born: a 'white Caucasian' born in twentieth-century Britain might accept secular materialist values, keep his or her money in a bank which gives interest, and believe in equal opportunities for both sexes and for minority groups. An Islamic reader, by contrast, might insist on the supremacy of the Qur'an in determining moral matters, pointing out that bank interest is unearned income and hence unacceptable, and that the 'equal' status of women need not mean identity of treatment or equality of opportunity.

What, then, does one gain from the systematic study of business ethics? Should we not say that, at best, our ethical values are culturally determined, even matters of social convention, and leave it at that? It is understandable that someone who is new to the formal study of ethics might initially feel sceptical about its value, and, in the face of the many different views on business ethics which have no obvious means of resolution, believe that all we can do is to 'agree to differ'. If we cannot find a definitive answer to what ethically we should do in a given situation, then perhaps we should just 'plump' for a solution, taking the view that it is likely to be as good as anyone else's answer to the question.

The notion that people's ethical values are only different from each other, never better or worse, is a position which we will consider at length in the next chapter. It is sufficient to say here that this view is at best controversial, and that the study of ethics can do the student the service of helping to determine whether one is justified in feeling morally superior to someone else, and whether there is such a thing as 'moral progress' which is worth striving for. If there is no such thing as moral progress, then it would not matter how we behaved in business, or indeed anywhere else. Hence it is worth finding out whether moral standards merely change, or whether they can improve or deteriorate.

It will not do to say that we must 'agree to differ', simply because there are no agreed answers in ethics, or because our ethical codes stem from our culture and environment. First, although we may often fail to settle ethical disagreements, we still engage in ethical discussion: people can give reasons for their beliefs and defend them against criticism from those who disagree. It would be irrational to embark on the process of discussion at all if nothing could be gained. Second, it must be acknowledged that, in ethical debates, people *are* sometimes persuaded. It is salutary to examine one's own ethical thinking and ask oneself whether all of one's beliefs are really identical to those of one's parents; as a child grows up, he or she becomes able to think independently. It is not uncommon for a student who has left home for the first time to be persuaded by some new 'cause', such as vegetarianism or environmental protection, or to become converted either to or from a religion. For some new 'converts' it may seem as if one has 'seen the light' and that these new discoveries are self-evident, if others would only take the trouble to 'see'. But for the most part, proponents of causes can give reasons, appeal to fundamental principles, answer objections and even on occasion persuade those who have thitherto thought differently. Although a study of business ethics does not set out to persuade the reader of any one set of truths, enquiry into whether there can be a quest for truth in such matters is useful in determining the value of ethical debate, both in business and in everyday life.

One can give a number of additional reasons for studying business ethics. Although we will not be offering recommended solutions to ethical dilemmas, one function of business ethics is to clarify one's concepts. What do we *mean* when we talk about 'equality', 'justice', 'democracy', 'going green', indeed 'right' and 'wrong' themselves? Asking questions of the form, 'What is the meaning of X?' has a long history in Western philosophy. The philosopher Socrates was particularly famous for analysing concepts which everyone took for granted, such as 'beauty', 'truth', 'knowledge' and 'justice'. The Socratic dialogues were written by Plato, his student,[2] and in each of them Socrates examines a definition which one of the parties to the debate puts forward. Although in most cases there appears to be an 'obvious' definition, Socrates always succeeds in showing that things are not so simple. For example, when Glaucon in *The Republic* suggests that *justice* means 'to everyone his or her due', Socrates asks whether this definition means that one should return a weapon one has borrowed from a murderer:[3] Glaucon must either accept an unpalatable conclusion (a *reductio ad absurdum*, to use philosophers' jargon) or else withdraw or amend his definition.

This example illustrates the point of debate about ethical matters. Before embarking on formal study our views may be woolly, inconsistent, even confused. Formal study can help to iron out confusions, to see more clearly the principles which lie behind our ethical thinking, and to clarify the fundamental concepts which we employ in ethical reasoning. In this respect the formal study of ethics is no different from the formal study of any other subject: we may feel, for example, that we know something about car mechanics, because we can carry out basic repairs on our car; but a formal study of automobile engineering will enable us to understand the principles behind what we are doing, and no doubt thereby improve our skill and understanding of car maintenance.

We noted the fact that there are wide disagreements on ethical matters, and it is useful to return to this point once again. We considered the view that wide disagreements provided a possible reason for dismissing the study of ethics as inconclusive and unproductive. However, the vast disparity between people's ethical judgements is precisely a reason *for* studying ethics rather than avoiding it. In the business world we are likely to encounter people with widely different moral stances; a government official in a Third World country may ask for a bribe for granting a necessary permission; a trade union official might, for example, press for paternity as well as maternity leave for workers. Business decisions cannot be postponed indefinitely—and in reaching a decision the process is much enhanced if one can understand the basis of one's opposite number's ethical outlook. (Understanding, of course, is not the same as agreeing.) One important function of business ethics is to show how it is possible to hold different views on such matters, and where one can locate the points of disagreement.

Finally, recent times have heralded the rise of the 'ethical consumer'. Many consumers are becoming increasingly aware of issues such as irresponsible marketing, support of oppressive regimes, respect for the environment, political donations, trade union relations, animal rights and so on. Consumer's ethical views are therefore now very much a part of companies' market research: what sort of standards do consumers expect and why? No doubt there are companies who think of appeasing the ethical consumer as a public relations exercise; indeed Friends of the Earth give an annual 'green con' award to companies they regard as the most notorious villains. Nevertheless, whether targeting the ethical consumer as a sector of one's market is mere window dressing or genuine ethical concern, to do either demands an awareness of the issues and of what will satisfy an ethically responsible sector of the public.

In many cases, public and political concern about ethical issues has been sufficiently great as to cause certain professions (such as advertisers, accountants, mail order firms, to mention only a few) to formulate codes of practice which define the limits beyond which a professional in the business world may not go. Where professional codes of practice are in operation, business ethics is no longer an 'optional extra': the professional must at least know what these codes require and how to conform to them.

Last, but not least, one fundamental reason for embarking on any activity is that it is enjoyable. Few people would demand reasons for sporting activities, going to the cinema or having a dinner party. True, there may be extrinsic reasons, such as sport keeping one healthy, cinema-going assisting relaxation, or dinner parties encouraging us to clean and tidy our houses! But we all know that these are not the prime reasons for such pursuits; if we enjoy them, that is sufficient reason in itself. Unfortunately, many books on ethics are 'heavy' and cause the reader to struggle; although there may be some enjoyment in feeling that one has 'conquered' the weightier tomes, we feel that this is a deterrent to many students. By writing a short introduction such as this, which does not presuppose any previous knowledge, we hope that we have popularized the subject sufficiently for readers to agree that ethics need not be an 'ivory tower' activity, but something which is intelligible to and indeed enjoyable by the first-time enquirer.

WHO ARE THE EXPERTS?

Since business ethics is a field of study which has very recently come to the fore in universities and colleges, it may be asked who 'owns' the subject. What specialisms are needed to teach it, and what are the traditional subject disciplines on which it draws?

At a recent business ethics conference attended by one of the authors, participants included specialists in philosophy, theology, sociology, personnel management, marketing, international business, accountancy, law and environmental science, as well as a few individuals who had set themselves up as professional consultants on business ethics.

There is no straightforward answer to the question of who 'owns' business ethics. From the time of Socrates (469–399 BCE), Western philosophers have debated what concepts like 'justice' meant and how it relates to conducting one's affairs in society, including business dealings. People like Moses, Solon, Hammurabi and Muhammad were in effect lawyers, and their law codes encompassed business transactions among most other aspects of living.

Religion has had an important role to play too. Moses and Muhammad, of course, gain recognition as religious leaders, and people like Jesus and the Buddha made pronouncements about how one's business affairs should be conducted. The history of Roman Catholic thought has made a particular contribution to business ethics, with concepts such as the 'just wage' and the 'just price'. It is clearly important for anyone who professes allegiance to a religion to know its implications for living one's life, including how one conducts one's business affairs. It is important, too, to remember that on a world-wide level, this includes the vast majority of professional business men and women.

Environmentalists have also made an important contribution to the field of business ethics. Organizations such as Friends of the Earth and Greenpeace have helped to lead the environmentalist attack on business policies which are potentially damaging to the environment, and we have devoted an entire chapter in this book to the environmental impact of business policies. Environmental issues are not new to business ethics, however: even as far back as the second millennium BCE, Hammurabi found it necessary to legislate on the preservation of palm trees. God's instruction to Adam in the Book of Genesis is to till the ground and to look after the land. One of the central concepts in the teachings of Jesus is 'stewardship'.

The notion of stewardship has an important link with economics, which is essentially the science of how to optimize the use of finite resources. The economist's role in business ethics is an important one, for maximization of profits, sales turnover and market share, if ruthlessly aimed for without regard to human and environmental consequences, are dubious ethical policies. For many decades now, the study of 'social economics' has been an important field of study for economists, in which it is recognized that social costs must be identified and taken into account in business and governmental decisions, as well as financial outcomes. More recently, the study of 'environmental economics' has emerged as an important area of study, in which consideration is given to the sustainability of economic growth, and the implications of economic matters on the planet as a whole. (We shall return to such matters in Chapter 8.)

Other academic inputs to business ethics have come from specific fields in which policies and decisions have important ethical dimensions. In personnel management one is faced with questions related to selection of applicants, equal opportunities, psychological testing, wages and wage differentials, management styles and management of change. Marketing has clear ethical implications regarding the quality of goods and pricing, as well has how goods and services are described and promoted. The ethics of advertising is a field which has itself generated several entire books, and is given a chapter in its own right here. Accountancy has a stake too: the way we invest has clear implications regarding what business ventures are enabled to take off and which are not, and how one presents one's accounts also raises important ethical questions.

It is important to acknowledge the stake of computing specialists, in the present era of high technology. The world of computing has its own special dilemmas. How ethical is it, for example, for a firm to store data about its customers? When, if at all, is it permissible to pass on such data to other firms? Computerization has enabled firms to 'black' individuals and bar them from credit. For what reasons might a firm legitimately take such action? And, with the advent of the new information superhighway, computerization has enabled the facility of a wide range of material, including pornography. Is this acceptable, or should there be controls on this? How feasible is it to have 'filters' which screen out such data from clients?

The role of the lawyer has importance too, since there are specific ethical issues which relate to the practice of law. For example, are there specific types of work which should not be undertaken, such as advising the pornography industry on whether entertainments and magazines are in breach of the law? (There are law firms who do exactly this.) Should one defend clients who are clearly guilty and likely to endanger society if their punishment is too lenient? Are there ethical and unethical ways of persuading judges and juries? There are wider questions too concerning ethics and law. Should good ethics invariably be enshrined in law, or should there remain an area where certain categories of action are matters for individual moral decisions? What might be the implications, consequentially and ethically, of changes in a country's statute books?

All of the above suggests that no single area of study can claim exclusive rights of expertise on business ethics. Each traditional discipline adduces its own specialist skills and knowledge and has a vested interest in its own particular areas of business ethics.

THE ROLE OF THE ETHICAL CONSULTANT

Despite the fact that business ethics is such a diverse subject area, with no obvious single qualification of expertise, there are a few people in the business world who have set themselves up, in effect, as 'experts' in business ethics. The role of the ethical consultant is therefore worthy of some comment.

It is easy enough to see what entitles someone to set up as a computing consultant, an environmental consultant or an engineering consultant: computing, environmental science and engineering are areas where there are clearly 'experts' whose body of knowledge is superior to that of the average lay-person, or indeed business person. Is there such a thing (or person) as an 'ethical expert'?

At the time of writing there are no constraints on individuals setting themselves up as ethical consultants. This is not, however, to imply that those who do so are necessarily charlatans. On the contrary, most have had some fairly substantial experience of the business world; indeed an ethical consultancy is itself a business organization. While one cannot necessarily expect ethical consultants to be ethically superior to their clients (as one might expect the computer consultant to be better at computing than the client), the ethical consultant can nevertheless bring to bear some of the following skills to the problems with which he or she has to deal.

First, the ethical consultant can reasonably be expected to have identified the various principles of ethics which might serve as a foundation for ethical behaviour. By presenting these to clients, clients may be helped to clarify the thought processes which underlie their ethical decision making. Second, the ethical consultant can be expected to have some superior knowledge of the consequences of the various courses of action which lie open to the consultee. For example, what kinds of management behaviour do employees typically resent? About what matters do they welcome consultation, and what are the consequences of open and more democratic management styles?

The third component of ethical consultancy is an acquaintance with the various areas of ethical concern. An organization such as the Ethical Consumer Research Association (ECRA), for example, identifies a number of categories under which products and firms are scrutinized, such as trade union relations, wages and conditions, land rights, environment, armaments, animal testing, political dona-tions, whether they have been the subject of boycott calls and so on. An ethical consultant should be in a position to know what to check, although at the end of the day it is the consultee who must decide whether an identified factor is a genuine cause for concern.

Allied to this, an ethical consultant should be in a position to undertake an 'ethical audit' of a firm—something which is increasingly in demand by firms who have a concern for sound ethics. An ethical audit, like an 'environmental audit'(see Chapter 8), entails a complete overhaul of the production processes of all goods and services, as well as of the internal organization of the firm. A complete audit will entail examining what suppliers a firm uses, as well as the destinations of goods and services. (Workers might manufacture steel pipes, but not realize that they were being used as armaments components—as happened in the Iraqi 'supergun' affair in 1991.) An ethical consultant, therefore, can be expected to know the track record of the various firms with which his or her consultees has to deal.

Most importantly, an ethical consultant should be able to advise a firm that is striving to be ethical on how to implement such policies. What mechanisms are needed to ensure that ethical policies are actually put into practice and do not merely remain as good intentions or empty words? An ethical consultant can advise on how a firm's ethical policies can be monitored, whether changes are needed to a firm's management structure in order to do this, and how ethical policies might be encompassed within any existing quality assurance system. Good business ethics needs to be planned for.

WHAT IS BUSINESS?

Before we embark on specific issues in business ethics, one further, apparently simple piece of ground-clearing is necessary. What exactly is meant by 'business'? The narrowest possible definition would confine the term to the standard capitalist or entrepreneurial firm, with ownership vested in private hands, a clear-cut division between employer and employee, and the latter very much out to make a profit out of sales to customers. In contrast, the widest definition would include any organization engaged in supplying goods and services. Consequently this would count as businesses not only the standard capitalist or entrepreneurial firm—be it a multinational corporation or a sole trader—but also the likes of government departments, churches or even charities.

Such breadth is clearly not irrelevant to business ethics. There will be issues to do with service to the public, employment, personal conduct and so on that will apply to any kind of organization that is, in some way or another, meeting the needs of society. But it is also very clearly stretching the word 'business' to the limit in allowing a government department, a church or a charity to be so described.

On the other hand, confining the word to only the standard capitalist or entrepreneurial firm seems unduly restrictive. It would exclude state-owned firms, employee-owned businesses and worker co-operatives, as well as mutual corporations such as building societies and consumer co-operatives that are run for the benefit of customers. The point here is that while these firms have a different form of ownership from the standard capitalist or entrepreneurial firm, they are just as much 'in business' as those standard firms—indeed, are normally in competition with them. More importantly, if we refused to count as businesses anything but the standard capitalist or entrepreneurial firm, we would exclude the possibility of different forms of business from the standard—possibilities which are very much the concern of business ethics.

For the purposes of this book, we intend to make the defining feature of a business the fact of its being engaged in *trading*. That is to say, there is not only the supplying of goods and services but also an exclusive—or at least predominant—dependence on sales to customers for income. This would exclude such obvious non-businesses as government departments and charities that depend on taxes or donations for income. But it would include such decidedly business-like entities as building societies, worker co-operatives, or (presently) state-owned firms such as the Renault motor company.

There can, of course, be a trading dimension to organizations that are not predominantly businesses. The charity Oxfam, for example, derives part of its income from running retail shops. English cathedrals typically run gift shops on their premises. State-funded bodies are increasingly required to operate within a marketplace: schools and universities, for example, have their funding linked to their ability to attract students; hospitals have to tender for patient referrals. There is throughout the public and voluntary sectors an increasing reliance on business-like approaches to marketing and costing. In so far as trading exists, at least some of the ethical dilemmas discussed in this book will arise for these organizations.

Altogether, then, there are good grounds for being less rather than more restrictive about what we are willing to call a 'business'. Even so, a line still has to be drawn between businesses and non-businesses if the study of business ethics is to have any coherence. Where we have drawn that line provides, we think, the best balance of coherence and flexibility. Arguably, where business ethics has resonance for non-businesses, this can be understood through recognition of their trading dimension or, more generally, by acknowledging that business ethics is part of a wider study that might be called 'organizational ethics' or, even more broadly, 'work ethics'. This wider study would involve the ethical dimension to all institutions' arrangements for supplying goods and services (outside the purely domestic) as well as business ethics proper. To the extent that the two overlap, therefore, this particular investigation into business ethics proper is also a contribution to that wider study.

IS BUSINESS ETHICS EASY?

All of the above might suggest that business ethics is a formidable subject. The issues raised in this chapter have taken us a long way from supposing that business

Case study

ISS—good ethics or bad business?

ISS is a success story. This Danish-based multinational is the world's largest supplier of cleaning and ancillary services (linen, catering, security and so on). In 1993 its turnover was nearly £1.4 billion and it had over 125 000 employees world-wide. In five years from 1988 its sales had increased by more than 100 per cent.

What is perhaps most remarkable about ISS is that in an industry notorious for low pay and a high staff turnover, it tries to offer its employees the best pay and conditions possible. It not only accepts but positively favours employees joining trade unions. It supports the idea of a statutory minimum wage—particularly in Britain where, unusually, there is no statutory minimum. It accepted the consequences of the European Union's acquired rights directive (guaranteeing existing pay and conditions when a business is taken over or work transferred to new undertakings). Its annual staff turnover is 20 per cent compared to an industry average of around 100 per cent. Its shareholders, dominated by institutions including the ISS pension fund, have been content with relatively low profit rates—compensated by increases in volume because of the growth in turnover. In an industry where price competition based on low wages is the norm, ISS has a policy of competing on the basis of quality. To quote the *Financial Times*,[4] 'ISS operates on a business culture that works on the theory that the well-rewarded and well-motivated perform their jobs better than those who are not.'

One of the jewels in ISS's crown was winning the cleaning contract for Heathrow Airport Terminal One in 1993. The company running the airport, BAA, awarded the contract to ISS after experiencing poor-quality service provided by other cleaning companies. With ISS providing the service the result was a dramatic increase in customer satisfaction with the standard of cleanliness in the terminal. Staff were even trained to give passengers directions. In a television interview[5] the BAA manager responsible for overseeing cleaning services stated catgorically that the company was finished with awarding contracts on the basis of price: quality would be the determining factor. Very soon afterwards ISS lost the cleaning contract for Terminal One. It was awarded to a company which would be paying new staff around 30 per cent less than ISS.

Is ISS's policy good ethics or bad business? The moral of the story, according to the chief executive of ISS, is that Britain needs a minimum wage. Does the ISS case show that good ethics is not always good business, and hence that the coincidence theory is flawed?

ethics is a subject with which we already have a good acquaintance and in which we are all perfectly capable of reaching our own conclusions. Perhaps the reader may now feel that the contrary is the case, and is in danger of despairing about ever being able to surmount all the issues and areas of expertise which are subsumed under the heading 'business ethics'!

A few words of encouragement may therefore be appropriate. Every subject contains much more material than any single individual can potentially assimilate. The non-specialist in computing, for example, will often comment on how formidable—indeed incomprehensible—much of it seems! However, this does not matter, so long as one knows all that one needs to know; there is no need to go further, unless one simply wants to dazzle one's colleagues by becoming a computer whizz-kid! So long as there are experts to turn to when our limited expertise fails, all is well.

The same can be said for business ethics. No one can be expected to know everything about the subject, but those who enter the business world can at least be expected to recognize the ethical implications of what they are doing, to see what the problems are, and to be able—with help, as appropriate—to reach an appropriate conclusion. It would be a realistic expectation that, say, a marketing student should be reasonably well acquainted with ethical problems surrounding the areas of marketing, sales promotion and advertising, and be in a position to adjudicate between the various competing views on the subject. Such a student may quite legitimately decide that his or her knowledge of the ethics of accountancy or personnel management can be left at a more rudimentary level. Unless it is one's goal to set up practice as an ethical consultant, to write books on the subject, or to apply for a professorial chair in business ethics (of which there are a few), detailed knowledge of all the several areas of the subject is strictly optional.

The present book offers a fairly broad introduction to a wide range of issues, encompassing those which we consider to be currently the most important fields within the subject. Our aim is to provide readers with a feel for the variety of topics which have implications for business ethics, together with the variety of views which are possible. The most important thing in business ethics, however, is not encyclopaedic knowledge or highly opinionated views, but an ability to recognize when a business matter is in part an ethical one. The student who can do this has a head start over those who do not: to recognize an ethical problem is to realize that there is a specifically ethical dimension to be addressed, and that there are likely to be differing views on the topic, for which in all probability a cogent case can be made. The recognition of such a problem alerts the manager, employee or student to the issues that are involved, the ethical theory which needs to be brought to bear, as well as any facts which need to be ascertained in order to resolve the moral dilemma. In short, the successful student of business ethics sees the problem and knows the means by which to arrive at an answer. This books aims therefore to alert the reader to where some of the most common problems in business ethics lie, and to provide readers with at least some of the expertise which they need to resolve business ethics problems for themselves. Readers will not necessarily find all the answers, but if in the course of reading this book they discover the means to find them out, then the authors will have been more than successful.

DISCUSSION TOPICS

1. The authors stated at the beginning that no one was a stranger to business ethics. Consider some of the scenarios described in the early parts of this chapter: selling a car or fridge that needs repair; being undercharged in a shop; buying Chinese goods; animal testing on perfumes; 'whistle blowing' if the work place is unsafe; getting a job through the old boys' network; whether to use 'ethical' or conventional investment funds.

   What would you do, and—most important—why? If you want to say, 'It depends,' on *what* does it depend? The circumstances? Further information? A moral or religious standpoint?

2. Why do you think that business ethics seems to raise more questions than it answers? What is it about ethical questions which makes them so puzzling?

3. Consider the five views of business ethics set out in this chapter (pages 7–9). Consider their merits and weaknesses.

4. What do you think of the idea of having business ethics consultancies? Are there people who are better qualified in business ethics than others, or is each person's opinion equally valid on such matters?

NOTES

1. SWOT stands for 'strengths, weakness, opportunities and threats', while PEST means 'political, economic, social and technological'.

2. It is doubtful whether Plato records actual dialogues in which Socrates engaged, but this question is irrelevant to our present argument.

3. Plato, *The Republic*, Book I, trans. H. D. P. Lee, Penguin, Harmondsworth, 1966.

4. *Financial Times*, 22 February 1995.

5. BBC2, 23 September 1995.

2 *Ethical Theory*

Ethical theory is perhaps less popular among students of business ethics than case studies. Cases are real, and can be readily envisaged. More often than not we can imagine ourselves in similar situations and agonize about what we might do if we found ourselves in such ethical dilemmas. By contrast, ethical theory often seems arid and abstract. It appears to be about principles rather than people, and, since ethical theories have traditionally been formulated by philosophers, it often seems as if proponents of such theories try to make over-subtle distinctions and to pursue a debate like a dog with a bone, long after it has ceased to interest the average citizen.

The criticism that ethical theories, as traditionally propounded by philosophers, are arid and lacking in relevance to everyday affairs may have some point to it. But this is to present a case for doing ethical theorizing well rather than badly, not for refusing to do it at all. Every subject needs a theoretical underpinning: no student of the sciences can remain content simply to make observations and connect up equipment in a laboratory; he or she must make inferences, look for patterns, and—above all—try to explain *why* things appear to happen as they do.

When it comes to ethics, *explaining why* we should act as we believe we must is fundamentally important. If our actions lack an underlying rationale, then we are likely to act inconsistently, and we are likely to have no basis on which to make future moral decisions on situations which we have not yet encountered. Just as a scientific theory tells us what will happen in the future in given circumstances, so a moral theory can enable us to decide what we *ought* to do in new situations.

RIGHTS AND DUTIES

One piece of ground-clearing is important at the start. In the previous chapter, we claimed that business ethics was not synonymous with acting within the law. It is important to emphasize that the ethical theories with which we shall deal serve to explain why certain types of action are ethical or unethical, as the case may be, not why they are legal or illegal. We will recognize a tripartite distinction, which will reappear in subsequent discussion, between (i) ethical rights and duties; (ii) legal rights and duties; and (iii) 'role-specific' (sometimes called 'institutional') rights and duties.

The distinction between rights and duties is reasonably straightforward. For the most part, rights and duties are, as it were, opposite sides of the same coin. If an employer has a duty to ensure reasonable standards of health and safety for workers, workers have a right to expect it. If it is believed that workers have a right to a minimum wage, then employers have a duty to pay it. General rights and duties are moral entitlements in which everyone shares: a duty not to cheat, for example. At their most fundamental (an area we will return to) they concern what are described as 'human rights': a right to life, for example.

Legal rights and duties are more circumscribed. They only apply within particular jurisdictions, and in the United Kingdom are defined through statutes passed by parliament, through 'common law', and through legal judgments given in courts which establish precedents ('case law'). Although, as discussed in Chapter 1, there is an overlap between law and ethics (it is both illegal and unethical to sell unmerchantable products, for example), some actions are unethical but not illegal, and (less commonly) vice versa. Breaking a promise made to a friend is (usually) not illegal, but is unethical—unless some very good reasons can be found to the contrary. In some cases, it has been argued that violating the law can sometimes be ethically acceptable, e.g. animal rights protesters attempting to prevent lorries transporting live animals for slaughter. (Whether or not one supports them, the example suffices to show that, even if something is illegal, it is still an open question whether or not it is ethical.)

Role-specific rights and duties are different again. These are rights and duties with which we are endowed by virtue of the specific roles we assume. The student has the 'role-specific' right to use the campus sports facilities; the business executive may have the 'role-specific right' to the much coveted key of the executive cloakroom. Examples of role-specific duties would be the students' obligation to hand in work on time, or the sales managers' task to promote the company's goods and services.

It is essential to point out the overlap between these three sets of rights and duties. Thus, a role-specific duty may also be a legal duty: for example, the sales manager who failed to promote the company's goods and services would also probably be in breach of contract. In contrast, a student who fails to hand in work on time will be failing in a role-specific duty, but is not acting illegally. While in so far as any role-specific right or duty is moral as opposed to legal, it derives its moral force from being a restricted instance of a *general* right or duty. Our manager and student, for example, could be demonstrating a role-specific failure of a general moral duty of fidelity.

A SPECIMEN CASE STUDY: BRIBERY

In what follows in this chapter, we shall consider what underlies our moral obligations. As a matter of fact, we probably all already possess at least rudimentary moral theories. That is to say, not only do most of us have convictions about *how* we ought to behave, but, if asked, we could give *reasons* for these convictions. Let us take a very familiar scenario in business ethics, and consider a number of equally familiar responses. We shall then attempt to draw out from these commonly heard comments the moral theories which lie behind them.

> *A well-known educational charity wishes to set up an office in an Indian city. Having employed an architect to draw up plans, its officers seek planning permission. The planning department indicates that, in order to obtain approval, it will be necessary to offer a bribe to the relevant officials.*

To bribe or not to bribe? Faced with this moral dilemma, consider these possible responses:

- *Response 1* It is up to the individual. If you can live with the decision, then go ahead. If it worries you, then do not pay and risk the consequences.
- *Response 2* Everyone does it—at least in India. This charity's problem was that, as a Western organization, it was simply unused to demands of this kind. You cannot get anywhere in countries like India without offering bribes.
- *Response 3* Bribery is simply wrong. The end does not justify the means: even if bribing would enable the charity to undertake important and commendable work, this does not make bribery right.
- *Response 4* In a developing country, where there is malnutrition, disease and a low literacy rate, humanitarian work should always take precedence over 'principles'. Although it might be better if one did not have to bribe one's way into setting up a branch in the city, it is the better of two evils.
- *Response 5* The planning officials have no *right* to the charity's money. Money belongs to those who have earned it, and the planning officials have done nothing which entitles them to it.

RESPONSE 1: SUBJECTIVISM ('It is up to the individual')

The first response seems to suggest that there is no objective right answer to the moral dilemma: it is up to the individual to choose among options, none of which are intrinsically right or wrong.

The theory that moral judgements are 'up to the individual' has taken various forms in the history of ethical theory. One type of theory that gained some support in early twentieth-century Britain was based on the concept of 'self-realization'. Exponents of such a theory included F. H. Bradley (1846–1924), who claimed that there is some kind of 'ideal self' to which each individual should endeavour to aspire. This may vary from one self to another: the important thing, however, is to find what that 'ideal self' is and to strive to attain it.

The existentialist movement, which until recently proved very popular in Europe outside Britain, tended to recommend that in matters of ethics the important thing was not *what* you decide but *that* you decide. We all like to seek advice and ascertain what the majority opinion is about important issues (ethical and non-ethical), but unless we have the moral courage to decide things for ourselves we are in danger of simply drifting along with the crowd and losing our own individual identity. Crowd following has its dangers, as was well evidenced in the persecution of the Jews by the Nazis, and it is important that the individual does not simply drift into an 'inauthentic' way of life by being swallowed up in some mass decision by a 'crowd' of people. Existentialism is therefore the complete antithesis of the position to be considered later in this chapter, that what is morally right is to be identified with what is approved of by society.

Another theory which bears some similarities to the previous two has been influential in shaping British moral philosophy. This is the theory known as emotivism and propounded by the celebrated philosopher A. J. Ayer (1910–1989). Ethics (and also religion), Ayer held, were rather different from the sciences. If a scientist makes a claim, such as that there is a planet beyond Pluto in our solar system, then such a claim can be verified.

Can we do the same thing with regard to ethical statements? The reader might be tempted to say yes: 'Thou shalt not steal', might be verified by noting the amount of human suffering that is caused by acts of theft. However, what about the ethical statement that 'It is wrong to cause human suffering?' It does not seem that we can 'verify' a statement like this any further, but yet it seems a perfectly meaningful statement, and not merely a tautology, 'Causing human suffering causes human suffering.'

If the expression is not verifiable, then how does it have meaning? Ayer's answer was that ethical utterances have a different kind of meaning from the factual meaning of scientific assertions; ethical statements have 'emotive meaning', and simply serve to evince our emotions. Just as a football supporter who chants 'Up the Rovers!' or the campaigner who bears a banner saying 'Down with censorship!' does not literally tell us anything about the Rovers or about censorship, so someone who says 'Stealing is wrong!' is saying something (very roughly) like 'Down with stealing!'—an utterance which expresses our emotions about the subject, but which yields no factual information at all. Ayer's theory has sometimes been labelled the 'boo–hurrah' theory, since it entails that moral expressions are nothing more than sophisticated ways of booing or cheering about types of action.

Later ethical theorists refined Ayer's emotive theory of ethics. The American philosopher C. L. Stevenson contended that ethical statements were more akin to commands (imperatives): 'I approve of X; do so as well.' The Oxford analytical philosopher R. M. Hare developed Stevenson's theory by formulating a 'logic of imperatives'—a system by which one could be deemed to have given good or bad reasons for espousing ethical positions, even though the statement of that ethical position does not give information which is capable of being true or false.

All this is technical stuff, and readers who wish to pursue the topic further can safely be referred to Stevenson's very readable *Ethics and Language* and Hare's very lucid book *The Language of Morals*. At the risk of dismissing either of these writers without having given them a fair hearing, we may state that opinion is divided as to the adequacy of the account of ethical discourse which they have given. One very serious criticism which subsequent writers have offered is that it is difficult to account for 'moral seriousness' if there is no such thing as *truth* in ethical matters. We debate issues such as abortion, euthanasia, feminism, animal rights and so on, assuming that such topics are of great importance. Yet it is difficult to see why any importance whatsoever should be attached to such controversies if neither party to such debates has a greater claim to truth.

RESPONSE 2: CULTURAL RELATIVISM ('Everyone does it')

The second response might be interpreted as an appeal to what is commonly done in one's own social group. This type of theory is known as 'cultural relativism': what is right and wrong is relative to the circles in which one moves. How wide that circle is may be a matter for some disagreement. It is possible to suggest, for example, that the rightness or wrongness of an act relates to what is deemed acceptable by society at large. For other relativists, such a circle is too large and it may instead be argued that there is no universal set of societal norms, but a series of 'subcultures', of which one's 'work culture' might be one. Thus the acceptability of petty pilfering, for example, on this last criterion, might depend not on what society at large approves of, but on the consensus view of either blue-collar workers in general, the prevailing view within the car industry, or the norms which are accepted within the particular factory.

For the purposes of this discussion, we do not intend to adjudicate on how wide the cultural relativist's concept of a 'culture' should be. Instead, we shall make some comments on relativism in general. Like the first theories we have discussed, the second set acknowledges a subjective element in morality, but, unlike Ayer, Stevenson and Hare, the theory accepts that ethical beliefs can be true and false—meaning that they are in accordance with the norms of our culture (or not in accordance, as the case may be), rather than, as with the natural sciences, that they reflect a reality outside social conventions.

According to the cultural relativist, moral truth can vary with time as well as place. For example, we believe that slavery is wrong because we live in twentieth-century Europe, but, if we had lived in the times of the slave trade, we would have seen nothing wrong with it. (Even an ardent Christian like St Paul instructed a runaway slave to return to his owner.) Thirty years ago it was quite commonplace to find separate 'male' and 'female' columns of situations vacant; in Europe today this would not be tolerated. Hence, the relativist might say, slavery was ethically acceptable in the ancient world of Greece and Rome, but is ethically unacceptable today; sex discrimination is unethical in twentieth-century Europe, but not (say) in Victorian England or in many Islamic countries, where the practice prevails.

Relativism is inspired by several considerations. First, it acknowledges that our beliefs and practices are indeed shaped by the environment around us, which varies from one time and place to another. Second, it is a reaction against the arrogance of any one culture which brashly claims to have a monopoly of truth, such as the West did in the heyday of Christian missionary enterprise or when Europe and America were beginning to reap the benefits of the West's technological revolution. Third, in the area of ethics, relativism accommodates the fact that there are important moral differences between cultures which seem impossible to resolve.

Although there may seem to be advantages in relativism, the theory has some very serious problems. It implies that ethical standards never improve or worsen; they only change. If relativism is true, then modern-day Europeans and Americans cannot say that they are morally superior to the slave traders; they are only different. The anti-Semitism of Nazi Germany, the relativist seems to imply, although morally quite unjustifiable now, was ethically acceptable then. (It was not that it was merely *believed* to be ethically right: it *was* ethically right, the relativist must affirm.)

On this logic, then, the German people have become no better since World War Two—only different. Further, anyone who sought to oppose the Nazi regime, according to the cultural relativist, far from being a brave dissenter who deserves our praise, must have been acting immorally, since he or she was going against the culturally agreed trend of anti-Semitism. Cultural relativism therefore has no place for commending the dissident or the reformer: anyone who seeks change in a society must at the outset be in the wrong. Indeed, if the relativist is right, no reforms can ever be needed in any society, since whatever is generally agreed is *ipso facto* right.

RESPONSE 3: NON-CONSEQUENTIALISM ('Bribery is simply wrong')

Religious morality

The third response to the 'bribery' scenario resolutely rejects the previous two theories. It suggests, unlike the emotivist, that there are indeed right and wrong answers to moral questions: stealing, in most if not all of its forms is wrong. Unlike the relativist, this respondent suggests that fundamental moral principles do not vary according to the prevalent moral climate, but stand for all time and in all places.

This type of theory is sometimes labelled 'non-consequentialism', although again the label applies to a number of different ethical theories. One important type of 'non-consequentialism' comes from traditional religious morality. Someone who says that bribery is 'simply wrong' may be thinking of the Judaeo-Christian scriptures or the Qur'an, where it is strongly condemned,[1] and one of the fundamental Buddhist precepts is 'to avoid taking the not-given', which encompasses all acquisitions in which there a lack of voluntariness on the part of the contributor.

At first appearance there seems much to be said in favour of the view that morality should be based on religion. What higher authority could there be to adjudicate on matters of ethics? If there is a God who is all-knowing and who wants to make its will known to humanity, surely the believer could not go wrong in basing his or her ethics on divine commandments? Indeed, many businessmen and women would claim that their ethics comes from the Jewish Torah, the Christian Bible, the Qur'an or some other religious text.

Obviously, if one disbelieves in or doubts God's existence, a religiously based ethic is unappealing. But, if there is a God, what objection could there possibly be to a believer basing his or her morality on God's will, however that will is revealed?

It is that last qualification ('however that will is revealed') which poses the problem, for unfortunately religious believers cannot achieve unanimity on the question of what God wills. The practising Muslim might claim that God's will is revealed with its final authority in the Qur'an; the fundamentalist Christian, by contrast, will claim that God's will is seen in the Bible (particularly the New Testament). This might not be a problem if one or both of two conditions held: (i) that a religion's sacred scripture is only binding on the adherents of that faith; or (ii) that the sacred scriptures of the various world's religions are in virtual agreement.

With the exception of the Jewish faith, where it is held that complete Torah-observance is a special obligation for Jews alone, religious believers tend to claim universal scope for their religious ethics. The Muslim's 'five pillars'[2] are for all people; lack of Christian love cannot be excused on the grounds that one does not accept Christianity. This would not be a problem if the various sacred texts were in agreement, but this is not the case: Christianity permits the eating of any food, whereas the Muslim is instructed to avoid pork and alcohol. For the Muslim, women are to be treated 'equally' but differently: a woman, for example, may inherit only half the legacy which accrues to a man, and the testimony of two women in a law court gains credence equivalent to that of one man. Many

Christians, by contrast (although by no means all), see Christianity as giving women equal status to men in a sense more conducive to Western feminism.

However, there are more fundamental problems about basing morality on religion. If we say that God's will is the ultimate guide to ethics, then what would we say if God commanded men and women to commit genocide, to commit robbery with violence, or to deceive people? Supposing God had decided to remove the word 'not' from each of the Ten Commandments which contained it, and added the word 'not' to those that did not. Would that then have made killing, stealing, adultery and perjury right, and sabbath observance and respect for parents wrong?

When one of the authors recently put this suggestion to a group of students, he encountered the response, 'But then that would not be God; that would be the devil.' Fair enough, but how could we tell the difference between God and the devil? If we suggest that God is the being who commands us to do what is right, and the devil who tempts us to do what is wrong, then we must already have independent standards of right and wrong in order to distinguish the two beings.

An analogy may help to clarify this point further. In our role as teachers, we are 'authorities' on what pieces of work deserve good grades: we can tell our students that essays must be clearly written, well argued, show good under-standing of the relevant issues, show evidence of appropriate background reading and so on. But suppose someone (perhaps a rather naïve fresher) believed that Chryssides and Kaler were the final authorities on these matters, and that students should only emulate these qualities 'because we said so'. It would be quite a valid retort to ask this fresher whether the observance of *any* set of instructions from Chryssides and Kaler would automatically result in a good essay. What if it were rumoured that we awarded good grades for the funniest essays, or the most confused essays, or to students who offered bribes or sexual favours?

It is not sufficient to retort, 'Ah, but the authors are not like that.' That response misses the point totally. *If*, contrary to fact, the authors *were* like that, this would not turn hitherto bad essays into good ones, or vice versa: it would merely show that we were corrupt, or incompetent, or both! Similarly, if Moses' tablets of stone had read, 'Petty pilfering is acceptable', this would not make stealing right, but would rather suggest that Moses had not been communing with a righteous god at all. However, in order to make such a judgement, we must already have a knowledge of what is right and wrong, in order to judge what comes from God and what does not.

What we have said so far may seem to imply that a religious understanding of morality is not possible, or even that we are against religion. This is far from the case. Most business men and women—on a world-wide level—espouse some form of religion, which provides moral guidance and inspiration in the form of legends, myths and parables. These often provide followers with concrete illustrations of how to live a moral life—an ingredient that is often missing in abstract ethical theorizing. A religion, too, can provide specific ways for practising one's ethics. For example, Christian Aid enables Christians (and others) to give at least some of their possessions to the less fortunate, and thus follow the teachings of Jesus Christ. The *zakat* (alms) box placed in the mosque is an obvious means whereby Muslims can donate the prescribed 2.5 per cent of their savings to the poor. A religion can also give a community a sense of identity, and offer teachings about reality—where life has come from, why we are in the world, where we are going, what one might expect after death and so on. What is believed about such matters cannot fail to affect one's moral values, of course, but while religions can inform their followers about standards of right and wrong (just as Kaler and Chryssides can inform students about academic standards), the religion itself cannot be the *ultimate* source of authority, any more than the present authors are the ultimate authorities about standards in universities.

Another kind of non-consequentialism: 'respect for persons'—Kant's ethic of duty

If morality does not depend on divine command, on what else might it depend? The late eighteenth and early nineteenth centuries saw Europe's 'Age of the Enlightenment'. The Age of Enlightenment was marked by an emphasis on human reason. What this meant was that truth of any kind—not just in matters of morality, but in science and the arts—was not to be accepted simply because of divine authority or the authority of the Church; rather, human reason could be trusted as the arbiter of truth.

The adjective 'human' in the phrase 'human reason' is also important, for the Age of Enlightenment signalled an emphasis on the worth of humanity, in contrast with a blind obedience to a supreme being. Accordingly, much moral theory in the Age of the Enlightenment marked an increased emphasis on humanity rather than God.

It is in this context that we encounter one of the most celebrated philosophers and moral theorists of the Enlightenment, the German thinker Immanuel Kant. Kant believed that the essence of morality was to be found in *reason*: it was by a process of rational deduction (as distinct from religious faith) that one could discover the basis of right and wrong.

What, then, is the essence of morality? The first thing that reason tells us, Kant argued, is that one's duty is to be done for duty's sake. Morality is not the same as self-interest, or even benevolence. If we do what is right in order to gain other people's approval, or because we like someone and want to do him or her a good turn, we have not acted wrongly, but—according to Kant—we have not acted from the correct motive, which ought to be fairly and squarely the motive of having recognized that the action *is one's duty.*

Kant's ethic sounds austere, and has often been misinterpreted by later commentators. It is therefore important to set the record straight. Kant does not mean that we should not entertain feelings of friendship or compassion for others, or that we should never think of our own self-interest. What he is insisting is that these of themselves cannot constitute truly moral grounds for acting. If the fact that Jones is our friend were the reason for treating him well, then we would be let off the hook if, say, we were to quarrel with him, and our friendship were to come to an end. Nor is it the case that we should show kindness to people because it promotes human wellbeing: the moral law, Kant held, was to be obeyed *because it is the right thing to do,* not because of any consequences which accrue to moral behaviour.

The second point which Kant noted about the moral law was that it is by nature *universal.* If we say that it is wrong for George Chryssides to accept a bribe, then it follows that it is wrong for John Kaler to do so also, and indeed for anyone else. That is, of course, unless someone can show that there is some relevant difference in his or her circumstances which might make us more inclined to recognize an exception, e.g. an Indian civil servant who earns low wages, and whose low wages are possibly justified on the grounds that they are able to be topped up with bribes.

The fact that the present authors' circumstances are different from our hypothetical Indian civil servant would have been important to Kant, for if we, who do not have to struggle for bare subsistence, were to accept a bribe we would be acting on a different principle from the civil servant, who *ex hypothesi* has no other means of survival. According to Kant, if we contemplated theft we would be acting on different *maxims.* A 'maxim', for Kant, is the personal principle on which we act. Thus, our civil servant's maxim might be, 'When my basic wages do not provide the bare means of subsistence, and there are no other means of providing for my family, I propose to accept bribes from my clients.' If we—the authors—were to accept bribes in our present set of circumstances, our maxim might be something like, 'When the opportunity arises to supplement our incomes and there is little risk of detection, then we propose to accept bribes.'

The first maxim could be 'universalized': that is to say, in a society where some people were so impoverished that they had no other means of subsistence, we would be prepared to accord them the permission to accept bribes—although, obviously, society would be much better if this were not necessary. The second maxim, however, could not so readily be universalized: a society where it was always necessary to 'grease people's palms' would be one in which few of us would choose to live.

Accordingly, Kant's first formulation of the 'categorical imperative' was:

I ought never to act except in such a way that I can also will that my maxim should become a universal law.[3]

We mentioned the Enlightenment's emphasis on humanity and on human reason. Kant goes on to affirm the value he places on the human self in his second formulation of the 'categorical imperative' as follows:

Act in such a way that you always treat humanity . . . never simply as a means, but always at the same time as an end.[4]

Some commentators argue that this second formulation follows from the first ('Disrespect for persons cannot be universally willed'), while others contend that Kant's second principle is different. This issue need not detain us now. What is important is to recognize that Kant is according supreme worth to the human self, and that he does so because—in the true spirit of the Enlightenment—he sees humanity as possessing the 'distinctive endowment' of reason. For Kant this is supremely important; the ancient Greek philosopher Aristotle (384–322 BCE) had defined 'human' as 'rational animal' and the French Renaissance philosopher Descartes (1596–1650) had contended that humankind was distinguished from the animal kingdom because of its powers of reason. ('I think, therefore I am', was Descartes' famous dictum, in which he asserted, among other things, the importance of thought or reason.) Kant is thus following in the tradition of Aristotle and Descartes.

Apart from the endeavour to find the basis of right and wrong, Kantian moral theory has implications for issues such as animal rights—an important topic in research and manufacturing processes. By stressing reason, Kant—in line with Aristotle and Descartes—is setting humanity on a pinnacle above animals, with the possible implication that humans are more worthy of respect than the animal kingdom. Compared with the average human, the average animal lacks reason: it is therefore less important, it might be argued, for an animal to suffer in product testing, than that humans should suffer as a result of an undiscovered product defect.

For some modern-day critics of Kant, this elevation of humanity above the animals might be reason in itself for rejecting his moral philosophy. Some readers will no doubt see it as latent 'speciesism'. ('Speciesism' is the view that one species is superior to another, just as 'sexism' is the view that one sex is superior to the other.)

However, there are other reasons for being dissatisfied with Kant's moral philosophy. First, there are problems surrounding Kant's notion of the maxim and its universalization. We agree that for stealing to be right in one set of circumstances but wrong in another there must be a relevant difference in those circumstances and hence in the maxims on which the various parties are acting. But why cannot the authors of this book suggest that it is acceptable to act on the maxim, 'If you are a university lecturer, then you may steal goods when the risk of detection is low.' The maxim is perfectly universalizable: we could certainly imagine a society in which only university lecturers were allowed to steal. Of course, it may be pointed out, being a university lecturer is *irrelevant* to the question of the rightness of stealing, whereas being a single parent with starving children is decidedly relevant.

The authors would not wish to deny that the latter circumstances are relevant whereas the former are not. What is important is the reason why this should be the case, and it is difficult to give reasons which do not introduce additional principles to those that Kant has identified. For example, we might suggest that stealing is (usually) wrong for university lecturers and (sometimes) right for impoverished single parents, because these respective prohibitions and permissions enhance human welfare. But Kant insists that his moral theory is independent of the consequences, and hence this possible reason cannot apply. Alternatively, we might suggest that the reason for the difference has something to do with human rights: the owners of a store have property rights, which hold irrespective of university lecturers' desires for their goods. On the other hand, everyone has a right to life, and an impoverished family has a right to live, which, arguably, supersedes any other rights such as the right to property.

We have therefore a suitable cue for considering two further types of moral theory, one based on human welfare (utilitarianism) and another based on human rights (natural law theory).

RESPONSE 4: 'CONSEQUENTIALISM' ('Human welfare is best served')

There is another type of theory which may help us to adjudicate on the 'bribery' problem. To suggest that it is more important for the charity to commence its relief work than to avoid bribing corrupt officials is to contend that the circumstances surrounding a moral problem can and should make a difference to our decision. Perhaps a bribe would not have been so justifiable if we wanted to build a set of offices or a night-club. On this way of thinking, humanitarian aid, which relieves much human misery, is much more important than personal profit or entertainment, and hence may well justify giving a few rupees to someone who has not strictly earned them.

In making a moral decision, one might balance one person's welfare against someone else's and reach a decision on the basis of which course of action achieves the greatest good. To argue in this way is to adopt a 'consequentialist' approach to morality. Unlike Kantianism, what is important, for consequentialists, are not moral principles that seem to be carved in tablets of stone—for these probably do not exist—but *outcomes* of ethical decisions.

Among consequentialist theories, probably the best known is that of utilitarianism. Traditionally, the utilitarian holds that actions are right in so far as they are conducive to the greatest happiness of the greatest number of people, and wrong in so far as they are not. The term 'utilitarianism' was first used by the philosopher and social reformer Jeremy Bentham (1748–1832) and further developed by John Stuart Mill (1806–1873).

Utilitarianism finds the seat of morality in humankind, rather than in God. It thus differs markedly from a religious morality, although Mill was at pains to argue that producing the greatest human happiness was not inconsistent with obeying God's will. Neither Bentham nor Mill were ever able to subscribe to traditional Christian belief, and therefore it was important for them to devise an alternative source of moral authority.

There is another important respect in which utilitarianism differs from Kantianism. Kant based his theory on reason; by contrast, the utilitarians, by emphasizing human happiness, were basing their theory on *feeling*. Thus immoral acts were not those that failed to respect people as rational self-determining agents; the trouble with immoral actions, they held, was that they harmed people by making them suffer pain (either physical or psychological).

Bentham believed that humankind was subject to 'two masters'—pain and pleasure, which 'govern us in all we do'.[5] All human beings, he held, had a natural tendency to want to experience pleasure and to avoid pain. Not only did Bentham believe that, as a matter of psychological fact, humans are driven by these two forces, but these forces also determine what ought to be the case, and form the basis of a sound ethical theory.

Although the utilitarians at their inception emphasized *human* happiness, their feeling-based morality paved the way for later animal welfare supporters, who were subsequently able to point out that animals experienced pleasure and pain also, and were therefore worthy of consideration in determining which actions were right and wrong. This point has obvious implications for business ethics. For example, those who are opposed to animal testing in product development will no doubt point to the fact that animals and humans commonly share the potential to experience suffering; those who condone animal testing might find greater support for their views in a Kantian theory which asserts important differences between humans and animals. If animals cannot reason and humans can, then maybe there is a case (at least on Kantian theory) for treating animals differently.

Although it is impossible in a single section to do justice to all the complexities of the debate which continues to surround utilitarianism, it is important to clear up one or two basic misunderstandings of the theory. First, to state that the maximization of human happiness is the goal immediately raises the question of what happiness is. For Bentham, happiness was the same as pleasure, and Bentham contended that one ought not to rate one pleasure any more highly than another: the pleasure from reading poetry, he contended, was in no way superior to the pleasure derived from 'pushpin'. (Pushpin was a non-intellectual nineteenth-century game rather like shove ha'penny.) Mill found this less than satisfactory, and claimed that there were at least two types of pleasure—physical and intellectual—and that the intellectual pleasures were invariably superior to the physical ones. (This refinement of the theory, formalized by G. E. Moore (1873–1958) was subsequently called 'ideal utilitarianism', since it gives greater status to the intellect—to 'ideas'.) We cannot attempt to settle this debate here: ideal utilitarians will allege that Bentham was non-discriminating, whereas Benthamites will no doubt see Moore as an élitist, and claim that one has no right to say that the pleasures derived from sitting in a Cambridge library are superior to those which come from drinking beer or watching a football match.

Second, the utilitarian is not recommending that right actions must invariably produce large amounts of happiness. This is not always possible. The word 'greatest' in the phrase 'greatest happiness of the greatest number' is crucial, for in some cases the greatest happiness might simply mean the least misery. Let us suppose that a management team notes that their firm is losing its market share because it has not kept pace with technological innovation, unlike its competitors. The management will not have an easy choice. If they introduce new technology, they will probably have to declare redundancies (let us assume), or alternatively have to suggest reductions in wages. If they do not make technological innovations, they will probably continue to be uncompetitive and will run the risk of total closure, which will have much worse consequences than these other two alternatives. No decision will produce vast quantities of happiness; the least one can do is to miminize the misery.

This brings us to a third comment which has sometimes been made about utilitarianism. Surely, it has been argued, there are so many variables which are relevant to a situation. How can one possibly calculate the consequences of an action before deciding how to act? If we made a precise calculation of all the degrees of human pleasure and misery that accrued to each alternative course of action open to us, then by the time we had finished the calculation (if we ever could), the opportunity would have been lost.

It is true that situations are often complicated, and that therefore there is not time to make precise calculations. However, this does not mean that a certain amount of calculation is not possible. As a rough analogy, one might compare calculating the consequences of one's possible choices with the calculating that is involved in crossing a road. Our decision whether it is safe to cross depends on a number of variables: how fast we can walk, how far away is the relevant traffic, how fast it is travelling, whether the road surface presents hazards such as slippiness, and so on. In theory, one could calculate most of these factors with mathematical precision, but this would be unduly time consuming, and indeed unnecessary, since our past experience of crossing roads enables us to perform rough but serviceable calculations which, the vast the majority of the time, take us across safely.

In the case of a moral decision, it may not be possible to ascertain precisely how many individuals are affected, and what degrees of satisfaction or misery they will experience as the result of a decision, but at least it is possible to know roughly.

The management team that introduces the new technology will know something of the misery involved in lay-offs, the difficulties which are entailed by seemingly ungenerous wage settlements, the possible longer-term effects of soldiering on with lower technology and the ensuing risks of being unable to compete with those firms who have successfully implemented similar technological innovations. Although a complete calculation of the consequences would be unrealistic, one would hope that the management would make a rough estimate of the probable consequences into account (modern cost–benefit analysis purports to do just that), and not merely guess, or—worse still—ignore their employees' welfare altogether.

There is a problem about adopting a utilitarian solution to the bribery scenario. If it is simply a matter of weighing the potential benefits of the money to me against its potential worth to its present owners, then is it not the case that on any occasion in which we could use a sum of money more advantageously than its present rightful owner, we should feel constrained—indeed, obliged—to resort to whatever means it takes to acquire it: extortion, deception, theft or whatever?

It may be suggested that the weakness in the utilitarian solution is that it treats actions in a piecemeal way. If we consider the consequences of the one single act of proposed theft, we may well come up with an answer in our own favour, but yet one which runs counter to our normal moral sense. The trouble, it has been alleged, with this kind of utilitarian is that it considers acts in the absence of any moral rules.

This is where we encounter the theory of 'rule utilitarianism'. Rule utilitarians are unhappy with considering individual actions in this piecemeal sort of way. What is needed, it has been suggested, is the introduction of *moral rules* into our deliberation. What rule does the proposed act of theft fall under? The obvious rule is 'Do not steal.' Now consider whether the greatest happiness of the greatest number would be achieved by (a) everyone keeping such a rule, or (b) by everyone breaking such a rule or abandoning it at will when simply when it suited them. There can be little doubt that the greatest happiness would be achieved by (a) rather than by (b).

However, it may be argued that things are not so simple. How do we know that we have formulated the moral rule correctly? It might be suggested that 'Do not steal' is really too simple a rule and does not truly reflect what our normal moral consciousness dictates. How many of us can truly say that we have never appropriated goods which were not ours? Have we really never taken the occasional packet of paper-clips home from work, and used them for our own private purposes? It may therefore be suggested that the rule 'Do not steal' requires some modification. An employee might be prepared to appropriate a small item from work but not a large one: few of us would regard it as acceptable to steal, say, a computer; and few of us would regard it as acceptable to steal goods from private individuals—even a friend's packet of paper-clips! So perhaps a more realistic rule would be, 'Do not steal anything large from business organizations, and do not steal anything at all from private citizens.' In the case of bribery, the relevant rules are not so clear. Should the rule be, 'Never accept any bribes', or should it be, 'Always ask for a bribe if you can gain more happiness from the money than its present owner'? How we actually formulate a version of utilitarianism which has a place for unequivocal and acceptable moral rules seems a serious problem.

The idea that human welfare lies at the heart of moral matters may seem attractive, and there can certainly be no doubt that human happiness has something very important to do with ethical decisions. But is human happiness the only consideration to be taken into account when deciding what is right and wrong? One criticism which is commonly made about utilitarianism is that it fails to account for the principle of *justice*. In speaking of the 'greatest happiness of the greatest number' the utilitarian appears to emphasize the *amount* of happiness to be produced, and to say nothing about its *distribution*. A community could exist, for example, in which the majority of citizens enjoyed a high standard of living, but at the expense of an underprivileged minority. This would seem to satisfy the greatest happiness principle, but the situation would be objectionable, because it is unjust.

It may be suggested that the law of diminishing marginal utility provides a prima-facie case for justice. Suppose shopfloor workers are earning £8000 a year and the mangers £800 000. The firm, let us imagine, has improved its performance so that substantial wage rises are possible. The management has a choice: it can award themselves another massive increase with a meagre pay rise for the workers, or it can endure a self-imposed wage freeze, allowing only the workers to reap the benefit. (Various intermediate solutions are possible too, of course.) It is more likely that a 'bottom-loaded' improvement would maximize human happiness. Suppose, for the sake of argument, everyone is given a £2000 rise: workers on £8000 a year will probably notice a substantial increase in their quality of life and resulting happiness, whereas to a manager on £800 000 a year, the sum of £2000 is a drop in the ocean.

Let us consider these arguments. First, although no one's happiness is either more or less important than anyone else's, it does not follow that giving everyone equal degrees of wellbeing will maximize the *total* quantity of happiness. Indeed, it may be argued that creating inequalities can even optimize human happiness on a wider level. One possible example, it might be argued, is the issue of performance-related pay (PRP). PRP deliberately sets out to create inequalities, but supporters of such a policy might argue that such inequalities create incentives for employees to work better, thus ensuring that their customers and the firm's shareholders get a better deal. If this is indeed the case, then the utilitarian has to concede that there are situations where utility and equality conflict. One cannot have one's cake and eat it: both principles cannot be supported simultaneously.

Similar arguments could be used against the point about 'diminishing marginal utility'. Equal treatment in the form of equal pay may result in the optimum happiness among the workforce. But utilitarianism does not advocate the greatest happiness of one's immediate circle, but the greatest happiness of the greatest number of people who are affected. Many arguments have been employed to suggest that pay differentials create a better system of employment than a strictly egalitarian society. It has been argued, for instance, that workers need incentives, that extra rewards are appropriate for overtime, unsociable hours, dangerous jobs and so on. Reconciling the claims of equality and human welfare is certainly not an easy task, but it is important to recognize that equality and utility are two different moral principles. Each is relevant to determining what is right or wrong, and it is by no means self-evident that the principles coincide anything like as perfectly as the utilitarian might wish.

RESPONSE 5: NATURAL LAW—AN ETHIC OF RIGHTS

The final response we itemized at the beginning entails a rather different approach to ethical reasoning. Thus far we have considered moral principles and con-sequences of one's actions; we have not considered concepts such as *rights* or *entitlements*. It may be suggested that one compelling reason why an organization, however humanitarian its purposes, should not resort to bribery is that those who accept bribes are not entitled (have no right) to monies acquired in such a way.

Because of its emphasis on the welfare of society at large, utilitarianism seems committed to sacrificing the welfare of individuals or minority groups for the welfare of the majority. The concept of rights, arguably, can show why individuals' wellbeing should not be sacrificed for the greatest happiness of the greatest number. What is missing is the recognition that everyone has certain entitlements which may not be set aside simply in the interests of the greatest happiness principle.

The type of ethical theory which acknowledges the supremacy of rights is known as *natural law theory*.[6] According to this theory, rights rather than duties are primordial: duties can only be defined in terms of rights. Thus, *your right* to property generates *our duty* to refrain from stealing it; *our right* to disclosure of information gives rise to *your duty* to tell us the truth. In recognizing rights, natural law theory sets limits to the degree to which law may intrude upon people. Not all laws are just laws, and when the state deprives its citizens of any of their funda-mental rights ('natural rights'), we might say that this is contrary to natural law.

Where, then, do these 'natural rights' come from? They cannot come from state law, because they exist independently of state legislation, and at times may override it. It has been suggested that such natural rights are given by God. However, the very same claim was made by the opposing doctrine of the divine right of kings—a doctrine that was often used as a rationalization of tyranny. In any event, the alternative of a non-theistic natural law theory was on offer. This entails that humans have rights that are inherent in 'nature', irrespective of whether God exists. The requirements of human nature and society demand, it is said, recognition of certain fundamental rights that may not normally be taken away from us. However, whether these rights are God-given or not, they always exist, and in this respect natural law theory differs sharply from 'conventionalism', since human conventions lack permanence and objectivity. Natural law doctrine thus provides the individual with a theoretical basis for protection against a state which usurps excessive authority over the citizen.

There are a number of famous declarations of human rights which set out what these inalienable rights are, e.g. the Declaration of the Rights of Man and of the Citizen (1789), the Universal Declaration of Human Rights (1948) and the European Convention on Human Rights (1950). According to all these charters of human rights, every citizen has the right to life, liberty and possessions. All individuals have a right to protection under the law, to freedom of assembly, and to freedom to manifest their religion and beliefs.

This reflects natural law theory in that these rights stand above national law. With the European Convention on Human Rights, for instance, a citizen of a signatory country can appeal to the European Court of Human Rights and have legal decisions made by the highest courts in that country overturned.

Perhaps the most influential philosopher to propound natural law theory was John Locke (1632–1704). Locke considers what life would be like in an ungoverned state, which he calls a 'state of nature'. Although lacking the benefits of organized society, and in particular the means of enforcing proper standards of human behaviour, in a state of nature one would still have moral laws to observe, in the form of pre-existing natural rights. Locke believes that even in the state of nature there are several fundamental human rights which are paramount. As Locke writes:

> To understand political power aright, and derive it from its original, we must consider, what state all men are naturally in, and that is, a state of perfect freedom to order their actions and dispose of their possessions and persons, as they think fit, within the bounds of the law of nature, without asking leave, or depending upon the will of any other man.[7]

This passage identifies two important 'natural rights' for Locke. First, there was, he believed, a right to *freedom*, in so far, of course, as that freedom was compatible with respect for the natural rights of others. Second, Locke held, there was a right to *property*. The right of property, Locke explains, does not simply mean physical possessions. We have a 'property in our own person'.[8] This notion of a 'property in our own person' has several implications. In European law, it is generally recognized, for example, that 'property' includes intellectual property: copyright and patent laws, for example, serve to ensure that those who invent ideas are the ones who benefit from their invention, and that others may not copy or plagiarize, without the consent of the owner of that intellectual property.

Locke connects the notion of the 'property of one's own person' with the ownership of physical objects. When the first men and women began life on earth, there was no private ownership and all the earth's resources were held 'in common'. It was the fact that certain individuals 'mixed their labour' with natural materials that made them *theirs*. Locke, however, would not have endorsed the views propounded later by Karl Marx and twentieth-century communists: Locke's criterion of having mixed one's labour with something only determines who subsequently owns goods which have been previously held in common. In modern society few such commodities remain, and ownership is therefore determined by a further property right which Locke identifies, namely the 'right of inheritance'. We appropriate goods from others, by gift, by bequest or—more commonly—by purchase. Also, for Locke, the labour of servants belonged to their masters— something Marx radically challenged.

For completeness, it is worth mentioning the third 'natural right' which Locke identifies: the 'right to punish'. Natural law must be upheld, otherwise society degenerates into a 'state of war'. Consequently, Locke believed, it was important to ensure that due sanctions were imposed against any violators of natural law, even though in Locke's hypothetical pre-organized society there would be no codified legal system. In organized society, of course, this right to punish has been handed over by individuals to the state. In contemporary European society it is normally considered inappropriate to 'take the law into one's own hands' by taking direct action, organizing vigilante groups, or having private individuals or companies enforce the law. The recently formed 'Guardian Angels' organization that aimed to combat crime on the London Underground has not met with universal favour, to say the least.

It might be suggested that it is Locke's discussion of property that provides the solution to the bribery dilemma. A bribe is simply not one's property and officials who accept bribes have not 'mixed their labour' with anything for which they have not already been paid: they are already paid by the authorities for scrutinizing architects' plans and adjudicating on them, and the requested bribe is not freely given, bequeathed or exchanged for any additional service.

Does a theory of natural rights, then, solve all our problems in ethics? Alas, this is not the case. One serious problem with natural law theory is that it provides no obvious means of determining what one's natural rights are. Does the individual have a right to employment? Does someone have a right to life after committing a serious crime? Does one have a right to convert from one religion to another? Do women have the same rights as men? While some champions of human rights would claim all of these are entitlements of a citizen, they are by no means universally agreed. Few states can guarantee employment for life for each citizen; many countries still practise capital punishment (and justify this policy);

some Muslim states make it illegal to convert from Islam to any other religion, on the grounds that rejecting Islam is tantamount to rejecting God; in countries such as Saudi Arabia women may not drive cars or show their faces in public. At the end of the day, it looks as if natural rights are either matters of faith, or those entitlements which are ultimately upheld in international courts of law.

Presumed rights, too, can conflict. The suggestion that British citizens should carry identity cards is controversial precisely because of the conflicting rights issue which it generates. British citizens value freedom of passage, which is often thought to demand that citizens are not stopped for ID checks. On the other hand, if ID cards can be used to reduce crime—as some suppose—then some forfeiting of one's right to free passage could, arguably, be a price worth paying to secure one's right to property and personal safety.

A further problem about natural rights theory is that it cannot account for situations in which everyone's natural rights have been respected and a proposed course of action goes beyond mere observance of human rights. For example, suppose a firm sets aside a certain proportion of its annual budget to support some charity: which good cause (or causes) will it promote? No individual charity has a *right* to support, even though companies and wealthy individuals may regard it as a moral duty to become benefactors. Faced with a decision about who should be the object of one's charity, individuals and companies cannot therefore appeal to any natural rights, but will be more likely to resolve such questions by utilitarian considerations. (Perhaps legitimately, there may be self-interest involved in such choices too: a company wishes to select a beneficiary which can be connected with its company image. For example, in its television advertising Kimberly-Clarke recently supported the campaign, 'A dog is for life, not just for Christmas', since the dog who unravels the Andrex toilet tissue had won the hearts of many viewers!)

SOME CONCLUSIONS

All the theories we have considered have their advantages and their defects. Are we really any nearer finding a basis for our ethical decision making? Given that there are attractive and unattractive features alike in all the theories we have considered, it is not untypical for a student of ethics to ask whether we might not combine all the good features of the theories we like, and discard the unattractive material. There is certainly no objection to doing this, the only proviso being that the elements which we combine must not be mutually contradictory. We cannot suggest, for example, that we should always promote the greatest happiness of the greatest number *and* always recognize, say, the fundamental natural right of property, for, as we have seen, there are situations in which these two components conflict (as in the example of stealing to avoid starvation).

When considering what is right and wrong, factors relating to all three types of theory (Kantian, utilitarian and natural law) all seem to have an important

Case study

Insider dealing—'victimless crime'?

In the European Union and the United States 'insider dealing' in stocks and shares is illegal, although the situation is different in Australia, where 'insiders' are expected—even encouraged—to make use of their superior knowledge of the stock market's likely trends.

The logic behind such prohibitions is that all who speculate on the stock market should be on an equal footing—a presumed entailment of the principle of justice. However, insider dealing has its defenders, who adduce two lines of argument in its favour.

First, it may be argued that, although prohibitions on insider dealing put all potential investors on an equal footing, insider information is a particular piece of expertise that the insider possesses, and should be used in exactly the same way as financial advisers use their knowledge of investment and trends in financial markets.

The second argument is that, if insider dealing is a crime, it is a victimless one. If the insider is able to make a fast buck through superior knowledge, why should this be so deplorable? The insider is not like the bank robber, who causes human suffering and who walks off with monies that clearly belong to others. When commenting on his transactions in Barings Bank in 1995, Nick Leeson pleaded that his actions only involved figures on computer screens, and hence were only a technical offence.

If the 'victimless crime' argument has weight, then we must draw one of three possible conclusions. The first conclusion is that of the non-consequentialist, who may conclude that for an action to be wrong there need not be deleterious consequences; 'insider dealing' may simply be inherently unethical. The second line of response is to exonerate insider dealers, and to support their financial astuteness—or luck: if there are no victims, a consequentialist might conclude, there is damage to human welfare, and hence no moral blame.

There is a third possibility, however. It might be suggested that there are indeed victims of insider dealing, even if they cannot be individually identified. Privileged gains on the stock market must entail losses for others (or at least reduced profits); if insiders rush to buy promising shares, this increases the price at which other investors will come in; if they have to sell other holdings in order to buy, this depletes their value. The repercussions may not be great, but they are not non-existent, and hence it can be argued that there are indeed consequences for other investors. In the case of more serious financial frauds, there have

> indeed been victims, as has been witnessed in the collapse of the Bank of Credit and Commerce International (BCCI) in 1991.
>
> For the consequentialist, there can of course be no such thing as 'victimless crime'. Those who deplore insider dealing and other supposed financial malpractices must therefore either support a non-consequentialist ethical theory (in which actions can sometimes be wrong even if no one is harmed) or else demonstrate that people suffer adverse consequences from such practices.

bearing. Determining the proper course of action therefore demands that we consider, first, the bearing our proposed action has on the wellbeing of others (its 'utility'). Second, we must consider our motives in so acting: is it from a 'sense of duty' (as Kant insisted we should) or are we acting from ulterior motives? (A firm might, for example, want to be seen to adopt 'green' policies in order to increase its profits, rather than from genuine concern for the environment.) Third, we must show 'respect for persons' by taking into account their fundamental moral rights, which can only be overridden if rights conflict, or if there is some overwhelming good which will result.

This 'blend' of the various factors does not give us a tidy solution to the question of what we ought to do, and in some situations what is deemed to be the right outcome must be 'a matter of judgement', on which those who disagree may well have to agree to differ. The study of ethics may not provide us with clear unequivocal answers to all moral dilemmas, but having a preferred theory at least enables us to determine the relevant factors which must be taken into account.

DISCUSSION TOPICS

1. Does ethical theory place one in an better position to consider issues in business ethics? If so, how?
2. Consider the relationship between general, legal and role-specific rights and duties. What legal and role-specific rights and duties attach to (a) being a student; (b) being a teacher; (c) being a company director; (d) being a shop-floor worker?
3. Do you think that religious people show greater integrity in business dealings than those who profess no religion? Why is this (or this not) the case? What difference does a religion make to the way in which one conducts one's business?

4. Consider the bribery example discussed in this chapter. Does any particular moral theory offer a better solution than the others?
5. Can you think of an ethical dilemma in which the outcome would be affected by the ethical theory to which you subscribed?

NOTES

1. See, e.g., Amos 5.12; Qur'an 2: 188.
2. The Qur'an enumerates five principal obligations: belief in God and the prophethood of Muhammad; prayer five times daily; giving alms to the poor; fasting during the holy month of Ramadan; and making the pilgrimage to Makkah at least once during one's lifetime.
3. H. J. Paton, *The Moral Law: Kant's Groundwork of the Metaphysic of Morals*, Hutchinson, London, 1964, p. 70.
4. Ibid., p. 96.
5. Jeremy Bentham, *Principles of Morals and Legislation*, in John Stuart Mill, *Utilitarianism*, ed. Mary Warnock, Fontana, London and Glasgow, 1965, p. 33.
6. This traditional use of the term 'natural law' must be clearly distinguished, of course, from that of the recent 'Natural Law Party', which is a product of the Maharishi Mahesh Yogi and transcendental meditation.
7. John Locke, *Second Treatise on Civil Government*, in Ernest Barker (ed.), *Social Contract: Essays by Locke, Hume and Rousseau*, Oxford University Press, London, p. 5.
8. Ibid., p. 24.

3 *Business and Justice*

We have already mentioned the notion of justice in our discussion of utilitarianism, and have seen how central justice is to morality. Justice takes several forms and, in one form or another, is an element in almost any moral situation. Put briefly, it is what people deserve, or what they have a right to. This can be a matter of receiving a particular kind of treatment, being in receipt of certain goods, or enjoying certain prerogatives or freedoms. These can be required of specific people or of society in general. They can be beneficial or, in some cases, harmful.

When rights are at issue, then it is almost certainly a benefit that is involved; no one ordinarily demands a right to be harmed. What people deserve, however, can be either: one's just deserts can be prizes or penalties, credit or blame, reward or punishment. Whether dispensed through deserts or rights, and whether dispensing for individual good or ill, justice amounts to nothing less than the entire operation of morality in relation to the things people ought to have—whatever these are.

FOUR KINDS OF JUSTICE

We can distinguish different sorts of situation in which justice figures, and on that basis separate out different forms of justice. Traditionally, four main forms are identified: procedural, retributive, remedial and distributive.

PROCEDURAL JUSTICE

Procedural justice deals with the treatment people ought to receive in connection with the application of rules that govern or control them in some way. It is about applying those rules in a consistent and even-handed way. Consequently, it involves not being arbitrary in decision making, sticking to the rules, following agreed procedures, and not arbitrarily discriminating between people when applying the rules.

In a legal context, procedural justice entails allowing people a fair trial, assessing the evidence properly, following due process of law, and the like. Lawyers use the term 'natural justice' in this context. The fundamental principles of natural justice are said to be enshrined in the maxims, 'Hear the other side' (both parties must be allowed to put their case) and, 'No one shall be judge in one's own cause' (judgement must be impartial).

Although originally principles governing court proceedings, they have along with considerations of procedural justice in general, come to be legally required of any organization that exercises power over people. For example, an employer might be deemed to have unfairly dismissed an employee if that person was given no opportunity to rebut charges against him or her—thereby contravening the 'Hear the other side' principle. A failure to follow agreed or usually recognized disciplinary procedures might also offer grounds for regarding a dismissal as unfair.

Procedural justice only encompasses the application of rules, but not what those rules themselves are. Accordingly, it is perfectly possible to have a meticulously fair application of a monstrously unjust rule. For example, a rule excluding members of a particular group—say, black people—from congenial, well-paid jobs within an organization might be scrupulously observed, and black people excluded regardless of their aptitude for the work or any personal preferences of the persons doing the selecting. It is scenarios such as this that can cause people to say that law and justice are not the same thing.

Thus, quite apart from mistrials and miscarriages of justice, a particular rule can be unjust even when applied fairly. Procedural justice must therefore be distinguished from *substantive justice*, i.e. what people actually receive under the rules. For example, English law permits the dismissal of two or more employees when only one has committed an offence but the employer cannot decide which one has done it. Here, no matter how scrupulous the employer is in trying to determine the guilty party, and whatever other considerations might justify the rule permitting collective dismissal, the fact that the rule permits the innocent to be punished along with the guilty is a clear breach of substantive justice.

RETRIBUTIVE JUSTICE

The other three forms of justice which we shall now consider are all forms of substantive justice. The one that is breached in the collective dismissal example is retributive justice. This involves punishment for wrong-doing. It concerns what punishment is appropriate for what offence and how to maintain a correct balance between severity and leniency; in short, requiring the punishment to fit the crime. Retributive injustice occurs when a punishment is too severe or too lenient for the offence, such as an employee being instantly dismissed for some minor misconduct, or a company director being awarded a token prison sentence for a multi-million pound fraud.

Before questions of appropriate punishment arise, one must be guilty as charged. A precondition for retribution is the committing of the relevant offence: that is why collective dismissal for an offence committed by one person is a breach of retributive justice, whatever else might be said in its favour.

REMEDIAL JUSTICE

Our third type of justice is remedial justice (sometimes also called 'rectificatory' or 'compensatory' justice). Remedial justice might be regarded as the converse of retributive justice. It deals with wrong-doing with respect to the victim, rather than, as with retributive justice, the perpetrator. It involves putting things right, making amends, restoring what was unfairly lost, or at least providing an equivalent. In law, it entails awarding damages, costs or criminal compensation.

Remedial injustice exists when people are inadequately compensated or overcompensated. Many would say that this occurs in the United Kingdom when relatively small sums are paid out for serious or fatal industrial injuries, compared with the huge sums sometimes paid out as exemplary damages in libel cases.

DISTRIBUTIVE JUSTICE

With this fourth and final form of justice there is no necessary connection with wrong-doing. It concerns the way in which benefits and burdens are to be shared out among people. Its aim is the morally correct division of things such as wealth, power, property, obligations and so on, whether between pairs of individuals, within groups of people, between groups, within whole societies (then called 'social justice'), or even between societies (as in the North–South divide between rich industrialized countries and poor Third World countries).

It would be wrong to think of the four forms of justice as discrete: they clearly overlap. For example, the retributive principle that someone must be guilty of an offence in order to be punished is also a procedural principle: it too has to do with how rules are applied. Likewise, the notion of exemplary damages combines retributive and remedial elements in that they are awarded to punish the perpetrator as well to compensate the victim. Clearly, too, any award of damages is distributory—as a transfer from perpetrator to victim it is a sharing out of benefits and burdens.

JUSTICE AND EQUALITY

What people deserve or have a right to roughly divides into two obvious categories. There are things to which everyone is entitled, and those to which only some are. With the first there is universal eligibility; with the second, eligibility depends on meeting certain qualifying conditions.

Generally speaking, matters of procedural justice fall into the first category.

The whole point of fair and consistent application of rules is that everyone is treated according to the rules without arbitrary exceptions being made. Universal eligibility is therefore built into the very notion of procedural justice: we are all entitled to it. No special virtue is demanded; we accept that everyone, even the most notorious villain, deserves a proper hearing and has a right to a fair trial. This is because in a court of law or at a disciplinary hearing, the prime objective is to establish whether people really are as villainous as we might suppose.

With retributive and remedial justice, we find ourselves in our second category (benefits or impositions to which only certain people or groups have a right). The issues of retribution or remedy only arise if someone has been guilty of wrong-doing or has suffered harm as a result of someone else's wrong-doing. Consequently, both are very much forms of justice where dispensing is done on the basis of meeting specific qualifying conditions.

Distributive justice presents a more varied picture. Where it encompasses human rights and their corresponding duties, it is a matter of universal eligibility. As we saw in Chapter 2, a defining feature of human rights is that they are possessed simply by virtue of being human. Therefore, they are possessed equally: everyone has the same rights to life and fundamental freedoms, with no one having more or less of a right to them than anyone else. As the Universal Declaration of Human Rights (1948) puts it, 'All human beings are born free and equal in dignity and rights.'[1]

We have to admit some qualifications to this. It is accepted, for instance, that children and mentally impaired people can lack the capacity to exercise certain freedoms or assume certain duties. We accept, too, that rights can be justifiably taken away from someone who has failed to respect the rights of others. Imprisonment for theft, for example, takes away the right to liberty. Sometimes particular social roles can make the duty to protect rights particularly onerous: a manager, for example, might have very specific duties relating to the right to life because of responsibilities for the health and safety of staff. Also, some rights can only be exercised within particular forms of association. For example, although the right to vote is very properly seen as a universal human right, it very obviously requires citizenship of some specific national state in order to be realized. However, neither this nor any other qualification which might be listed can alter the basic commitment to equality in the distribution of human rights. This equality lies in the fact that their defining feature is their common and equal possession by all humankind. A presumption of equality is therefore the necessary starting point to any distribution of human rights. The most that can be allowed is that there are partial exceptions or practical limitations to an otherwise fundamental rule.

Where any such general presumption of equality becomes questionable is in the sharing out of material resources, principally wealth, income and property. Here we find a broad division of opinion between egalitarians and anti-egalitarians. The debate centres around three interrelated issues: (i) the relationship between equality and efficiency; (ii) the nature and extent of any qualifying conditions for receiving a share in material benefits; and (iii) the relationship between equality and liberty.

The 'efficiency' argument is conducted on essentially utilitarian lines. We value efficiency to the extent that it maximizes human welfare through improvements in the quantity and quality of the goods and services available to us. Anti-egalitarians might claim that for maximum efficiency there have to be financial incentives in the form of unequal rewards; human nature being what it is, people might easily become complacent or unmotivated if there were no inducements to achieve more than the bare minimum that is required.

All but the most uncompromising egalitarians would accept the broad outline of this argument and would agree that a degree of financial inequality is a price worth paying for productive efficiency. Where they part company with anti-egalitarians is on how much inequality they are prepared to accept. They would want to keep it down to the absolute minimum. In assessing that minimum, they would want to take into account the disadvantages ('disutilities') associated with inequality. It can depress and demotivate those who, perhaps through no fault of their own, must lose out in any unequal distribution. Also, the egalitarians might claim, these things are not just bad in themselves, but harmful to the unity and sense of collective purpose that seem so essential to the efficient working of organizations and of society in general. This means that any gains in efficiency from a system of unequal rewards must be offset against efficiency losses from the resultant disunity. Thus, if efficiency is to be maximized, inequality must exist only to the extent that it interferes as little as possible with organizational and social harmony.

Just how high must incentives go to maximize efficiency? Egalitarians will claim that quite narrow bands might well suffice. They will point to the fact that in the lower levels of organizations, quite fine gradations seem to provide enough of an incentive. That they suddenly become enormously large gradations at the very top would seem to indicate that executives are taking advantage of a lack of accountability by effectively fixing their own pay (see Chapter 4), rather than a need for very high incentives to attract them to their jobs. In the case of privatized utilities in the United Kingdom, top managers showed a readiness to accept their post before their salaries were increased to astronomical proportions—telling evidence against the use of an 'incentives' argument here.

Moreover, any utilitarian calculation about salaries must allow for diminishing marginal utility. In other words, the more people have of something, the less utility they derive from it. Food, for example, has more utility for a starving person than a well-fed one. On this basis, provided that efficiency is sufficiently catered for, material goods should be shared out as evenly as possible for utility to be maximized.

In relation to the second focus of the debate—the issue of 'qualifying conditions'—egalitarians stress the claims of *need* while anti-egalitarians stress the claims of *merit*. Need is an egalitarian concept because it is about relieving deficiencies. If people are poor, sick or otherwise deprived, they have a need for some form of help. However, this does not mean that they are entitled to more than other people, it is simply that the quality of their lives must be brought up to some acceptable minimum or agreed average. This applies not just to their general standard of living but also to their opportunities in life, their chances to succeed and fulfil themselves through education or work.

Here egalitarians can use the efficiency argument to their advantage. They can claim that only if there is fully equal opportunity for everyone will all the available talent be used, and hence efficiency maximized . They can also point out that inequality stemming from inherited wealth may be a barrier to maximizing efficiency, since it entrenches people in privileged positions regardless of their talents. Some people may, for example, end up running businesses simply as a result of inheritance or family influence, not because they are the best people for the job.

Merit is an anti-egalitarian concept because its allows that some people can deserve a bigger share of material rewards than others. It is the converse of need, being based on (positive) contribution rather than (negative) deficiency. If some people merit more than others, it is because they contribute more—they make more effort, take on more responsibility, demonstrate superior ability and so on. Consequently, the anti-egalitarian will assert that they deserve more. On top of this, by rewarding these qualities we will generally be encouraging greater efficiency: by and large, the harder people work, and the better they are at their work, the more efficient they will be.

Again, the usual egalitarian response is not to reject the argument but to question how far the resultant inequality needs to go. Just how much difference is there in effort, responsibility or ability among different people within the same organization? Effort is fairly widespread at all levels of society. One can put great effort into fairly menial tasks. Much the same is true of responsibility. A train driver, for example, is responsible for the safety of hundreds of people. Ability certainly does vary considerably, but for the most part is likely to be a matter of marginal difference. Even when there is truly outstanding talent, it is not at all clear why, though such people might merit more than the merely marginally talented, they should merit so much more.

In short, there is no obvious way of deciding just how much more the outstandingly talented truly merit. It could be suggested that the outcome should be left to market forces, and that whatever someone earns is what they merit. However, not even the most fervent supporter of market forces supposes that they correlate with just deserts in any systematic way. Market forces are too much a matter of luck and circumstance—being in the right place at the right time. They may even reward the ruthless and unscrupulous, such as Robert Maxwell, or bring rewards for morally dubious activities such as pornography. Finally, the egalitarian can again point out that the criterion of merit is one which excludes inequality based on inherited wealth: clearly, that is unmerited.

With the third area of dispute—the relationship between equality and liberty—anti-egalitarians have an opportunity to argue for unlimited economic inequality. In a nutshell, their argument is that if left at liberty to conduct their economic exchanges within a market framework, people will inevitably end up with differing accumulations of material goods. Thus liberty inevitably leads to inequality. The prevention of inequality means interfering with the freedom to engage in market transactions—an erosion of personal liberty. As liberty is a fundamental right, attempts to impose equality are thus seen as violations of human rights and therefore judged to be morally wrong. If, as some anti-egalitarians argue, liberty is an inviolable right, then no matter what degree of inequality results, no matter how wide the gap between rich and poor, it will still be morally wrong to intervene.

This anti-egalitarian argument is open to attack on several fronts. As an exclusively rights-based argument, it ignores considerations of utility; and, as we have already argued, rights are only one factor impinging on ethical matters. However, it seems hardly credible that there can be a right to liberty which is so inviolable that no gap between rich and poor, however large, warrants interference with it. In any case, rights have to be ranked in order of importance. A right to a minimum standard of living, for example, surely outranks liberty. Arguably, there is even an overriding right to as equal a share of material goods as is consistent with optimum efficiency and productivity.

The debate continues. In the meantime we can note that with egalitarianism versus anti-egalitarianism we have a central dividing line not only between theories of justice, but also between political parties and even people's whole moral attitude to social and organizational problems. Certainly it tends to be the greatest dividing line in fundamental issues of business ethics. There the choice is very often between a broadly egalitarian and interventionist approach as opposed to a broadly anti-egalitarian and free market one.

JUSTICE AND ECONOMIC SYSTEMS

What fundamentally determines the distribution of benefits and burdens within a society is the economic system. For example, an agrarian feudal system has a very different way of distribution from an industrialized capitalist system. Accordingly, questions of social justice—justice between groups in society—are to a large extent synonymous with questions of the distributive justice of different economic systems.

In the context of modern industrialized societies, the choice of economic systems is sometimes presented as lying on a continuum from *laissez-faire* capitalism at one extreme to Soviet-style communism at the other. (Economics textbooks are particularly fond of presenting the choice in this way.) This presents the options as a choice between a combination of private ownership and unrestricted market forces at one end, or an opposing combination of state ownership and central planning at the other. It is allowed that gradations are possible; in fact, it is often insisted that no actual society can perfectly represent the two extremes. Most pertinently, given the collapse of Soviet-style communism, a modern capitalist economy is usually not devoid of a certain element of central direction at the macro-economic level or of an often very large public sector.

Even so, the continuum model is still perhaps too restrictive. It presents the choices as a package deal between private ownership *and* free markets or state ownership *and* planning. This does not allow for a range of more complex options. There can be private ownership combined with central planning, as in wartime Britain. There can be state ownership with markets, as was attempted—not very successfully—in the former Yugoslavia. In addition, there is often the assumption that 'private ownership' has to mean the classic capitalist situation of businesses being run for the benefit of owners as distinct from employees or customers. But this (as we noted in Chapter 1) is not necessarily so. Businesses can be owned by the people working within them, as in worker co-operatives or employee-owned firms in general. They can be run for the benefit of customers, as in consumer co-operatives or mutual corporations such as building societies and some insurance companies.

There are therefore more options for running an economy than are dreamt of in a crude continuum model. The significance of this for an examination of social justice is that there are many more options for reaching a desired moral end than that model supposes. In particular, there is no longer the implication that egalitarians are stuck with the undeniably inefficient combination of state ownership and central planning. That particular combination certainly had egalitarian aspirations—although how egalitarian it was in practice is quite another matter. The idea was that by vesting ownership in the state everyone had an equal share in ownership. By instituting central planning it was hoped that production would be directed at meeting the needs of society, rather than simply to generate profits for the few. (Need is, as we saw, an egalitarian criterion of distribution.)

However, only the most blinkered adherent to the continuum model would suppose this combination (state ownership and central planning) to be the only way of attempting to reach egalitarian ends. Egalitarians could tolerate private ownership and markets but use taxation to redistribute wealth more evenly—the Scandinavian option. Alternatively, they might just try to ensure that the private ownership is more evenly spread—the wider share ownership option. Another way might be to have markets and private ownership but spread the wealth by enabling the vast numbers of employees to do the owning. Alternatively, businesses could be organized on a mutual basis so that profits benefit consumers (i.e. the whole of society) rather than a relatively select band of owners.

None of these options is of course exclusive: they can be used in any combination. Nor need the aim be anything like that total equality towards which Soviet communism was allegedly directing itself. The society's aim might simply be to reduce the scope of the inequalities so that extremes of relative wealth and poverty are avoided. It might even be simply to avoid anything resembling absolute poverty at the bottom but leaving people to be as rich as the market allows at the top. Conversely, the imposition of a wage ceiling (at one time suggested by the British Labour Party's left wing) would flatten out inequalities at the very top, but allow significant variations in wealth below.

CATHOLIC SOCIAL THOUGHT

One important contribution to debates about social justice, which seeks to avoid extremes of inequality, is Catholic social thought. Although relatively little discussed—at least in most of the English-speaking world—it is an undoubted influence on one of the world's most successful economies: Germany. Partly as a consequence of German economic strength it is also having some impact on the European Union. The influence shows itself in the area of what is called 'social' legislation. This deals with workers' rights—matters involving pay and working conditions as well as, most controversially, workers having the right to consultation, and even to participation in management decisions. The latter is the most distinctive feature of the German system, and it is also the aspect to which the present UK government is most opposed. Perhaps more than anything else, it prompted that government's opt-out of the provisions of the Social Chapter of the Maastricht Treaty. This, in keeping with the general thrust of EU social legislation, promised a strengthening or workers' rights, including rights to consultation and participation.

What Catholic social thought offers is a middle way between the supposedly excessive individualism of *laissez-faire* capitalism—as represented by political liberalism—and the excessive collectivism of socialism in general and Marxist communism in particular. The most celebrated Roman Catholic statement concerning modern social issues was Pope Leo XIII's encyclical *Rerum Novarum* (15 May 1891). The encyclical was critical of both types of economic system: collectivism, Leo asserted, denied the right to private property; individualism could militate against the common good, by creating gross inequalities between rich and poor.

While the encyclical deplored state control over the individual and the workplace, society was not an extraneous addition to the individual. Ever since the time of creation, human beings have lived in social groups, have inherited the legacy of previous generations, and will leave an inheritance to subsequent generations. Society is a requirement of human nature, offering opportunities for service to others, and demanding loyalty and respect for the authority that governs it. Civil authorities serve to ensure the common good: respect for persons, social wellbeing and peace. Associations of individuals, and human institutions within society are to be encouraged—hence Roman Catholic thought is not opposed to trade unions. Roman Catholicism asserts a *principle of subsidiarity*: the state devolves authority to such organizations, many of which are run independently of the state. One such organization is a business company.

Private ownership is therefore lawful. Human beings have a right to ownership of possessions, and such possessions may legitimately exceed those consumable—and hence impermanent—goods which are needed for survival. Humans can possess stable things like houses, furniture and indeed businesses.

With business, of course, comes the opportunity for profit. Again, Roman Catholic thought has no inherent objection to making profits. Pope John Paul II later spoke of the 'legitimate role of profit as an indication that a business is functioning well',[2] and affirmed that a free market is the best method of providing a meeting place for resources and needs. (This papal encyclical was called *Centesimus Annua*—'The Hundredth Year'—commemorating the centenary of Leo XIII's *Rerum Novarum*.)

The fact that businesses tend to create a distinction between owners and workers, with the potential inequalities that this creates, is accepted. Unlike collectivism, Catholicism does not aim at strict equality among individuals, and indeed recognizes that there exists a 'natural inequality' among human beings, who differ from one another in their capacities, skills, state of health, strength and hence fortune. Inequality is not seen as an intrinsic evil; on the contrary, differences belong to God's plan. Differences can have positive advantages too, by encouraging generosity, sharing and mutual enrichment. (We shall leave readers to evaluate this last argument.)

However, there can be 'excessive economic and social disparity'. As the *Catechism of the Catholic Church* puts it:

> Their equal dignity as persons demands that we strive for fairer and more humane conditions. Excessive economic and social disparity between individuals and peoples of the one human race is a source of scandal and militates against social justice, equity, human dignity, as well as social and international peace.[3]

The acceptance of inequalities within a divine plan entails that employers and workers are not inherently hostile, so long as both parties recognize their mutual obligations. In contrast with *laissez-faire* individualism, neither party ideally aims to secure the maximum wealth for oneself; but, unlike the collectivist system, there is no desire to abolish the distinction between owners and workers. The model of the business company that arises from the Roman Catholic model is that of mutual *co-operation* between owner and worker, between management and trade unions: the two parties regard themselves as social partners, with mutual obligations. (The influence on EU social policy is clear.)

The employer has a right to expect the worker to be honest, to work according to one's contract, not to damage property, or to cause injury to the employer. Although workers are entitled to belong to trade unions, their right of assembly may not include violence or riotous behaviour: workers are to 'shun evil principled agitators'.

Employees, likewise, have their rights. Since humans are made in God's image, they have a right to be respected. As Leo XIII reminded the Church, workers have souls, and hence the employer must not merely exploit their physical bodies for their strength. Workers must be allowed sufficient time away from work to fulfil their religious obligations, and employers have a duty to guard workers from sin. (Although these requirements may sound quaint over a century later, we do of course recognize the need for sufficient recreation, and the undesirability of employers putting temptation in workers' way.) However, the employer's prime duty is to give the worker what is just.

It might be observed that giving workers what is just is easier said than done, and indeed Leo XIII himself recognized that there was no simple principle which could be implemented which might evaluate the worth of someone's work. *Rerum Novarum*, however, enumerates a number of principles which might profitably be taken into account in assessing what is just remuneration for a job.

First, a wage must be the result of free consent between the two parties involved. A wage which is the outcome of threats on the part of either party, or which is agreed merely because one party is in desperate need, is unjust. An agreed wage constitutes a contract (even if the contract is merely verbal), and such agreements must be honoured. Once a wage has been agreed, it is ethically unacceptable for the employer to pay less, even if he or she claims to be unable to afford more. Of course, at the time of entering into the contract, the wage must be affordable by the employer; there is simply no point in agreeing a sum which one is unable to pay. (The criterion of affordability takes credence from modern 'parity' arguments. When workers seek a wage increase on the grounds that employees doing similar work elsewhere are earning more, it is sometimes a hard economic reality that some firms are simply in a better position than others to pay generous wages.)

Second, a wage must entitle the worker to life's basic necessities—at least enough 'to support a frugal and well behaved wage earner'. (Employers are not obliged to subsidize a prodigal lifestyle on the part of their workforce!) Such basic necessities must include adequate provision for one's wife and family: a working mother, Leo asserted, was a disgrace—'a most wicked abuse . . . to be abolished at all costs'. (Most Western business people would no doubt wish to reappraise this aspect of Catholic social teaching today, but it must be remembered that in 1891 the housewife lacked the benefits of modern technological assistance and childcare facilities.) Employers who held down wages solely for their own private financial advancement were in breach of Catholic law.

When determining what was a fair rate for a job, the employer should also consider the price at which the goods or services were being sold, and the employee should receive a due proportion. This criterion ensured that there were not undue differentials between a company owner and a worker, and that large inequalities were prevented.

In general, Catholic social teaching has endeavoured to reduce the gap between owner and worker. Workers should in fact aspire to become owners, and this should be reflected in their pay. They should receive enough not merely to cater for their basic subsistence, but to enable them to save and invest. If workers can acquire a financial interest in the firm that employs them, then they will have a greater incentive to work harder, and greater wealth and equality will result. Leo, however, rejected the collectivist view that workers have rights to all profits and products of their labour. Profit sharing, likewise, is not an obligation under Roman Catholic canon law.

Rerum Novarum stipulates that the good of a country as a whole must be taken into account in wage determination. If wages are too high, the price can be unemployment; if they are too low, human misery results, with its accompanying temptations, even crimes. Finally, the state has an obligation not to erode the just wage by means of excessive taxation. Although governments need to raise revenue, overburdening citizens with high taxation constitutes undue state intrusion on individuals, who should as far as possible be permitted to decide how to spend the products of their labour.

CAPITALISM AND PROTESTANTISM

The Protestant Reformation had tremendous import for business ethics, and indeed ethics more widely. It would be a mistake to think of the Reformation exclusively as a set of liturgical and theological reforms. When Martin Luther (1483–1546) felt obliged to deny that the Pope of Rome had supreme authority, he paved the way for jettisoning the whole system of canon law, which the Roman Catholic Church had developed over the centuries. (The word 'canon' means 'a standard' or 'a measure', and Roman Catholic canon law therefore serves as a measure by which the believer might compare his or her own behaviour. This system of 'law' continues, in theory at least, to be binding on those who subscribe to Roman Catholicism.) No more could supporters of the Reformation feel constrained by doctrines of the 'just wage' and the 'just price'—matters on which the Church had pronounced.

It has been commented, by the sociologist Max Weber (1864–1920) among others, that there was an important connection between the rise of Protestantism and the spirit of capitalism. The Reformers themselves did not actively promote the 'spirit of capitalism', Weber argued, but they provided a number of implicit incentives in this direction.

Weber's suggestion might seem initially implausible to those who are well acquainted with the Christian faith. After all, it might be argued, did not Jesus of Nazareth himself warn against accumulating personal wealth. The rich young ruler who asked Jesus what he must do to 'inherit eternal life' was told that he should give away all his belongings to the poor and that it was easier for a camel to go through a needle's eye than for a rich person to enter the kingdom of God.[4] A contemporary Protestant might also insist that salvation does not depend on one's works, but on divine grace.[5] Indeed, one of the principal doctrines which was revived by the Reformers—especially John Calvin (1509–1564)—was the doctrine of *predestination*. The doctrine of predestination acknowledges the fact that God is omniscient (all-knowing), and therefore at the very moment of creation must have been able to predict the course of human events and, particularly, which individuals would gain salvation and which would not. Being omnipotent (all-powerful), God had the power to bring about whatever outcome of natural and human events he considered to be best; consequently, God must have actively willed that certain individuals should be the beneficiaries of his grace ('the elect') and that certain others should not ('the damned'). If it seems unfair that God should make an apparently arbitrary choice between the 'elect' and the 'damned', preventing them from altering his plan by doing right deeds, Calvin taught that God has his reasons for doing so, although, being human, we do not know what these are.

This rather abstruse piece of theology may at first sight seem quite unconnected with business studies. Yet there is a very important connection as certain Protestants in the sixteenth and seventeenth centuries held that, although men and women could do nothing to alter God's choice, if they were fortunate, they might find certain reassuring signs that they had indeed been elected as citizens of God's kingdom. Certain Christians—known as the Puritans—believed that material prosperity was a sign of God's favour. Material prosperity, they believed, could be gained through work, and accordingly the Puritans held a very high regard for hard work and its resulting fruits of material prosperity.

There is a further connection between Protestantism and what has become known as the 'work ethic'. The Protestant Reformation was, among other things, an attempt to get back to the Bible as the 'supreme rule of faith and life'. What, then, had the Bible to say about work? To the Puritans in particular, the Bible indicated that God worked unceasingly: he 'neither slumbers nor sleeps',[6] and the whole creation was a result of six days of God's work.[7] However, the creation story ends with God viewing the results of his work and then taking the seventh (sabbath) day as a day of rest. The Puritans inferred from this that six days of the week should be devoted to hard work, with the minimum time for sleep and recreation, and strict cessation of work on Sunday (the Christian sabbath). As the famous Puritan Richard Baxter (1615–1691) said:

> Keep up a high esteem of time and be every day more careful that you lose none of your time, than you are that you lose none of your gold and silver. And if vain recreation, dressings, feastings, idle talk, unprofitable company, or sleep, be any of them temptations to rob you of any of your time, accordingly heighten your watchfulness.[8]

Statements such as these were not merely homilies; they contained implicit critiques of Roman Catholicism. St Thomas Aquinas (1225–1274), for example, who is still regarded as Catholicism's most eminent theologian, had equated works with 'prayer and choral singing'—a definition which was too 'churchy' and other-worldly for the likes of Baxter. Aquinas had also claimed that certain people could legitimately be exempt from earning incomes through work, such those who had private incomes (notably the 'landed gentry') and those in contemplative orders. For Baxter and the Puritans, however, *all* should be liable for work: relaxation was 'sloth', and activity 'increases God's glory'.

Baxter's teachings may seem to have affinities with Benjamin Franklin's maxim, 'Time is money.' But the Puritans, of course, did not extol the virtues of work merely for utilitarian reasons. Work was to be engaged in because it was God's will, and hence by working one could become more 'god-like'. The Puritans' way of thinking about work had important implications, however, for the development of capitalism. A system which encouraged its followers to work but not to spend entailed that people saved their money, which thereby became available as investment. This in turn enabled the infrastructure of capitalism to be built up.

The Puritans, then, extolled the virtues of work as a god-like activity, but their 'work ethic' extended to more than the desirability of labour for all and a hostility to those who did not earn a wage. Any kind of labour which earned a wage was encouraged, even if it involved repetitive mechanical tasks—the Puritans had no concept of 'job satisfaction'. Low wages and exploitation were condoned on the grounds that work was decreed by God; indeed Luther had taught the importance of 'keeping to one's station', and the doctrine of predestination tended to imply that one's lot in life was willed by God in any case. As a later Protestant writer put it in a verse of the well-known hymn:

> The rich man in his castle,
>   The poor man at his gate,
> God made them, high or lowly,
>   And order'd their estate.[9]

There was certainly no concept of a 'just wage', and indeed the Reformers had abandoned the system of religious ethics which entailed such concepts.

ADAM SMITH AND THE 'INVISIBLE HAND'

The Protestant Reformation allowed a further development in wage and price determination. With no system of canon law to determine the price of goods and services, the moral vacuum created by Protestantism meant that prices and wages were determined by market forces rather than by religious or moral considerations. The notion that market forces should freely determine the outcome of economic matters is known as *laissez-faire*, a phrase which literally means 'leave to do', and might be paraphrased in the popular maxim, 'Leave well alone.'

The notion of the 'price mechanism' was developed by the eighteenth-century economist Adam Smith (1723–1790). Smith was faced with the problem of how wages and prices were, as matter of fact (not as a matter of ethics), determined within an economic system which did not impose legal or ethical controls on the prices of goods and services. Theoretically, it seems that the aims of the vendor and the purchaser are poles apart. The farmer who wants to sell potatoes wants to obtain the highest possible price; the housekeeper who wants to purchase them, on the other hand, wants to pay the lowest possible amount. How, then, do the two manage to meet? For Smith, the answer lay in the laws of supply and demand. If the farmer sees that there are other suppliers competing to sell, he or she will recognize that a slightly reduced price will facilitate the sale; equally, if the housekeeper sees that there are others who are trying to purchase potatoes, he or she will recognize that a better chance of securing potatoes is gained if he or she is prepared to pay a little more than those who are potentially competing for the purchase. In the face of competition, the vendor thus—in theory at least—seeks to meet demand at the lowest possible prices; the purchaser, likewise, will have to bid the highest price that will fend off competition for the purchase. The respective self-interest of buyers and sellers is thus reconciled by an 'invisible hand': competition among vendors and among buyers moves prices away from the prices at which the buyer and seller would ideally like to buy and sell. State intervention is not needed to ensure that buyers and sellers find mutually agreeable prices: a commodity's price or a worker's wages are simply what the market will bear. The price mechanism, then, determines the price at which goods and services get bought and sold, and enlightened self-interest serves the common good by recognizing that markets are (in the main) competitive, and that in the face of competition one must meet demand at the lowest possible, rather than the highest possible prices.

It should be mentioned that the laws of supply and demand, which Smith described, present a theoretical model of the price mechanism, and only apply fully to 'perfect markets'. Markets may be 'distorted' for many different reasons:

consumers may not know that there is a cheaper product in the adjacent shop; they may prefer the service in the more expensive shop; or indeed they may decide that the dearer product is preferable because it is a more 'ethical' purchase. (It may be 'greener', or the manufacturers may have a better track record on trade unions or animal testing.) It is interesting that in a *laissez-faire* system, ethical considerations become 'market imperfections'!

FREEDOM OR EQUALITY?

In a *laissez-faire* system it is inevitable that some entrepreneurs will fare better than others, and that inequalities will be the inevitable result of determining prices and wages by means of Adam Smith's 'invisible hand'—the price mechanism. Does this then mean that a *laissez-faire* system should be rated ethically inferior to, say, a state-controlled economy or a system where there is significant state intervention to fix the prices of goods and wages, or at least to prevent significant increase in prices or decreases in wages (e.g. by means of some kind of prices and incomes policy)?

Not necessarily, proponents of *laissez-faire* would argue. Justice can be defined as what the market bestows. Allowing markets to operate freely allows full scope for the liberty of those who engage in business, enabling them to buy and sell, to employ and be employed without undue state interference. For proponents of *laissez-faire*, liberty is supremely important, and, they would argue, having a free market is the best way to achieve this. Freedom is thus more important than greater equality of wealth distribution.

SOME CONCLUDING COMMENTS ON THE JUST WAGE

We have considered two views on wage determination that stand in stark contrast to each other. *Rerum Novarum*, being a papal pronouncement, tends to sound authoritative—which is what is intended, of course—rather than that its ideas are matters that can be debated. The Protestant position, which gave rise to the doctrine of *laissez-faire*, seems to suggest that there is nothing to be discussed in the first place: market forces can and should decide what people earn, irrespective of any other considerations we may wish to bring to bear on questions of wages.

Part of the problem, however, with allowing market forces solely to determine wages is that it can allow exploitation. During the system of apartheid in South Africa, it transpired that white employers were paying black miners a mere £2 per week. When interviewed on television, the employers defended their policy on the grounds that the workers continued to present themselves for work: market forces, apparently, were such that the miners could not better their employers' deal by shopping around for more lucrative employment, and their employers were evidently getting an adequate supply of labour at this price. This argument, however, was unpersuasive to the many critics of apartheid. At best, arguments

Case study

The Social Chapter—too generous to workers?

When the Maastricht Treaty on European Union was signed in 1992, the United Kingdom reinforced its image as the maverick nation who wanted to 'go it alone' on important aspects of EC policy. The British government was not prepared to commit itself to the final stage of economic and monetary union, unless a separate decision to do so was taken by a future British parliament. Britain insisted on retaining its power to determine its own monetary policy. In the areas in which the United Kingdom has opted out, its MEPs will be barred from voting.

One highly controversial section of the Treaty from which the United Kingdom opted out was the much discussed Social Chapter. The present Conservative government has found itself unable to sign it, although the Labour party has stated that, on gaining office, they would be willing to sign.

On the surface, the policies defined within this part of the Maastricht Treaty may seem innocuous. The 'protocol on social policy' (to give it its official title) commits its signatories to improving workers' health, safety and working conditions, to ensuring sexual equality in the workplace, and the rights of 'third country' workers residing in the European Union.

More problematic for British employers, however, is the Social Chapter's commitment to the 'protection of workers where their employment contract is terminated'.[10] Since an employee on a temporary contract automatically becomes permanent after two years under current British legislation, it has become a practice for certain employers to lay off workers after their term has run for around 23 months.

A further British reservation about the Social Chapter concerns the rights of worker consultation, which are set out in the protocol, e.g. 'representation and collective defence of the interests of worker and employers, including co-determination'.[11] Additionally, the European Commission would have 'the task of promoting the consultation of management and labour at Community level', requiring that any future proposals in the Social Policy field would entail consultation of management and labour on the Commission's part. Such consultation, where appropriate, could lead to legally binding agreements.

Perhaps the most controversial issue surrounding the Social Chapter has been the proposal that there should be a minimum wage for all workers. The British Labour Party is sympathetic to the idea of a minimum wage as a means of avoiding worker exploitation, although at the time of writing Labour will not commit itself to a definite figure. Opponents of the minimum wage argue, however, that if employers are obliged to pay at least £4.15 an hour (a figure often quoted in this connection), they will be obliged to reduce the size of their labour force, or even go out of business altogether.

The Treaty shows clear influence of Catholic social thought, being moderately egalitarian, and supportive of interventionist measures to achieve greater levels of equality. The emphasis on free markets, *laissez-faire* and anti-egalitarianism on the part of British Conservatives stands in stark opposition to such policies—hence their reluctance to endorse the Social Chapter.

based on market forces might determine what employers can afford and what workers will accept; further considerations are needed to determine whether a wage is *just*.

The idea of a Just Wage raises all the problems of *distributive justice* dealt with earlier. The basic issue of how a finite amount of a commodity (money) should be distributed among workers, either nationally or within a company. Assuming that there are good reasons for different workers deserving different rewards for their labours, then we can expect, and indeed justify, differences in levels of income—the only question is how far they should go.

What might such reasons be? Qualifications, skill and experience are often cited as qualifying conditions for extra remuneration. Working conditions form a further set of grounds for defending inequalities between workers. Jobs that are unpleasant, dangerous or involve unsociable hours might be agreed to deserve more than jobs which do not have such characteristics. This is partly to redress a balance: if someone has an unpleasant job, then the most obvious form of compensation is enhanced remuneration. There is a further consideration, namely that in order to attract people to jobs with negative features, some incentive needs to be offered—otherwise everyone would be attracted to the more pleasant ones. Likewise, jobs that carry a high degree of responsibility might deserve high pay.

There are also considerations of utility. Arguably, workers and job seekers need to be encouraged to optimize their abilities, and to have incentives to aspire to more demanding ones. Again, cash incentives are an obvious way of doing this.

Some writers have emphasized the importance of acknowledging the more egalitarian concept of need. Marx and Engels are particularly renowned for the *Communist Manifesto*'s famous dictum, 'to each according to his [or her] need'.[12] The question of *needs* is, however, fraught with problems. There are biological needs (what someone requires to keep physically alive); basic needs (what someone requires to achieve a minimally acceptable standard of living, such as a home and basic furniture); occupational needs (the tools of the trade that a worker needs to carry out his or her employment); and 'social necessities' (items such as a radio, and, some would say, a telephone and even a television). Beyond these, one might say, anything else is a *want*.

Different people may of course have different needs as a result of past actions. A couple with a large family will clearly need more to support their children. Gamblers may say that they 'need the money' to pay off their debts. Aspirants to a lavish lifestyle may claim to need extra money for high mortgage payments or the hire purchase of a BMW.

It could be invidious for employers to assess the needs of workers when determining what they should be paid—though this is done, for instance, in Japan. Also, it might be counterproductive, since employers would be less keen to employ the needy if they were obliged to pay them more. The issue of needs is therefore perhaps best dealt with by a country's taxation and social security systems rather than directly by employers. When organized in this way, people are on a more equal footing when they apply for jobs, and government policies can determine which particular needs of citizens ought to be met, and which ignored. A taxation system also has the obvious effect of addressing the issue of accumulated wealth: as people have different levels of consumption, and as some citizens inherit wealth from others, a government can decide whether to allow such inequalities to remain, or whether a greater levelling of wealth is desirable. Whether the state should close or widen the wealth gap, however, is something that will continue to divide the political left and the political right, the egalitarian and the anti-egalitarian.

In practical terms, people's wealth patterns are related to the types of political-economic system we identified at the beginning of this chapter. Free markets will generate inequalities, since one's remuneration will be dictated by what market forces will bear. A state-controlled system is in a better position to impose nation-wide wage policies, which traditionally have been slanted in favour of much greater equality. (This need not necessarily be so, of course: a state-controlled economy could decide on sharply rising echelons of wealth, if it so wished.) Particular circumstances will also, in practice, determine wages. We have already noted that a firm can only pay its workforce what it can afford, and wages can also be determined by the degree of unionization enjoyed by the workforce. Where workers are not unionized, wages are more easily kept down. At the other end of the scale, where executives are not accountable to shareholders, then there exists the much criticized opportunity for them to set themselves astronomically high 'fat cat' salaries.

These final points take us on to issues of how firms are structured, and the ways in which managers and staff are accountable for their actions. These are issues which will be dealt with in the next chapter.

DISCUSSION TOPICS

1. Consider the various criteria that might be used for determining a fair wage: hours of work, responsibility, qualifications, experience, special characteristics of the job (e.g. lack of safety, unsociable hours, unpleasantness). In the light of these criteria, what should be the ideal pay differentials between a doctor, a lecturer, an electrician, a miner and any other job you may wish to consider?
2. Why might earners of 'fat cat' salaries 'need incentives'? Consider possible arguments in their favour—not merely against!
3. The key to the executive cloakroom is the legendary prize possession of the ambitious manager. To what extent can these class distinctions and symbols of authority be justified? Consider arguments for and against segregation in common rooms, canteens, cloakrooms. (Students might consider to what extent staff–student segregation exists in their college or university, and what can be said for and against the practice.)
4. What difference is the Maastricht Treaty likely to make to British workers? What additional differences would be introduced if the Social Chapter were accepted? How desirable are such changes, in your view?
5. What elements of the Social Chapter echo Catholic social thought?

NOTES

1. Universal Declaration of Human Rights, Article I.
2. T. I. White, *Business Ethics—A Philosophical Reader*, Macmillan, New York, p. 76.
3. *Catechism of the Catholic Church*, Geoffrey Chapman, London, 1994, para. 1938.
4. Mark 10.17–22.
5. Ephesians 2.9.
6. Psalm 121.4.
7. Genesis 2.2.
8. W. G. Runciman (ed.), *Weber—Selections in Translation*, Cambridge University Press, Cambridge, 1978, p. 141.
9. Cecil Frances Alexander, 'All things bright and beautiful', in *Hymns Ancient and Modern*, Clowes, London, 1904, no. 573.
10. *The Treaty on European Union*, Agreement on Social Policy, Article 2, para. 3.
11. Ibid., Article 2, para. 3.
12. K. Marx and F. Engels, *The Communist Manifesto*, Penguin, Harmondsworth, 1967.

4 *Responsibility and Business*

THE NATURE OF MORAL RESPONSIBILITY

Issues of moral responsibility take two basic forms. The first concerns *duty*. We speak of 'having responsibilities', meaning duties owed to other people, or perhaps organizations. These duties might be the general moral duties that human beings owe to one another (being honest, keeping promises, having concern for their welfare), or the additional 'role-specific duties' that come with particular social roles such as parent, police officer, manager, company director or whatever (see Chapter 2). In either case, whether the duty is general or role specific, we have responsibility in what we might call a 'duty owed' sense. With it, there is an essentially forward-looking perspective. To 'have a responsibility' is to be committed to behaving in certain ways in the future: to fulfil the duty constituting that responsibility. If someone can be relied upon to do so, he or she is commended as a 'responsible person'.

With the second basic form of responsibility, on the other hand, the perspective might be described as backward looking. It is 'being responsible' in the sense of bearing responsibility for things that did or did not happen. This requires, of course, that we somehow brought about the situation in question. Events must in some way be consequences of our previous action or inaction for us to be responsible for them; indeed without some such causal link, there can be no responsibility of this second sort. Accordingly, we have responsibility here in what might be called a 'causal' sense.

Within this causal form of responsibility there is an obvious, but yet very important distinction between being responsible for harmful as opposed to beneficial situations. Responsibility for what is harmful makes us liable for blame and punishment; while responsibility for the beneficial makes us eligible for praise and reward. It is the same specifically causal responsibility which would be traced back in both cases, but it is clearly for very different ends. Where a harmful situation prevails, the process is one of fault finding. We are, in a phrase, 'being held accountable'. We can evade blame and possible punishment only to the extent we can show we are not responsible. In contrast, when beneficence prevails, our usual interest is in maximizing the extent to which we are responsible. The more we can be seen as responsible for the situation, the more we are eligible for praise and perhaps even reward. Holding someone responsible can therefore entail giving credit as opposed to fault finding: people can 'gain due recognition' rather than 'be held accountable'. Accordingly, we can recognize these contrary approaches to causal responsibility by saying that when liability for blame and punishment is at issue, the matter is one of 'accountability'; whereas when eligibility for reward and punishment is at issue, the matter is that of 'due recognition'.

From whichever of the two directions we approach matters of causal responsibility, we eventually have to end up considering questions of moral responsibility in the 'duty owed' sense. This follows for accountability because what makes us morally liable for blame and punishment is not simply that we brought about a harmful situation but also that in doing so we failed to fulfil a duty. Just what duty this might be can vary enormously: it might be general or role-specific. In either case, since we can be blamed and punished for mistakes as well as misdeeds, our obligation may be to display some due level of care or competence as well as to refrain from intentional wrongdoing. Whatever form it takes, a failure of duty must be present for blame and punishment to be applicable. It is not enough that our action or inaction somehow brought about the harmful situation, or that if we had acted differently it could have been avoided. Our action or inaction must also involve a breach of duty—only then can we be held morally accountable for what we did or did not do.

For example, someone might very well be held accountable for failing to summon an ambulance for a colleague after an accident at work, when it was easily within her power to do so. This follows from a general duty which we all have to preserve life. However—excluding the possibility that there are role-specific obligations that might suggest otherwise—the colleague cannot be held responsible for the heavy metal rod that fell on the employee, or the fact that the victim was not wearing a hard hat at the time. Supervisors or managers may well be in a very different position, having duties towards rank-and-file staff that their colleagues do not. If they had failed to indicate the possible danger, or omitted to provide hard hats, then they can be held responsible for the accident occurring in the first place. Either way, it is duties owed that determine accountability: the colleague has the general duty to give assistance; the managers have this general duty, as well as a definite role-specific responsibility (it is a legal requirement, in fact) to make the workplace as safe as possible.

Duty thus sets the parameters within which accountability operates, and this is no less true for matters of 'due recognition'. What gains us recognition depends on what our moral duties are, and how we have responded to them. The difference here is that we are now talking of success rather than failure in carrying out one's duties: we become eligible for praise and reward because we have not only fulfilled our duties but done so in an exemplary fashion, displaying some higher than usual level of care, competence or moral virtue. In the most credit-worthy cases, we may indeed have exceeded what duty strictly demanded, having gone above and beyond its call. In all cases, though, it is only by first specifying duties that we can know whether, and to what extent, someone is worthy of due recognition. Winning orders, for example, is no more than a sales manager's role-specific duty. Winning a particularly big order in the face of fierce competition is quite another matter. Praise will certainly be appropriate, and perhaps a special bonus or even career advancement.

In these respective examples of accountability and due recognition, we can see that moral responsibility in the causal sense depends upon moral responsibility in the 'duty owed' sense, whether the duty is general or role specific. The colleague who fails to summon the ambulance is accountable because she owes to others a general duty of care and respect for human life. The sales manager who clinches the prestigious deal deserves due recognition because she has performed a role-specific duty in an exemplary fashion.

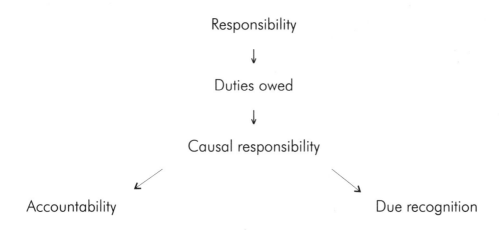

Fig. 4.1 The nature of moral responsibility

The 'duty owed' sense of responsibility is therefore primary. It is only by first deciding what duties were owed that an analysis of causal responsibility will enable us to assess whether and to what extent someone is to be held accountable or receive due recognition (see Fig. 4.1).

ISSUES OF RESPONSIBILITY IN BUSINESS

On the basis of the above analysis, a general account of moral responsibility in business can be given. First and foremost are considerations of duty. What are the duties which people involved in a business owe to each other: staff to managers, managers to staff, directors to shareholders, and so on? More generally, what are the duties which these groups owe to the business as a whole: to the business as an organization which links their separate and possibly conflicting interests? Looking outwards, what are the duties which, as organizations, businesses owe to their customers and suppliers? What, also, of duties to the environment? What of duties to the local communities within which businesses are located? More widely still, what are the duties which business organizations owe to society as a whole—to the national and sometimes transnational communities within which they operate?

SOCIAL RESPONSIBILITY

This last and broadest question about duty—about duties to society as a whole—is the most fundamental in business ethics. An answer would amount to nothing less than an account of what the nature of business activity should be. It would be prescribing the essential character of that activity. This is because duties of any kind are always relative to some wider purpose which they are designed to fulfil. For example, since doctors are duty bound to treat the sick, the wider purpose their duty fulfils is that of the relief of sickness. So too with businesses: to explain their duties in relation to society is to prescribe their function in society. It is to say what purpose or purposes they should fulfil within the workings of society. Moreover, it is clearly the case that, whatever else they might be, businesses are, above everything else, purposeful. They do not just happen—they are consciously created and, however confusedly, are directed towards certain ends. Like tools, they are defined by their function. What they *are* is defined by what they are *for*. Obviously, at the level of any one business, those ends can be many and varied; as many and varied, it might be suggested, as the people directing individual businesses have mind to make them. However, over and above any merely local aim, is the wider consideration of how businesses should fit into the operations of society as a whole. This specifically social role is clearly the more general and important. It sets the moral standard against which the aims of individual businesses are to be judged. It is what, by and large, businesses ought to be doing as opposed to what, in any particular case, they actually are doing. So as duties define purpose, and purpose, in its turn, defines the essential character of business, it follows that to specify the duties which businesses owe to society is to say what the general character of business should be.

The different specifications of what those duties are will give rise to different accounts of what the nature of business should be. Unsurprisingly then, the issue of 'social responsibility' is an area of great controversy within business ethics. There is much at stake. The ultimate ends towards which businesses ought to be directed are being debated. Hence, the debate inevitably has profound implications about how businesses should be constituted and run. Depending on the ends specified, different structures will or will not be appropriate, with the rightness or wrongness of any particular form depending on how well it serves the social role laid down. If, for example, the ultimate aim of businesses is the maximizing of financial returns to their owners, then this will have profound implications for the role of managers, the position of employees, attitudes to customers and so on. Much, therefore, of what might be said about the particular duties which people involved in a business owe to each other, or to the business itself, or the duties a business owes to customers, suppliers, local communities, or to the environment—or whatever—will hinge upon what is decided about the general and overriding social duties of business. An account of those duties will provide a framework within which more particular duties can be assessed. For example, if it were decided that the overriding social aim should be the maximizing of benefits to employees, then this would have very different implications for the duties of managers as compared to an overriding social aim of maximizing financial returns to owners. Indeed, to varying degrees, almost all the duties linking people within businesses and linking businesses to the outside world could come out differently depending on what view was taken about the social responsibilities of businesses. Thus, opposing views on social responsibility are not just disputes about one area of duty among many, but about offering different models of what a business should be.

EXECUTIVE ACCOUNTABILITY

Business ethics also ends up having to consider different models of what a business should be when it deals with moral responsibility in that secondary sense of tracing causes, as opposed to specifying duties. We have seen that the myriad specific questions about the duties of businesses and the people connected with them converge on the single general question of the nature of businesses as social institutions. That same broad question reappears when we consider causal responsibility.

We shall start our discussion by identifying one single problem, which at first may seem rather narrow, namely the accountability of executives. The problem is narrowly based in four respects. The first is that the focus is only on corporate businesses—that is to say, companies rather than the unincorporated form of business represented by partnerships or sole traders. A second is that there is particular emphasis on public rather than private companies—that is to say, those that make a public offer of their shares rather than those that do not. A third restriction is that, in tackling executive accountability, it is only the causal responsibility of those in overall charge which is at issue. That of everyone below them is left out. Moreover , this exclusion is not even seen as much of a problem. In business ethics, the big and possibly only issue of causal responsibility is the one of executive accountability. (For our purposes, 'executive' refers only to the topmost layer of management within a business.) A fourth and final restriction is that it is only the accountability and not also the due recognition of these people in overall charge which is being considered. The latter is, in fact, treated as a problem arising from the issue of executive accountability.

One good reason for focusing on companies in general, and on public companies in particular, is their size and economic importance. Taken collectively, companies are the dominant form of business enterprise within an advanced economy. Most businesses within such an economy are not companies and the great majority of companies are fairly small. However, nearly all large or very large businesses have company status. In addition, most of the very largest, including giant multinationals, are public companies. Consequently, companies in general, and public companies in particular, play a dominant role in terms of goods and services produced. (For this reason, as well as to keep our account within manageable proportions, we shall follow custom and concentrate on companies in discussing the moral responsibilities of businesses.)

That dominant role is perhaps reason enough for concentrating on companies. But there are other, more integral reasons for treating them in isolation from other forms of business enterprise. They concern the peculiarities of a corporate structure and the peculiar place of executives within it. Put briefly, an organization, whether it is a company or anything else, has corporate status if it is treated in law as if it were a person in its own right. As such, a corporation is regarded as something quite separate from any of the people associated with it, whether they be owners, employees, members of governing boards, or whatever. It is deemed to be capable of owning property, entering contracts, committing wrongs, suffering damages and just about anything else that an individual can do by way of activities governed by law. The corporation, rather than any human person or persons linked to it, is the entity owning the assets, owing the debts, receiving the proceeds, employing the people and so on.[1]

In reality, of course, a corporation can do none of these things. It is a mere legal construct, a make-believe person for the purposes of legal identification. Its supposed activities are always those of real people acting on its behalf. Taking the corporation as a whole, its supposed activities are, in reality, those of the people in overall charge: they take the key decisions, work out strategies, determine organizational structures and so on. In so far as we can attribute activity to the corporation as a whole, it belongs to these people in overall charge. For nearly all practical purposes, they *are* the corporation. What they do is, generally speaking, what the corporation does; even if, from a strictly legal viewpoint, they are merely acting on its behalf.[2] This is a situation with possible conflicts of interest built into it. It inevitably presents the problem of how the interests of the corporation are, in practice, to be separated from the interests of those who control it. If what the corporation does is what they do, what can ensure that they act in the interests of the corporate body rather than their own individual interests? By what means is this to be done? How are they to be made answerable for the way they run the corporation? Here we encounter a problem of accountability. It is one that is specific to corporations, and resides in an inevitable tension—and even potential conflict—between what a corporation is in legal theory and what it is in working practice. For those corporations that are companies, it is the problem of 'executive accountability'. However, it is the same general problem of preventing the interests of the corporation from being subordinated to the interests of those controlling it.

For public companies, there is the added dimension that those doing the controlling are usually not even the same as the people doing the owning. The controllers are professional managers employed by the company; while those with the ownership rights are usually a quite separate and invariably much more numerous body of people who own company shares but otherwise play no other part in its operations apart from having the (normally unexercised) right to attend and vote at annual general meetings. In private companies, on the other hand, a separation between ownership and control is much less of a feature. They tend to be owner-managed; which, of course, eliminates the distinction between controllers and managers altogether. Even when this is not the case, there is usually only a relatively small number of shareholders—often members of the same family—and this usually makes for a much closer supervision of professional managers by owners than is possible in public companies with their often vast and varying body of shareholders.

Since a separation of ownership from control is much less prevalent and severe for private than for public companies, some people take the view that executive accountability is mainly a problem for public companies. This follows because, for them, the accountability is owed only—or at least primarily—to those with ownership rights over a company, namely shareholders. Thus, where there is little or no separation of ownership and control, it will seem to such people that there is little or no problem of executive accountability. However, it is possible to take a broader view. One can acknowledge the particular difficulties relating to public companies because of the separation of ownership from control, but at the same time deny that executive accountability is something which is owed only, or even primarily, to shareholders. It will be owed to other groups as well. On this latter view, the separation of ownership and control is not the sole or central issue. Hence the problem of executive accountability is not something largely confined to public companies; it will hold for any sort of company, public or private.

The relationship between executive accountability and the function of businesses will now become apparent. Those who take the broad view of that accountability are generally subscribing to some form of 'stakeholder' theory, i.e. that a company exists for the benefit of all those who have a 'stake' in it. The notion of a 'stake' can be variously interpreted, but what it means is having some kind of claim on the company as a result of one's interests being somehow connected with the activities of the company—usually in the sense of depending on it for your wellbeing. More important is the question of precisely who is to be included in the category of 'stakeholder'. Obviously shareholders and employees, but thereafter the list will vary, though it nearly always includes customers, suppliers and the local communities in which companies operate.

On the question of just how such varied interests are to be represented, there is a sharper division. Some—usually academic commentators—suggest board membership, with directors representing shareholders, being joined by directors who represent employees, consumers and local communities. Others—perhaps usually working executives—prefer to leave boards as organs of shareholder interest with executives simply taking on duties to these other groups as well to shareholders. On this model, the job of executives is to determine the balance between these various interests.

Those who would confine executive accountability to shareholders support a position which, by way of verbal juxtaposition, is referred to as the 'stockholder' theory. For them a company exists to serve the interests of its shareholder owners, and the sole, or at least overriding, duty of executives is to serve that interest. It is therefore solely or primarily to shareholders that executive accountability is owed. There are certainly people other than shareholders whose fortunes are tied up in the company, but that is beside the point: they do not own the company. The essential point—and here we get to the heart of the debate—is that from a stockholder perspective, a company is simply a piece of private property—no different, in principle, from land, houses, machinery or anything else that people can own. In contrast, from the stakeholder perspective, corporate status transforms a business into something closer to public property; something for which more than just ownership rights must be recognized. From both perspectives this is nothing to do with being 'public' or 'private' in the legal sense of whether shares are on public sale or not. What is crucial is being incorporated. For stakeholder theory this lifts a business out of the merely private property category; for stockholder theory it does not.

By way of a defence of their position, stakeholder theorists may sometimes question whether shareholders own a company. They contend that the company itself owns the assets of the business; all shareholders have is certain rather complex ownership rights relating to the income generated from the use or sale of those assets. Legally speaking, they say, no one 'owns' a company: it is simply a forum in which certain rights—including ownership rights of a peculiar kind—can be exercised. All of this may be true, but it does not seem to make much difference in legal practice—at least in Britain, where the interests of the company are equated with those of its shareholders. Thus, where the law requires directors and executives to act in the best interests of the company, they are in effect being asked to act in the best interests of shareholders. For all practical purposes, then, shareholders are treated as owners of the company whatever their nominal legal title may be.

In any case, the debate is centrally concerned with what *ought* to be the legal position, not what it is, as a matter of fact. It is about showing that one position is morally preferable to the other. To this end, each side can make use of both utilitarian and rights-based arguments. Stockholder theorists can talk of an inviolable right to property. To treat companies as anything but the private property of shareholders is, they might say, to abuse that right. Alternatively, they can appeal to utilitarian considerations, suggesting that serving the shareholder interest is the most efficient way of running a business. They might even make the 'invisible hand' claim that by following that interest we automatically serve all the others.

In reply, the stakeholder theorist can say that it is not the fact of any one particular interest being served that produces efficiency but having to pursue it within a competitive environment. As for one interest automatically serving all the others, this need be no more true of the shareholder interest than any of the others: they are all interdependent. In any case, it is unrealistic to suppose there can never be conflicts of interest. So if the objective is a utilitarian one of maximizing the benefits to all concerned, then stakeholder theorists can make the counter-claim that there must be accountability to all concerned if each conflicting interest is to receive due weight. Alternatively—perhaps even additionally—they too can use the language of rights, and speak of everyone whose interests are tied up in the company having a consequent right to hold to account those who run the company. These are complex arguments and we cannot, for reasons of space, go into the detail here (though we shall discuss the employee aspect in Chapter 5). We have largely to content ourselves with outlining the two contending positions. It must, however, be borne in mind that our remarks about executive accountability have different implications depending on whether they are seen from a stakeholder or stockholder perspective.

Following the focus on companies, and on public companies in particular, the third peculiarity in discussions of executive accountability lies, as we said, in the fact that the causal responsibility of all those below executive level is being ignored. This is no doubt because it is at an executive level that power is concentrated, and there is obviously a very close correlation between power and causal responsibility. At its most obvious, that correlation is simply a question of scale: the greater one's exercise of power, the greater one's impact on events and, consequently, the greater one's causal responsibility for the way things turn out. Thus, as a consequence of having that much more power than anyone else within businesses, executives will also have that much more causal responsibility for what happens in businesses. There is therefore that much more for which executives are accountable and, on that basis alone, we might be justified in concentrating on them. As it happens, however, there is more to the justification than that. We also need to look at the nature of executive power and not merely its comparative scale. Here, two factors are relevant.

The first is that executive power is largely a matter of power over people.

One can talk of power over resources, both physical and financial, but clearly this would mean very little without the power to direct people in the use of those resources. Ultimately at least, executive power involves directing of people in the use of resources. In that process, the people so directed inevitably lose some causal responsibility for what they do—not in the details of its execution, but at least in the broad outline of what they do. This does not mean they become automata without wills of their own, nor does it mean that they are absolved from any obligation not to act illegally, or immorally, or both. There are still obviously areas of individual responsibility in even the most tightly controlled businesses. However, in even the most loosely controlled, those areas are circumscribed by the exercise of executive power. The overall structure of activity will always, to some greater or lesser extent, be dictated by the executive level. To that particular extent, responsibility for the activity will belong not to the individuals carrying it out but to the executives in overall charge. Thus, the peculiarity of causal responsibility at the executive level is that because it is so much about controlling people, the causal responsibility of others diminishes and increases as it—respectively—waxes and wanes. The more causal responsibility executives have for what occurs in a business, the more tightly they control and, consequently, the less the causal responsibility of the people being controlled. Conversely, the less causal responsibility that executives have for what goes on, the less tightly they control and so the more causal responsibility there is for the people below them in the business. On this basis, it is not simply the scale of executive causal responsibility but also its inverse relation to everyone else's which gives priority to the executive level in any examination of this kind of moral responsibility.

The second factor about the nature of executive power which gives it this priority is to some extent the converse of the first. Just as the first was about what, for now, can be described as the downward flow of power from the top to the bottom within businesses (we will qualify this later—see p. 79), so the second is about the consequent upward flow of causal responsibility from the bottom to the top. The top is where that responsibility terminates. This is obviously and immediately so for matters to do with the overall conduct of the business. By definition, executives are the people ultimately responsible here. But this is also to some extent true of even very particular matters. Part of the blame for the surly shop assistant, for example, might lie with executives failing to implement a staff training scheme. Here too we can trace a line causal responsibility back to the executive level—albeit partial and indirect. We cannot do this in all cases, of course. Executives cannot be responsible for every single detail of what occurs in a business; and it is also true that the larger the organization, the more attenuated this indirect sort of causal responsibility must become. None the less, there is a 'terminal character' to executive responsibility which holds not just for the overall conduct of the business but for almost anything that happens there. It is where 'the buck stops'.

Use of this phrase acknowledges the essentially hierarchical structure of

Power

People

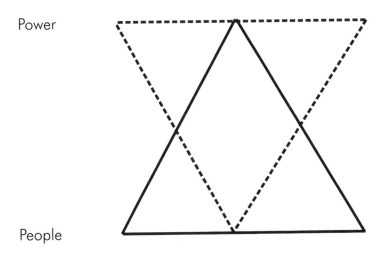

Fig. 4.2 The organizational pyramid

businesses. What we have here identified as the terminal character of executive responsibility is nothing more than a consequence of executives being positioned at the top of the organizational pyramid. The same is true of the other two reasons given for concentrating on the executive level. The greater scale of executive responsibility, and its inverse relation to subordinate levels, are also no more than different consequences of this same pyramidal structure. All three reasons for the concentration reflect a situation where a majority at the base of the pyramid have the least power and the most particular responsibilities, while a gradually diminishing number of people have powers and responsibilities that are correspondingly greater and more general until they reach their greatest and most general at an executive pinnacle constituted by just a few people or even a single individual (see Fig. 4.2).

There are variations on and exceptions to this paradigmatic case, of course. The steepness of the pyramid can vary with the size of the organization and whether there are many layers of administration or the now fashionable 'flat' structure with its minimum of layers. Some businesses will also escape being pyramidal by being just too small or by being composed of just a few co-equal partners. Generally speaking, though, no business of any size escapes being a hierarchy with an executive level at the top. It is, after all, probably no more that what it is to be 'an organization'; and any business of any size will be this.

With the fourth and final restriction on the problem of executive accountability, the concentration on accountability to the exclusion of due recognition, we find a straightforward reflection of where controversy now lies—at least in Britain (even more so in the United States) and at least with executives of large public companies. While many would argue for a lack of accountability in relation to these executives, few, if any, would argue for a lack of due recognition. In fact, those who argue that there is not enough accountability see its most visible proof in the seemingly *undue* recognition that has come to these particular executives in recent years. By this they usually mean hugely increased earnings which, it is argued, bear little relation to company performance, to what others in the company are getting, to the supply of managerial talent or even, given lucrative severance clauses in contracts, the risks of failure. This situation reveals an absence of accountability, critics claim, because it reflects a situation where executives are effectively awarding themselves the increases. They are being left free to use the company simply as a vehicle for their own self-interest. There is, it is said, no one to whom they are genuinely accountable and the consequence is unjustified pay increases.

It is important here to separate the issue of whether these pay increases are justified—a question of distributive justice (see Chapter 3)—from the issue of whether the underlying cause is a lack of proper accountability. From the point of view of those arguing for a problem of executive accountability, any widespread or blatant abuse of power could be offered as proof that the problem exists. For example, it could be found in the apparent ease with which corporate criminals such as Robert Maxwell have seemed able to perpetrate their wrong-doing. There may be no ultimate protection against such people, but arguably a more effective system of executive accountability would make their lives more difficult. Alternatively, and remembering that people are accountable for mistakes as well as misdeeds, proof of an accountability problem could be found in certain forms of business failure. For example, there is the phenomenon of corporate collapse following excessive borrowing which, in part at least, must be attributed to unrestrained executive egos. Not only that, but the case for a lack of executive accountability does not even need to be based on establishing any particular outcome, whether it is misdeed or mistake, undeserved pay increases, or anything else. It is enough that the accountability falls short of what people have a right to expect. As we have seen, accountability rises out of duties: we are accountable to other people because of duties owed to them; our accountability entails their corresponding right to hold us to account for the performance of our duties. A lack of accountability occurs when others are denied an effective means for exercising a right to disclosure of information. In themselves, untoward effects are simply proof of what happens when that right is denied—and why, of course, we have such a right in the first place.

Here we need to be aware of the difference between merely having duties towards people and actually being accountable to them for the carrying out of those duties. The first is something which holds no matter what we do or think about it. We have those duties whether we shirk them, evade them, deny them or whatever. Accountability, on the other hand, is something more concrete. Whatever right to accountability people might have, unless there is the means to exercise that right, there is no accountability. Accountability is something that must be embodied in mechanisms. There have to be procedures and structures whereby it is enforced. More than that, these mechanisms must include the means to impose sanctions of some kind. The prospect not just of blame but also, where appropriate, of punishment must be there for accountability to exist. Finally, these mechanisms must be effective. They must be capable of deterring those owing the accountability from abuse of power or dereliction of duty.

We need also to distinguish accountability from power. In itself, accountability is not so much about limiting or reducing power (although that may be a consequence) as of ensuring that there are effective penalties for situations where power is wrongly or incompetently used. We have accountability when the means for ensuring this are in place. Thus, although in practice accountability will almost always inhibit the exercise of power, all that it formally requires is that there is some form of eventual reckoning for the way power has been exercised. It is not so much the extent of power with which accountability is concerned, but rather the manner in which it has been exercised and, most importantly of all, its results. In principle, it is compatible with any degree of power—save that of evading an eventual reckoning.

This last point is important because scepticism about the need for greater executive accountability can involve the assumption that it must necessarily be accompanied by a loss of executive power and, as a result, a loss of business competitiveness. 'It's a tough, rapidly changing world!' supporters of this argument would say, and only if executives are given a free hand to take decisive action can businesses face up to competitive challenges. Increased accountability would inevitably limit the ability of executives to take decisive action, and with it the ability of businesses to compete effectively.

This need for a free hand can be exaggerated, of course. As we have suggested, it can sometimes be in the best interest of a business to restrain executive initiative. In any case, increased accountability might so concentrate the executive mind as to be as much a spur as a brake to initiative. None the less, it can be allowed that for organizations in general, and for competitive businesses in particular, there is an obvious need for some optimum level of executive initiative. Exactly what that level should be is obviously open to debate, but given our distinction between power and accountability, there is no reason to suppose that increased executive accountability must necessarily lead to a diminution in executive power and, with it, an undesirable loss of executive initiative. It depends on how the accountability is organized.

It is perhaps useful here to distinguish further between 'participative' and 'non-participative' ways of establishing executive accountability. Participative accountability is built into the operational structure of a business: executives are made accountable for what they do, while they do it. Their accountability lies in the fact that for certain of their decisions they must have the consent of those to whom they are accountable: there are things they cannot do without that permission.

(Shared decision making is the prime exemplar of participation—see Chapter 5.) This is a form of accountability which will diminish and restrict executive power. In principle, it is the kind constituted by a company's board of directors. This is meant to be a sort of standing committee of shareholder representatives set up to oversee continuously the conduct of company affairs between annual general meetings— which, in effect, means continuously overseeing the conduct of its executives. In practice, of course, things are somewhat different, a fact which might suggest further proof of a lack of executive accountability. In the United Kingdom, most boards, even of public companies, will have a majority of directors who are also executives of the company. Those who are not are usually the nominees of those that are, and will, in any case, be mostly executives in other companies. (All of this makes their title of 'non-executive directors' somewhat misleading.) However, in principle at least, a board of directors is an example of participative executive accountability in that it operates through (what is meant to be) a shared involvement in executive decision making.

With a non-participative form of executive accountability, on the other hand, there need be no such involvement. Here, the mechanisms lie outside the normal operational structure of the business. There is a body to whom executives are accountable for their actions, but this need only function after events, not during or before them. This is still accountability in that executives are made answerable for their exercise of power, but it does not, in itself, entail anything about the size and scope of executive power. In fact, it is compatible with them having a totally free hand—the only inhibiting factor being that at the end of the day they will face a reckoning. They need neither consult nor seek permission; the only restriction is their knowledge of the price they will pay for what might be considered mismanagement. This is therefore a kind of executive accountability which can fully embody in practice that distinction from power which, in principle, holds for accountability in general. By way of example, we can cite the accountability which executives have to the shareholders' annual general meeting. This is usually a post-event reckoning, and, as such, it is usually a non-participative mechanism for executive accountability. It therefore need not, and invariably does not, do much to diminish or restrict executive power—even if, as is rarely the case, shareholders were to attend annual general meetings and take any sort of active part in the proceedings. (The fact they rarely do is again taken as proof of a lack of executive accountability.)

We are obviously not dealing with a hard and fast distinction here. There is not an either–or choice of 'participative' as opposed to 'non-participative' mechanisms. Nor is it impossible to have elements of one in the other. The combination of a board of directors and an annual general meeting of shareholders is itself an example of where these two mechanisms work side by side (or at least attempt to do so). While the possibilities, for instance, of a board simply rubber-stamping a decision already taken by executives and of an annual general meeting being asked to give prior approval to an executive proposal demonstrates how elements of one sort of mechanism can be found in another. None the less, in so far as we can separate them out, there is the crucial difference that the non-participative model does not act directly to diminish or restrict executive power, whereas the participative does.

We can understand this difference in terms of the working of the organizational pyramid referred to earlier. The way accountability normally works here is as an aspect of hierarchical power; it attaches considerable importance to one level being answerable to the level above. Thus organizational power involves an upward flow of accountability as well as a downward flow of commands. Were this the only kind of accountability and were it also to terminate at the executive level, then, in organizational terms, executives would enjoy power without accountability. They would have a general causal responsibility for the organization without also being answerable to anyone within it. The device of having a board of directors, at least in theory, adds another level of upward accountability; a level above the executive to which it is answerable. (The fact the two levels are not kept separate is where the model breaks down.) Consequently, this is a mechanism for participative accountability which, even when it works, is fully compatible with a power structure. The most it does is extend that structure up a step; if not so much in its downward commanding aspect, then certainly in its upward accounting dimension. In contrast, were executive accountability to be participatory in the sense of involving employees in shopfloor decision making, then this would very much run counter to hierarchical power structures. It would produce a *downward* flow of accountability to be set up against the more usual upward flow (see Fig. 4.3). An example is the German system of works councils where managers need to obtain the agreement of an elected works committee before instituting certain sorts of changes in working practice.

The possibility of such very different kinds of accountability as in the third schema is certainly a reversal of normal hierarchical functioning—which is why managers generally find it so threatening. For example, leaving aside the rather dubious cost arguments, it goes a long way to explaining the hostility of most British managers to the establishment of German-style works councils in the United Kingdom. It must not be supposed though, as perhaps these managers do, that accountability to employees must necessarily take this hierarchy-threatening form. Executives can very well be made accountable to employees in ways which preserve hierarchical structures. As with shareholders, accountability can be through representation on boards of directors—something that would preserve a strictly upward flow of accountability. Again, we have a German example in the allocation of up to half of the places on company 'supervisory boards' to people elected by employees. Here the means, though hierarchical, are participatory. There is a sharing in decision making. Yet even this does not necessarily follow for accountability to employees: it could be through something like an annual general

Fig. 4.3 Power and accountability in organizations

meeting of shareholders—a mechanism which, like that meeting, could be nothing more than an eventual reckoning for what is otherwise a free hand. In practice, perhaps because of a greater sense of involvement, employees are unlikely to be quite as supine as the average shareholder. We do find something like a company annual general meeting, however, in the 'general assemblies' of members of worker co-operatives belonging to the Mondragon group—though combined with the very participative mechanisms of a board of worker-directors and a kind of works council.

Alongside this distinction between participative and non-participative ways of organizing executive accountability is the much more straightforward one between direct and representational mechanisms. For example, accountability to shareholders can take the direct form of facing them at an annual general meeting or the representational path of directors acting on their behalf. Again, and as actual business practice also shows, the two mechanisms can of course co-exist.

CORPORATE GOVERNANCE

Summing up then, we can say that executive accountability can be organized in a variety of ways which can also be variously combined. Some might, to differing degrees, be bound up with executive decision making; others might, to differing degrees, stand outside it. As a consequence, some might severely limit the freedom of action of executives, while others will barely affect it. Some will make executives accountable to shareholders, some to employees, some to both. (Others could no doubt involve quite different group such as, say, consumers.) Some will make

Case study

Shell admits responsibility

Oil spillages at sea have been a repeated cause of environmental disaster. In March 1967 the *Torrey Canyon* grounded off Land's End in England, spilling 34 986 000 gallons of oil, and causing serious marine pollution. Since then there has been a series of similar disasters, some of the best remembered being the *Amoco Cadiz* (France 1978), the *Atlantic Empress* and *Aegean Captain* (Trinidad and Tobago, 1979) and the *Exxon Valdez* (Alaska, March 1989).

On 19 August 1989, in the wake of the *Exxon Valdez* incident, and just after the formation of the National Rivers Authority (NRA), Shell discovered a discrepancy between the amount of oil being pumped from the Tranmere terminal on the River Mersey, and the amount arriving at the Stanlow refinery. Meanwhile, coastguards were observing substantial quantities of oil on the river.

Shell took action immediately. The Fire Brigade was informed at once, and a well was built under the damaged pipe, which was 'clipped' at the damaged point to make a kind of temporary repair. Vacuum tankers were brought in to flush out the oil between the terminal and the leak. Water was then pumped through the pipe to force out the oil, causing a large gush, as 7 tonnes of oil escaped through the pipe. The gush gave the television crews, who had now arrived on the scene, a dramatic piece of film to show to viewers, and at a later stage the NRA was able to use this clip as evidence when prosecuting.

Instead of waiting for the media to home in on the company, Harold Bardsley, the public affairs manager and environment officer, together with Bob Reid, the chair of Shell UK, and Sir Peter Holmes, chair of the Shell Transport and Trading Company, gave a press conference the day after the incident. They admitted liability—an action which enabled the clear-up operation to proceed more smoothly, since the local authority now knew that payment would be forthcoming, and that there would be no legal battle to recoup the expenditure. Shell was also seen to be taking the matter seriously, attempting to recover its desired image as a company that cared for the environment.

Although the spillage was only 0.5 per cent of that of the *Exxon Valdez*, Shell was none the less prosecuted and fined £1 million—an enormous sum, at which Shell executives were surprised. (Fines for comparable pollution incidents had generally not exceeded £25 000.) The cleaning-up operation cost Shell a further £1.4 million; £2.5 million to renew the pipeline, and a further

£2 million on monitoring for the prevention of any similar future incidents. Shell also spent £200 000 for a study group to advise on how any further incidents of this kind might be avoided.

The incident raises several issues. Although Shell's reputation was dented by the Tranmere spillage, their prompt action shows that damage and reputation can at least be minimized by prompt action which acknowledges one's accountability. Shell's fine was severe, compared with other offenders, and raises the question whether it was commensurate with the damage suffered, or whether the judge, Mr Justice Mars Jones, wanted to make an example of Shell, in the wake of previous oil spillages.

executives directly answerable to the chosen group or groups, some will do it through representative bodies. What they will all amount to, however, are different forms of 'corporate governance' (as it has come to be called). As the phrase would suggest, this much-discussed topic concerns how companies should be 'governed'. As in matters of political governance, the concern is with mechanisms whereby those in positions of overall power are to be accountable for the exercise of that power. In a political context this means elected politicians; in a business context, company executives. Because executives control companies, it follows that the way they are themselves controlled is, in effect, the way the company as a whole is controlled. Consequently, the issue of corporate governance is, in effect, identical to the issue of executive accountability. In practice, they come down to the same thing. The questions to be asked in both cases are about ways of making executives accountable for their actions: are they to be participative or non-participative, or a mixture of both, and to what degree is either option to be exercised? The search, in both cases, is for mechanisms that will ensure accountability while allowing executives the freedom they need to operate within a competitive environment. Most fundamentally, there is, in both cases, the crucial prior question: to *whom* should executives be accountable? Is it shareholders, or employees, or consumers? Is it to be all of these, only some or none at all? Having decided that, we can then go on to decide on mechanisms: whether direct, representative, participative, non-participative or whatever.

Any or all of these various ways of establishing executive accountability are, we can now see, also various forms of corporate governance. They are also, by implication, different models of social responsibility, as it applies to corporate business. In specifying the ways executive accountability is to be enforced and, most crucially, to whom it is to be owed, we are not only determining the structures for corporate governance, but are, at the same time, identifying what the social purpose of businesses should be. This follows because within an institutional setting such as a company, accountability is owed to those on whose behalf power is exercised, namely the people for whose benefit the institution exists. Consequently, by determining to whom accountability is owed, we are deciding for whose benefit the company is to be run. We are defining the interest or interests it should serve, and are thus defining the social purpose it should fulfil. We are saying that the allotted role of companies within society is to serve that particular interest group. There may, of course, be incidental benefits to other groups and things may not work out exactly as intended. It was never, for example, the intention that companies should be run for the benefit of professional managers, even if, as some critics contend, that is the way things turn out.

Whether or not it is frustrated, the intended social role is the one enshrined in structures of corporate governance which are, and have to be, structures for executive accountability. Take, for example, that most famous statement of stockholder theory provided by the Nobel Prize-winning economist Milton Friedman. In it he argues that the role of corporate executives is to be simply 'agents' serving the interests of shareholders. He further argues that their interest is in nothing but a maximum financial return on their investment. Accordingly, for him—and here we quote the title of his article—'the social responsibility of business is to increase its profits'.[3] In other words, Friedman passes from an account of executive accountability to an account of social responsibility. This, of course, is what he must do, for only by determining what those who control them should do can we determine what businesses should do.

The final link in the chain is provided by the fact—noted in our section on social responsibility—that to define the social purpose of business is to offer a model of what business should be. Accordingly, by inevitably involving the issue of corporate governance, and with that the issue of business social responsibility, what was acknowledged to be the rather narrowly based problem of executive accountability widens out, as predicted, into being about competing models of what businesses should be like. More specifically, given its corporate sector focus, it widens out into being about competing models of what a corporate business should be like. We have thus a conceptual chain which runs from executive accountability, to corporate governance, to corporate social responsibility, to corporate models.

DISCUSSION TOPICS

1. This chapter has given a framework for understanding power and responsibility within businesses. How might it be used to explain different styles of management?
2. What are the problems about saying that a 'company' is responsible for something? In what ways is it more difficult to hold *companies* accountable for their actions than it is to hold *people* accountable?
3. Imagine you are drawing up a code of practice for a firm. What categories of

duties, if any, might the firm be said to have (i) to its employees; (ii) to its shareholders; (iii) to its suppliers; (iv) to its customers; (v) to society more widely?

4. Consider the above case study of Shell UK. What lessons about corporate social responsibility and executive accountability may be drawn from it?

NOTES

1. George D. Chryssides and John H. Kaler, *An Introduction to Business Ethics*, Chapman and Hall, London, 1993, pp. 226–229.
2. The fact that their actions are, in law, the action of 'the company' can be very useful to executives when things go wrong. It can enable them to evade personal responsibility by hiding behind the 'corporate veil'. See ibid., pp. 240–241.
3. Milton Friedman, 'The social responsibility of business is to increase its profits', *New York Times Magazine*, 13 September 1970; reprinted in Chryssides and Kaler, *An Introduction to Business Ethics*, pp. 249–254.

5 *Employment*

EMPLOYMENT AND THE FUNCTION OF BUSINESS

During a recently televised discussion of unemployment, a leading industrialist commented that it was not the function of business to provide jobs. He was reacting to criticisms from unemployed people about plant closures and the resulting job losses. His critics, he somewhat condescendingly suggested, were simply confused about what businesses existed for. Exactly what they existed for he did not say, but what he meant was clear enough.

From the point of view of those running business, labour is pre-eminently a cost to be kept as low as possible. What businesses are generally set up for is to make a profit for their owners, and this is normally a precondition for their continued existence. Even not making *enough* profit is, under certain conditions, reason for closing an operation down. It might be better—i.e. more profitable—to concentrate resources elsewhere, e.g. to put capital into a new and expanding business rather than an old and contracting one.

There is, however, another perspective to that of those running businesses—that of the people employed within them. From their point of view businesses are very much about providing jobs. A business is not much good to them unless it does just that. Moreover, the better the jobs provided, the better, from their point of view, the businesses are working. The higher the pay, the more secure the job; the better the working conditions, the more they welcome it. Here, then, is a perspective that seems the very opposite of those who run businesses. It sees labour not exclusively as a cost but rather as a source of income. It gives wages for employees exactly the same status as profit for owners: both are monies derived from the operation of the business. From the employee's perspective, if anything is a cost it is the profit that diverts part of the income generated by the business into other hands.

Of course, things are not quite as simple as this somewhat stark contrast presents them. Those who run businesses are also very often employees within the business. They are professional managers rather than, or sometimes as well as, owners, and hence their interests are not entirely distinct from those of non-executive 'ordinary employees'. Professional managers also need jobs and want them to be as rewarding as possible. Conversely, even ordinary employees are not entirely divorced from an interest in profit. Most obviously, through share owner-ship they can also have a status as owners. Theirs is not usually a controlling interest, and their shares are not necessarily in the businesses for which they work. They are also usually held in a very indirect fashion through unit trusts, pension funds and other sorts of institutional holdings. None the less, through a direct or indirect involvement in shareholding, many ordinary employees will have an interest in profits as well as wages. In any case, is there not a necessary and more general overlap between the two perspectives in that profits and wages depend on each other for the system to work? Wages have to be paid for profits to be earned and, conversely, wages are only paid if profits are earned. So are not all contrasts and conflicts between the two perspectives automatically resolved by this fact?

It is all very true that people can have a financial interest in both profits and wages, and that the two are economically interdependent, but whether this is enough to resolve all differences between the two forms of income is quite another matter. There is still the question of where the *predominant* interest lies: in profits or wages? Do people benefit more through profits or from wages? To answer this we must look not just at the process and the way its different parts interact, but also at outputs. We must look to what businesses supply by way of benefits and ask whether it is mostly through the medium of profits or of wages.

Taking society as a whole, there can be no doubt that the benefits that people derive from business activity are very much more through the medium of wages than profits. This is amply demonstrated by the Central Statistical Office 'Blue Book' figures on income and expenditure within the UK economy. These show that on the average of recent years, nearly two-thirds of total UK income derives from wages and the wage-related benefits of social security and pension contributions paid by employers. (For convenience, we can lump this all together as 'wages'.) Not all wages are paid out by business, of course. Many people are employed by what can be called 'non-trading organizations'. Unlike trading organizations, their income is not principally derived from sales to customers, and hence do not count as 'businesses' for our purposes (see Chapter 1). This non-trading and therefore non-business part of the economy is mostly accounted for by public sector employment—by local government as well as by publicly funded services such as health and education. By discounting the wages they pay along with some small allowance for the private voluntary sector, we arrive at a figure of something like three-quarters as the proportion of total wages paid out by businesses. This means, therefore, that something near to one-half of total income takes the form of wages paid by businesses.

In contrasting this figure with the proportion of total income deriving from business profits, we have to distinguish between companies and unincorporated businesses. What might be thought of as 'profit' in the latter case is officially classified as 'income from self-employment'. At a tenth of total income it mostly just reflects the proportion of self-employed people with the workforce (about an eighth). What is left over after deducting what the self-employed might have been paid in wages could be called 'profit'. In the case of those larger unincorporated businesses where self-employed proprietors employ other people, it probably should. However, any surplus after allowing for the cost of the self-employed's own labour can never be more than a relatively small proportion of total income. For most of the income classifiable as 'profit', we must turn to the corporate sector. Here we find not only most of the profits, but also an unequivocal contrast between profit and wages, as well as the source of most of the wages paid to employees by businesses (about 80 per cent as opposed to 20 per cent for unincorporated businesses).

Particularly since privatization of most of the state-owned 'public corporations', corporate businesses are mostly within the 'private corporate sector', i.e. corporate businesses not owned by the state. This private corporate sector mostly consists of joint stock companies—the dominant form of business enterprise throughout the economy. The way in which such businesses convert profits into individuals' income is through dividend payments, and the official figures tell us that, on the average of recent years, dividend payments within the private corporate sector are exceeded by the amount paid out in wages by a ratio of somewhere between ten and twelve to one. This means that, in income terms, society has between ten and twelve times the interest in corporate wages than it has in corporate profits. Consequently, in a strictly financial sense, this dominant form of business enterprise produces overwhelmingly more wages than profits for individual members of society.

We are not, of course, the first to point out the quantitative dominance of wages over profits in the operations of business. Milton Friedman has noted that 'Something like three-quarters of all income generated in the United States through market transactions take the form of the compensation of employees, with about half the rest going to the self employed.'[1] Peter Drucker goes even further, claiming that, 'In every developed country, between 85 and 90 per cent of the economy's product is being paid out in the form of wages and salaries.'[2]

Where all this leaves the contention that businesses are not about providing jobs is fairly obvious. Whatever its truth from the point of view of those running businesses, it is profoundly untrue for society at large. From the point of view of society, business is very much about providing jobs, preferably well-paid jobs with good working conditions at that. Thus, employment emerges as a large part, perhaps even the major part, of that social purpose for business which we discussed in Chapter 4.

If those who run businesses identify profits rather than employment as their prime purpose, this does not necessarily mean that these managers and owners have diametrically opposed interests to the rest of society. It must be borne in mind that in order to have the sales from which profits are derived there must first be income to do the buying. Income which is, to a dominant extent, provided by businesses themselves is mostly, though not exclusively, through the payment of wages. Businesses are thus in the curious position of not only providing goods and services, but also the wherewithal to buy them. Consequently, businesses as a whole have a vested interest in providing as many well-paid jobs as possible and, in order to inspire consumer confidence, having those jobs as secure as possible. This is, however, only true for businesses as a whole. In order to secure competitive advantage, all things being equal, an *individual* business will have a vested interest in having as small and poorly paid a workforce as possible, as easily adjusted up and down as possible. How we are to reconcile the interest of the individual business with the wider interest of society and business at large is therefore a very vexed problem—indeed one of the central problems of business ethics. As usual, some would see market forces as sufficient to resolve the issue. The point they would make is that treating labour as a cost to be kept as low as possible is actually a good thing. It encourages maximum efficiency in the use of labour, thus boosting productivity and so increasing the overall level of prosperity for everyone—including employees. Others are less sanguine. They would opt for government regulation or even changes in corporate governance to bring the aims of business into line with those of society.

Whichever approach is adopted to resolve it, this fundamental tension between business imperatives and society's wider interest in secure, well-paid and congenial employment shows itself in a myriad of issues in business ethics. We have already discussed the right to a fair wage in the previous chapter, and identified several of the problems inherent in the notion. There is also a range of issues involving trade unions. These include the presumed right to belong to a trade union, whether having a 'closed shop' is a legitimate practice, whether employers should offer inducements for the work force to de-unionize, and the circumstances in which unions may legitimately bring workers out on strike. Conditions of employment form another area: hiring and firing policies, working conditions and contractual obligations can all raise important moral questions. To attempt to cover every issue relating to employment is clearly impossible; we therefore propose to focus on just three of them. The first is the issue of *equal opportunities* in employment. The second concerns the moral correctness of the exposure of malpractices by employees ('whistle-blowing') and its relationship to a supposed duty of loyalty to employers. Finally, we shall examine the rights and wrongs of employee participation and its connection with the notion of leadership in business.

EQUAL OPPORTUNITIES

In certain respects, equality of opportunity is no longer an option for employers. In Britain, they are required by law not to discriminate on the grounds of sex or race.

(In Northern Ireland, the situation is markedly different: sexual, religious and political discrimination is prohibited, but not racial discrimination.) To a lesser extent discrimination on other grounds is also prohibited. New legislation aims to remove the barriers to employment for disabled people, and there is the very specific right not to be refused employment on the grounds of trade union membership or lack of it. In the discussion that follows, we shall focus largely on the traditional issues of gender and race, although we shall give some pointers concerning other areas of possible discrimination.

The fundamental moral principle behind nearly all the legislation is that it is unfair to discriminate against people on grounds that are irrelevant to the jobs they are doing or for which they are applying. Gender and race are two such irrelevant considerations and are therefore generally excluded as grounds for employment. The few permitted exceptions, called 'genuine occupational quali-fications', are mostly to do with catering for needs of a specific gender or race, such as being an attendant in a single-sex changing room, or a community worker for a particular ethnic group. Other exceptions include acting roles, modelling and working in ethnic restaurants. Such exceptions aside, the initial presupposition is that individual merit, in the sense of how well a person can do a job, should be the only relevant consideration for recruitment and promotion. In all other respects, people must be treated equally, regardless of gender and race.

In so far as equal opportunities is about employment on merit it is mostly uncontroversial. Supporters of an extreme form of *laissez-faire* could possibly claim that employment is entirely the prerogative of employers, theirs to bestow or withhold entirely according to their individual preference or even prejudice. Hence, it may be argued, employers have the right to decide whom they want to work for them, and if they do not wish to employ women, Asians, older people, wheelchair users, gays, Marxists or Scientologists, then that is their privilege. Just as employees have an undisputed right to accept or reject employment just as they please, have not employers the same right to accept or reject whatever candidates they please? In the United States this doctrine is called 'employment at will'. The thinking behind it is that employment is an entirely private arrangement between employer and employee, and that it is an infringement of the human right to liberty to restrict either party's freedom of action in voluntarily agreeing to the arrangement.

Equal opportunities legislation runs very much counter to this idea—at least in so far as it applies to employers. Such legislation indisputably does restrict their freedom to hire, fire and promote whomever they wish. Rather than seeing employing people as a right, it is regarded as a privilege to be granted only under certain conditions. In this respect, equal opportunities legislation could be said to embody the social perspective on employment that we discussed in the previous section. In other words, it sees employment as a social benefit to be regulated in the public interest rather than going along with the managerial view that it is merely a means to an organizational end—notably profit.

Extreme *laissez-faire* notions aside, it may seem self-evident that employers should appoint staff according to merit. However, many would argue that groups that have been disadvantaged in the past are not now in a position to compete effectively in the job market. Women may have had their horizons limited by sex-role stereotyping. Members of certain ethnic minorities may have started school with basic deficiencies in the English language. (In a few cases, such children have even gone to school without any knowledge of English whatsoever.) Members of both groups may well have been victims of past discrimination, and hence less qualified or less advanced in their careers than their advantaged counterparts. A socially induced sense of inferiority may mean they are lacking in confidence, even in ambition. To compete effectively they arguably need special forms of additional assistance. Equal opportunities, it is argued, must therefore move to a stage beyond simple non-discrimination to 'positive action' (or 'affirmative action', as it is called in the United States, where the concept originated).

British law sanctions only two forms of positive action. The first is straightforward encouragement: recruitment and promotion may be targeted at underrepresented groups. Advertisements may be specifically placed where members of those groups will see, or they may be told their applications are welcome. The second form of legally sanctioned positive action concerns training. It allows employers and training agencies to run courses designed for, and even restricted to underrepresented groups. These courses aim to give members of those groups the skills and confidence to compete effectively for jobs. They can be directed at people already in a firm's employ where promotion is the issue, or at those not in a firm's employ where the concern is with recruitment. The Midland Bank, for example, has run summer work-experience programmes for ethnic minority students to encourage them to apply for posts with the bank after graduation.

An extension of positive action that is not explicitly sanctioned in law is that of setting targets for the recruitment or promotion of underrepresented groups. One example is the retail company Superdrug which aimed to increase its overall proportion of female managers by 25 per cent and the proportion at senior levels by 50 per cent.[3] Another example is the Littlewoods organization which aims to have a workforce reflecting the ethnic mix of the areas from which it recruits.[4]

Whether or not it is combined with the setting of targets, a step beyond officially sanctioned positive action would be to decide that where candidates are of approximately equal ability, a member of a disadvantaged group should be offered the job in preference to a member of an advantaged one. Taken a stage further still, a firm might decide that even when female or ethnic minority candidates appear to be less able than males or white persons, they should still be given preference. This preference is likely to have limits: the female or ethnic minority candidate would at least have to be minimally capable of doing the job, and the male or white candidate perhaps not overwhelmingly more suitable. But within limits at least, the preference might be exercised.

From   1   traditional discrimination to

          2   non-discrimination to

          3   positive action without targets to

          4   positive action with targets to

          5   preference for underrepresented groups where
                  equally able to

          6   preference for underrepresented groups even where less
                  able

Fig. 5.1   Spectrum of approaches to equal opportunities

One might present these various approaches to equal opportunities as parts of a spectrum, as shown in Fig. 5. 1.

With this last position (preference for underrepresented groups when less able) we gave a clear-cut case of what critics refer to as 'reverse discrimination' (since previously disadvantaged groups are now being advantaged) and defenders label 'positive discrimination'. The latter term is, however, something of a euphemism. It suggests advantage to some without disadvantage to others—which in the context of competition for employment is somewhat dishonest. We will therefore use the blunter term and talk of 'reverse discrimination'.

On the face of it, reverse discrimination seems ethically unacceptable. It has exactly the same morally objectionable features as the traditional discrimination against women and ethnic minorities: that of selecting people on the irrelevant basis of sex or race rather than individual merit. It is certainly illegal. The law prohibits discrimination on the grounds of sex or race, not specifically against women or ethnic minorities. The bodies charged with overseeing the legislation, the Equal Opportunities Commission (EOC) in relation to gender and the Commission for Racial Equality (CRE) in relation to race, are required to act on behalf of *all* victims of sexual or racial discrimination, whether they be women or men, members of ethnic minorities or of the majority white community. In fact, the EOC now receives *more* complaints of sexual discrimination from men than from women.

The fifth stage (preference for underrepresented groups where there is equal ability) may seem more innocuous. Under such a policy, candidates for a job would be considered on merit except where the final decision seemed equally balanced between candidates. Only at this point would the policy of preference for underrepresented groups be invoked: belonging to a disadvantaged group would be allowed to 'tip the scales' in that candidate's favour. Consequently, this is still reverse discrimination—albeit of a marginal kind—in that sex or race is ultimately deciding the issue rather than an admittedly finely balanced judgement based on an estimation of individual merit.

Some would see reverse discrimination as setting in earlier with our fourth stage (positive action with targets). Targets, it may be argued, all too easily convert into quotas, a system in which a particular proportion of jobs are set aside for women or ethnic minorities. In denying other groups (effectively white males) the opportunity to compete for those jobs, quotas constitute reverse discrimination and, as such, are illegal in Britain (although widely practised in the United States). Those who defend targets as intrinsically different from quotas see the difference as lying in their optional as opposed to obligatory nature. Targets are presented as outcomes that are aimed for but need not be met, while quotas are outcomes that have to be met.[5]

Opponents of targets would argue that this is too fine a distinction to hold in practice. What stops a target becoming a quota is that there is still selection on merit with a target. That way the target figure can stay as merely an aspiration rather than a requirement because no particular outcome with regard to sex or race is guaranteed. Merit and not the target figure will decide the final selection. This being so, targets place those who select candidates in a position where they are asked to do two incompatible things: (i) to aim for an outcome based on sex or race, in order to meet the target; and (ii) to use a criterion for producing that outcome, i.e. merit, not based on sex or race. In addition, the whole point about targets is that they are supposed to be met. So, particularly within a results-orientated managerial culture, the pressure—consciously or unconsciously—to adjust perceptions of merit to reach the desired target must be very considerable.

Critics of positive action need not stop at targets. Some would see a potential for reverse discrimination in anything that goes beyond straightforward non-discrimination (our second stage), and would therefore condemn all forms of positive action. The problem, as they would see it, is that anything beyond simple non-discrimination must involve attempting to increase the representation of previously underrepresented groups in certain areas or levels of employment. So even without targets, positive action inevitably involves pressure to compromise on the principle of selection on merit. In addition, even measures for encouraging application by women or ethnic minorities could be said to involve reverse discrimination in so far as they serve to discourage men or white people by excluding them. Likewise, training programmes exclusively for women or ethnic minorities could disadvantage men or white people if they also suffer from the handicaps of a lack of qualifications, confidence or ambition—as many do. By having access to programmes designed to remedy such deficiencies, women and ethnic minorities are given an advantage over similarly handicapped men or white people who have been denied access to those remedial programmes purely on grounds of sex or race—which makes them victims of reverse discrimination. In reply, defenders of positive action might argue that with sufficient care and attention all these problems can be solved. There can also be training programmes for those men and white people who need them. Sensitively handled, they would claim, encouragement for underrepresented groups need not discourage over-represented ones. The general aim of increasing the representation of women and ethnic minorities will not lead to reverse discrimination, provided one rigorously adheres to the principle of selection on merit.

In attempting to refute charges of reverse discrimination, defenders of equal opportunity policies are accepting that it is morally unacceptable. This can be questioned. A more radical defence would argue that reverse discrimination cannot be equated with traditional forms of discrimination. It is not, as past discrimination was, merely the securing of an unfair advantage. Rather, it is the redressing of a wrong; the wrong of that past discrimination against women or ethnic minorities. Those who take this line sometimes talk of reparations. White males have been advantaged to the detriment of women and ethnic minorities, and must now be discriminated against to compensate those groups for the damage done to them.

There are two very obvious objections to this. First, it relies on notions of collective guilt and collective harm that, whatever their applicability to entities such as nation states, would appear to have no applicability to something as unorganized as gender or ethnic identity. Have *all* males or *all* white people enjoyed an unfair advantage in employment? Have *all* women and *every* member of an ethnic minority suffered unfair discrimination? Clearly, the answer to both questions is no. So to talk of reparations is to condone punishing the innocent along with the guilty, and to compensate those have not been discriminated against along with those that have.

The second obvious objection arises from the fact that reparations can only be for wrongs already done. So not only are they confined to particular people, but also to the past. It is only within a present or previous generation of workers that there can be people who have been victims or beneficiaries of discrimination. Yet equal opportunities are to a perhaps major extent about the recruitment of new workers. The major losers from reverse discrimination would therefore be young white males; members of a generation that will not include beneficiaries from past discrimination and therefore cannot be under any sort of moral obligation to pay reparations.

Reverse discrimination is perhaps more plausibly defended when talk of reparations is dropped and it is accepted that some innocent people will suffer as a consequence. The defence then becomes the essentially utilitarian one of arguing that some unfair discrimination against (mostly) young white males is a price worth paying to overcome the legacy of past discrimination against women and ethnic minorities. This very obviously confronts traditional objections against the sacrificing of innocent individuals for the common good (see Chapter 2). Perhaps more decisively, it does not even seem to work as a utilitarian calculation. This is because for every woman or member of an ethnic minority that benefits by being advantaged through reverse discrimination there must be a man or white person harmed by being disadvantaged. On this basis, there is no increase in utility: the gains and losses cancel each other out.

The only way there could be any increase in utility is if there were advantages in reverse discrimination that were additional to gains and losses to individuals. One possibility is increased competitiveness. It is routinely asserted by proponents of equal opportunity policies that businesses can gain a competitive advantage from having a workforce that is more broadly representative of society at large. They make the general claim that by selecting from a wider range of people, a greater amount of talent is made available to businesses. Related to this is a more specific claim about what has come to be known as 'workforce diversity'. It is said that women and members of ethnic minorities can bring new perspectives and new abilities to the business: a distinctively female approach to management, say, or knowledge of non-Western cultures and languages. Also, those customers that are women or members of ethnic minorities will, it is said, react favourably to businesses that reflect their presence in society.

Both these claims must be treated with some caution. There is only so much talent a business needs, and there is a problem only if not enough is available— which is not always the case. Likewise, claims about the advantages flowing from diversity need to be offset by considerations of the possible disadvantages. What, for example, if a diverse workforce is a more divided and fractious one? Are there not organizational advantages to homogeneity? Despite such cautions, there is probably still a good case to be made for supposing that businesses and the economy in general will, on balance, benefit from drawing on that wider pool of talent and abilities that will come from having a workforce that more closely reflects society.

However, even if this is so, it will not do much to justify reverse discrimination, not even in that exclusively utilitarian way we are considering. This is because in selecting for reasons to do with talent and particular abilities we are still selecting on the basis of merit, and not sex or race. It is the fact of having that talent and those abilities rather than race or sex which is the deciding issue. The only partial exception to this is if the selection is being made simply to reflect the prejudice of female or ethnic minority customers rather than because of any special sensitivity to their needs which female or ethnic minority employees might bring to the job. Reflecting the prejudices of customers would, however, give an equally sound commercial justification for traditional forms of discrimination; so even setting aside moral scruples, it cannot be said that this partial exception does much to advance the case for reverse discrimination.

What arguments about utilizing a wider pool of talent and abilities will do is to justify positive action that stops short of reverse discrimination. If there are advantages to be gained from a more representative workforce, then, overall, the common good will be served by securing such a workforce. Moreover, because selection is still on the basis of merit, no one's rights will have been abused in the process. The difficulty, as we have tried to make clear, is in practising positive action without slipping over into reverse discrimination.

Our discussion of equal opportunities has focused on gender and race. The prime reason for resenting discrimination on the ground of gender or race is that this is irrelevant to selection on merit. However, this same criterion can equally well apply to other areas of discrimination. Some job applications fail because candidates have been blacklisted by the Economic League. (The Economic League is an organisation that compiled blacklists of left-wing activists, and made the lists available to subscribing companies.) Age is often a barrier to employment, as is religion. (One business studies student, who was a Mormon, told us that the University of Plymouth was the only institution to which he had applied that even gave him an interview.) Disabled people have to cope not merely with their disability, but with the popular myth that 'disabled' means unable to do things. Gays and lesbians will sometimes claim to be victims of discrimination in the workplace if they 'come out'. People who are unduly heavy have claimed to find greater difficulty in finding employment than their lighter counterparts (in fact 'sizeism' is a word which has now gained currency to identify presumed prejudice in this area), and there is some evidence to suggest that tall people are more likely to secure promotion than shorter ones. Particularly in the United States, discussion has been generated about discrimination on the grounds of one's physical appearance: attractive women are undoubtedly more merchantable than those who are 'homely' or even ugly.

A few brief observations will need to suffice. First, in at least one area we are all on an equal footing—we are born at the same age and get older at the same rate. However, although all are equally subject to increasing seniority, prejudice against older workers entails that there comes a 'cut-off point' (usually around 50) at which, if one is unemployed, or if one wishes to change careers, the chances of being able to do so are low. At the time of writing, the Labour Party has pledged itself to legislate against age discrimination, since it militates against securing employment through merit.

Second, the concept of 'meriting' a job is a somewhat nebulous one, which we have not attempted to define in the course of our discussion. It is clear that university lecturers must have specialist expertise, that plumbers must be able to mend pipes, and so on. But does a hotel receptionist need a good physical appearance? Some hotel managers will no doubt take the view that, since a hotel's reception area is its public front, its staff must look as pleasing as possible. A counter-argument to this is that society's predilections for 'good physical appearance' are simply prejudices, and that one ought not to pander to these any more than one should expect a hotel receptionist to be white rather than black, so as not to offend racist clients.

Perhaps most seriously of all, equal opportunities legislation fails to address directly the issue of social class. Do not equal opportunities policies aim to remove disadvantage so that there can be fair competition for jobs? What else is social class but a measure of relative advantage and disadvantage? Unless linked to social class, gender and race can only be very blunt indicators of membership of a disadvantaged group. Without that linkage we have, for example, the absurd (although, we admit, unusual) situation where the daughter of a millionaire Asian businessman may be deemed to be in need of the assistance of an equal opportunity programme more than the son of a white family living in a deprived council estate.

WHISTLE-BLOWING AND LOYALTY

With equal opportunities the focus is on the ethical obligations owed by a business to its existing and potential employees. With whistle-blowing, we turn to the duties of employees to the business. A firm will obviously look for a high degree of loyalty from employees, but does this extend to an employee remaining silent about wrong-doing? The employee who does not remain silent is known as a 'whistle-blower'. He or she is someone who exposes a malpractice within a business—a malpractice that may be either illegal or immoral, or both. It may be a malpractice perpetrated against the organization itself, e.g. other employees might be stealing stock or claiming expenses to which they are not entitled. In such cases the whistle-blower is in effect acting as an informer on colleagues, and the matter can usually be discretely dealt with through internal disciplinary procedures. Consequently, this is referred to as 'internal whistle-blowing'. It is contrasted with 'external whistle-blowing', which occurs when a malpractice is perpetrated by the employee's organization against an outside party—another organization, the local community, customers and so on. The other organization might be being defrauded, the local community exposed to hazardous pollution, or the public being sold unsafe goods. But whether internal or external, the function of the exposure is to do something towards righting the wrong: to forestall it or prevent its recurrence, permit the victims recompense, punish the guilty, and so on. Hence, the exposing must be to a person or body able to bring these things about—someone higher up in the organization in the internal case; the police, the media, regulatory bodies and so on, in the external case. (Because the external case involves issues of wider social and business concern, we will—as is customary—concentrate on it and assume that the exposure is public.)

As whistle-blowing involves exposing wrongs, it might not seem to present much of an ethical dilemma. After all, it is axiomatic that wrongs ought to be righted and, if all else fails, public exposure may seem to remain the only viable form of redress. However, there are considerable problems, both moral and practical, relating to whistle-blowing that must be considered. One very obvious practical problem is the risk. It is generally extremely brave or foolhardy employees who engage in whistle-blowing. The cost can be enormous. Their action will usually make them very unpopular with both bosses and colleagues, both of whom can lose out if the organization is damaged by the exposure. The whistle-blower is very often sacked, blacklisted or generally victimized. Nor is this problem of risk without a moral dimension. People have a right, and to some extent even a duty, to consider their self-interest. Being a martyr, although noble, is generally above and beyond the call of what is morally obligatory. According to an oft-quoted survey of 87 American whistle-blowers, half suffered such serious disasters as lost homes, divorce proceedings, bankruptcy proceedings, and even attempted suicide. The most harrowing example is the experience of Stanley Adams after he exposed illegal price fixing by the Swiss pharmaceutical firm Hoffman–La Roche: he was given a year's suspended jail sentence for industrial espionage. (As their selling of numbered bank accounts demonstrates, the Swiss are very keen on commercial confidentiality.) Following his arrest, his wife committed suicide.

Undoubtedly the most effective way of protecting whistle-blowers would be a law prohibiting their victimization and providing them with compensation for any suffering they might incur. At present, UK law provides little or no protection for whistle-blowers. In fact, given the assumption that employees have a duty of loyalty and confidentiality towards their employers, the whole thrust of the law seems to oppose whistle-blowing. The legal climate is somewhat more favourable in the United States where at least one state, Michigan, has a law protecting whistle-blowers from retaliation by employers and the federal government even pays out large sums to those who expose overcharging on government contracts.

Those who see the legalistic path as unwelcome state interference might opt for self-regulating measures. They might argue that it is in the organization's long-term interest not to be involved in malpractices. They may even see the whistle-blower as performing a service to the organization as well as to wider social concerns. They will probably favour some sort of internal mechanism whereby ethical worries can be reported freely and confidentially within the organization. This could be by delegating someone to handle reports of malpractices or even instituting an 'ethics hotline' that receives reports anonymously. Such facilities are, however, few and far between in the United Kingdom. To fill the gap, the charity 'Public Concern at Work' has been set up to handle enquiries in total confidence and to give advice. Sometimes it will itself approach the organization to see whether a solution can be found. It does not deal with private grievance but rather with matters of public concern (hence its name) such as bribery, corruption, fraud, consumer and workplace safety, abuse of people in care, social or sexual harassment, and so on.

Whistle-blowers do not only have themselves to consider, but also their families, colleagues, the local community and even the business itself—all of whom can be adversely affected by the disclosure. Because of the conflict between these very legitimate concerns and the general moral duty to expose wrong-doing, discussions of whistle-blowing tend to concentrate on the conditions under which whistle-blowing is both prudent and morally permissible (or even obligatory). Typical of the conditions invoked are the following:

1. The malpractice must be serious. A persistent leaking tap or poor canteen facilities may be irritating, but hardly matters on which to go public. By contrast, the production of unsafe vehicles presents possible grounds for whistle-blowing, if other conditions are satisfied (see below).
2. There must be proof of malpractice, not merely suspicion or hearsay. Without proof the whistle-blower will at best look foolish, but may well be guilty of defamation.
3. There must be a good chance that exposure will right the wrong. There is little to be said for empty gestures, particularly when people may get hurt as a result.
4. Sometimes it is held that internal procedures must be exhausted before going public. However, this is not always practicable—typically for reasons of urgency or because the person to whom the malpractice must be reported bears responsibility for it or is likely to be hostile to its exposure. However, while acknowledging that seeking internal remedies may not always be feasible or desirable, one might say that whistle-blowing can only be justified when internal means of righting the wrong have at least been considered.
5. The final potential criterion is slightly more dubious. Sometimes it is insisted that the whistle-blower must be acting from a sense of moral duty and not for personal gratification, vindictiveness or to gain attention. However, although this condition is relevant to our estimation of the whistle-blower's moral worth, even a strict Kantian (see Chapter 2) must acknowledge that base motives do not turn right actions into vices; if whistle-blowing is justifiable, then the whistle-blower's action is right, however much we may deplore his or her motives in doing it.

As the discussion has indicated, the issue that looms largest in discussions of whistle-blowing is that of loyalty. We mentioned the legal presupposition that employees owe a duty of loyalty to employers. There is a widespread belief that this holds as a specifically *moral* duty as well. On this basis, the dominant question in assessing conditions for legitimate whistle-blowing is the conflict between a duty to expose wrong-doing and loyalty to the organization to which one belongs. More than anything else, that conflict makes whistle-blowing a moral dilemma and not simply something that ought to be done if at all practicable.

However, this assumption of moral conflict is highly questionable. Are employers or businesses the sort of beings to which loyalty is owed? Ronald Duska makes the point that loyalty is based on relationships that go beyond self-interest.

'Loyalty', he says, 'depends on ties that demand self-sacrifice with no expectation of reward.'[6] It is owed to groups which 'are formed for the mutual enrichment of the members'. This, he contends, is not the case with businesses, which exist to make profit. From the business point of view, an employee's relationship to the business is a means to the end of profit. Conversely, from the employees' point of view, the business is a means to the end of wages and—if they are fortunate—satisfying work. The relationship is one of mutual self-interest: the very opposite of the kind of relationship to which feelings of loyalty are appropriate. To suppose otherwise, Duska says, is at best 'foolish romanticism', or at worst the cynical manipulation of misplaced emotions by the employer. 'There is', he writes, 'nothing as pathetic as the story of the loyal employee who, having given above and beyond the call of duty, is let go in the restructuring of the company.' Duska therefore concludes that whistle-blowing presents no conflict between a moral duty to expose wrongs and loyalty to the business, because no such loyalty is owed. He adds that while the same argument does not apply to non-profit organizations, here any malpractices to be exposed are probably perversions of the public benefits to which the organization is directed, and so exposure leaves loyalty to the organization intact.[7]

Whether or not one agrees completely with Duska it is obvious that his observations set severe limitations on notions of employee loyalty within a conventional business structure. It is therefore relevant to consider the extent to which those limitations can be overcome by the reconstituting of businesses through the aspect of employment which we shall now consider—that of participation.

PARTICIPATION AND LEADERSHIP

As applied to businesses, 'participation' is a wide, even ambiguous term. At its widest, it is used for almost any kind of employee involvement in the workings of a business beyond being paid set wages and simply carrying out orders. A narrower usage would confine the term simply to those forms of involvement beyond the minimal where employees share in decision making with managers.[8] The latter has the advantage of precision. However, it leaves no generally accepted term (beyond 'involvement' itself) for all the other forms of employee involvement and so we will employ the traditional wide usage. Likewise, while recognizing that managers are also very often employees, we will sacrifice precision to traditional usage by contrasting 'managers' with 'employees'.

Loose though the term 'participation' is, it does not normally cover mere bargaining between managers and employees. This is so whether it is collective bargaining between managers and trade union representatives, or, as is increasingly the case, 'individual bargaining' in which managers negotiate directly with individual employees over terms and conditions. Bargaining of any kind is about parties with different and possibly opposing interests attempting to arrive at an agreement. It presupposes the existence of different sides with different objectives. Participation is the exact opposite. By involving employees in the workings of businesses it unites managers and employees in a common endeavour. The root meaning of the word 'participation' is 'sharing', and hence participation suggests a sharing of common goals between managers and employees, in which both parties work together on the same side. This is not to say that all differences between them will automatically disappear. They will each bring a different perspective to the task and perhaps a different set of interests; but, to the extent that there is participation, the task will be the same one. Participation, therefore, is intrinsically different from bargaining, and we can sum up the distinction by stating that bargaining starts from differences that have to be reconciled, while participation starts from a reconciliation that has to accommodate differences.

The broadest distinction among all the various forms of participation is between those that focus on giving employees a financial involvement in the business as distinct from those that focus on involving them in its control. Within the financial forms, there is a further division between those relating to income and those relating to ownership.

The subdivision that relates to income includes arrangements for profit sharing with employees, as well as various sorts of bonus schemes for improved productivity. The ownership subdivision is confined to various sorts of employee share ownership schemes. The latter is a form of participation that is far more developed in the United States than the United Kingdom. It has been estimated that in the United States 12 per cent of employees are significant shareholders in the companies they work for and that this totals 3.5 per cent of the value of all shares.[9] Since the 1980s, this development has been greatly helped by the introduction of Employee Share Ownership Plans (ESOPs). These provide tax incentives for the sale of shares to a trust which sells the shares on to employees.

In the United Kingdom, neither employee share ownership in general nor ESOPs in particular are anything like as widespread. However, there are some notable examples. The privatization of bus services has produced a significant element of employee ownership. Until fairly recently, the privatized transport group NFC was predominantly owned by employees. (They now own a substantial minority stake.) Instances of employee ownership through ESOPs have included the Baxendale engineering company in 1983 and, more recently, the paper-maker Tullis Russell. In both these cases, a private company was sold to its employees as an alternative to a public sale of shares. In two earlier pre-ESOP instances, the John Lewis retail group and the Scott Bader engineering company were simply given away to trusts that exercise ownership on behalf of employees.

With all forms of participation that focus on employees having a financial involvement in the business (as distinct from an involvement in its control), the element that makes it participatory is that employees are being given a share in the financial rewards of the business. Whether those rewards are through ownership or additions to income, there is participation through a linking of fortunes beyond the fact of employees merely having a job and being paid the going rate for it. With forms of participation relating to control, on the other hand, there is employee involvement in the workings of the business at an operational level: employees acquire a portion of the control over business that has previously been the preserve of managers.

Here a further distinction is needed, namely between employees having control through delegation and having it through shared decision making. In the delegation case, management simply hands over some of its customary functions to employees. In the decision-sharing case, certain management functions are shared with employees: manager and employees jointly decide on matters that were previously the preserve of managers alone. It is participation in what was acknowledged to be its narrow and perhaps more precise sense. The most clear-cut example of such participation is provided by the German system of co-determination, noted in Chapter 4. Here employees jointly decide certain matters at plant level with managers through representation or works councils, as well as having a say in overall company policy through representation on the supervisory boards that ultimately govern companies. Examples of participation in control that function through delegation include quality circles where employees get together to decide on actions to improve quality, and also the use of 'autonomous' or 'self-directed' work teams in which groups of employees are left to decide for themselves how a job should be done. Allied to these are schemes of 'job enrichment' where previously routine jobs have been expanded to give employees more responsibility. In practice, these methods of delegated control can merge into each other. What they all have in common is that they concern day-to-day working procedures and directly involve individual employees. Conversely, as the system of co-determination shows, shared decision making can operate at both a firm-wide as well as a local level, concern working conditions as well as procedures, and operate through representatives.

This distinction between shared decision making and delegation is particularly worth making because the latter is sometimes given the rather grand title of 'empowerment'. This is something of a misnomer as there is no real handing over of power in delegation. In an essentially hierarchical structure such as a business, power is much more about an upward flow of accountability than a downward flow of responsibility (see Chapter 4). All delegation does is shift responsibility on to employees, leaving accountability intact. They are made accountable for getting the job done effectively rather than just for carrying out orders. Hence, whatever the benefits delegation bestows on employees, a transfer of managerial power is not really one of them.

Things are different with shared decision making, however. To the extent that employees share in decision making with managers, they cease to be account-able to managers. To that extent, then, managers surrender power to employees. It can even be that in certain areas, managers are made accountable *to* employees. For example, under the German system, managers are ultimately accountable to the supervisory board containing employee representatives.

Most discussion of participation concentrates on efficiency. The argument is that by increasing employee commitment to the business, participation improves the way they work, thus boosting quality, productivity and, eventually, profits. Discussion of the moral rights and wrongs of participation is less frequent, and the subject is not even much debated in business ethics literature. There seems to be an assumption that it just has to be a morally 'good thing'. In part, this is because the weight of evidence seems to show that participation *does* generally lead to greater efficiency, and not only that, but a happier, more contented workforce.[10] This provides a powerful utilitarian justification for participation. By increasing overall welfare it must, in utilitarian terms, be a good thing. Faced with this, any moral arguments against participation will probably find it more effective to appeal to the concept of rights rather than utility. They might suggest that employees have no right to participation or, conversely, that for them to participate in the workings of business is a transgression of property rights or even of management's 'right to manage'.

This last claim can be given short shrift. In so far as they are distinct from owners, managers derive their authority to manage from owners. It is the fact of being appointed to run the business on behalf of its owners that gives them the right to manage. Alternatively, if the managers *are* the owners, their ownership gives them this right. Either way, the right to manage is only as good as the rights of ownership from which it is derived. So if participation is transgressing any rights, it can only be the property rights of owners.

As we have noted, employee participation comes in two main varieties and four subvarieties. There is (1) sharing in the rewards, and (2) sharing in the control, with the former subdivided into (1a) participation through ownership, and (1b) additions to income, while the latter separates into (2a) delegation or (2b) shared decision making. Where participation is through ownership, property rights will only be transgressed when a transfer of ownership to employees is effected by force or fraud. If the transfer is voluntary and involves no deception—as it is in the case of ESOPs—then far from being a transgression of property rights, it is an affirmation of them. With participation through income additions there is, likewise, no transgression of property rights. Profits are shared and bonuses paid on a voluntary basis, and usually for the purpose of benefiting the owners of businesses through improved employee performance. As for participation through employee involvement in the control of the business, for either variety, this is by definition a separate matter from ownership and so it need not necessarily impinge on property rights. If it does it would probably need to be both forced on ownership and reach a scale where employees had taken ultimate control away from owners. In any case, control of businesses has long been placed in the hands of professional managers.

Case study

British Gas and the 'fat cat' salary

In December 1994 British Gas announced that its Executive Director, Mr Cedric Brown, was to receive a pay rise of 75 per cent. He already earned around £400 000 and this rise therefore brought his annual remuneration up to £700 000.

Timed in a mild early December, the winter cold had yet to set in, and it was likely that once again many old age pensioners would die of hypothermia, being unable to afford the costs of heating their homes. In addition, there was a likelihood that the Tory government was about to increase its 8 per cent VAT levy on domestic fuel to 17.5 per cent (although in the end this did not occur, owing to a revolt in the Tory backbenches).

Although there was a reprieve on VAT, gas prices were raised by 2.9 per cent, and British Gas announced that it was to withdraw the facility of customer payment afforded by British Gas showrooms. As a further economy measure, the rank and file workforce were faced with the prospect of lay-offs and decreases in salary—a move which was particularly galling, since it came only two weeks after Mr Brown's massive pay rise.

The British Gas controversy raises several important issues in business ethics. Interviewed in the media, Michael Heseltine, the Minister for Trade and Industry, maintained that such high salaries were necessary if a company like British Gas was to be 'world class'. Having obtained several foreign orders, it was in the same league as multinational firms, and therefore high salaries had to be offered to those at the top in order to attract the right people for the job.

Yet Cedric Brown presumably had obtained his job at a lower salary, thus proving that the even higher salary was not needed to attract him. The comparability argument, typically, compared his work with that of higher-paid chief executives, not with chief executives of Third World or Japanese companies.

Although egalitarians would wish to see some levelling down of people's earnings, non-egalitarians might argue that, although large, Mr Brown's salary is still a drop in the ocean compared with British Gas's annual turnover. If his salary had remained at its former level, it would not have enabled British Gas to lower a typical household bill by even a penny, and it would only have saved two or three jobs.

Egalitarians will argue that it is the principle of equality that entails that such great differences in wealth should be abolished, not the con-sequences of doing so. However, perhaps ironically, despite the widespread disapproval of Cedric Brown's large income, the majority of Britain's

ESSENTIALS OF BUSINESS ETHICS

population enter the National Lottery regularly—an institution that also creates vast discrepancies in wealth. Is it consistent to deplore Cedric Brown's pay, but approve of the National Lottery?

Where it is, participation merely extends the transfer of control to include employees other than just managers.

The merely negative claim that employees have no right to participation could probably be answered by an appeal to the Kantian notion of respect for persons: not to involve people in workings of businesses is to treat them as simply a means to an end—the end of profit—and so fail to respect them as persons. Denying people a say in matters that so affect their lives is failing to treat them as fully human beings; it is a denial of human rights to be compared to a denial of democratic freedoms. Consequently, so the argument goes, employees do have a moral right to participation.[11]

Quite apart from utilitarian justifications and any basis in human rights, participation has, we would suggest, two other arguments that could be mounted in its favour. Firstly, it perhaps offers a solution to the problem of employee loyalty. As we noted in the section on whistle-blowing, because businesses treat employees as merely a means to the end of profit, considerations of loyalty are arguably not appropriate to businesses. However, as was just noted, an argument for participation is that without it employees *are* treated as simply a means to an end. In other words, where there is participation, employees are *not* being treated this way. Rather, they are engaged in a common endeavour with employers. To the extent that there is participation, everyone is on the same side. If this is so, then it would, to the extent that there is participation, be appropriate for employees to feel loyalty towards the businesses for which they work.

The second area where participation might be beneficial is that of leadership. This is a much discussed area of business, with discussion usually couched in terms of leadership 'skills'. This implies that leadership solely consists of the aptitude and attitude of would-be leaders. There is, however, another more conceptual dimension. Just as loyalty is only appropriate to a certain kind of relationship, so is leadership. Here too it has to be the case that everyone is on the same side; that they are engaged in some kind of common endeavour. People who are being directed towards an objective they do not share are not being led, they are being used. These are two very different things. Using and being used do not demand a common endeavour. The two parties can have quite separate and even opposing ends in mind—a lender and a borrower, for instance. With leading and being led, on the other hand, there has to be an overriding objective common to both. To the extent therefore that participation presupposes a common endeavour between managers and managed, it permits managers to be leaders and not merely bosses.

Participation is not the only possible way for this to happen. A paternalistic concern for staff will also put managers on the same side as employees and so convert them into leaders. An example of this—although usually combined with participation at a shopfloor level—is provided by Japanese management, with its still largely intact commitment to lifetime employment and the general welfare of staff. Participation is, though, the other and perhaps better way of converting managers into leaders. A strictly non-paternalistic example of this is provided by the Rover car company. There a pledge of no compulsory redundancies was made in order to secure the shopfloor participation deemed to be necessary for improvements in productivity and quality. The result is that workers can now suggest cost-saving measures, confident that they will not lead to sacking. For such workers it is appropriate to say that their managers are also leaders.

It is important not to see this linking of leadership and participation as a plea for sensitive, caring management—although this might help! Managers can be tough and ruthless while still being leaders, provided they are on the same side as the people they manage. For example, a manager forced to cut staff in order for the business to survive can still be a leader. In contrast, a manager who cuts staff purely in order to boost profits by lowering labour costs is, however dutiful the service to owners of the business, in no sense a leader to the people he or she manages. Such a manager can be compared to a general for whom victory in battle is having as few of his soldiers left alive as possible. It would be as inappropriate to talk of 'leadership' in the management case as in the military one.

DISCUSSION TOPICS

1. What does a firm exist *for*? How does your answer affect its responsibilities to (a) shareholders; (b) employees; (c) society?

2. Is it acceptable for a firm to engage in (a) positive action; (b) imposing targets for underrepresented groups; (c) reverse discrimination? Examine the arguments for and against the various stages of the employment spectrum, mentioned in this chapter.

3. Are there categories of employee who still experience discrimination, such as small people, ugly people, excessively 'large' people, adherents to controversial religious groups? What do you think of the argument that belonging to certain groups is voluntary and hence the member should bear the consequences? (For example, it might be suggested that one could leave a religious group, or that a heavy person could go on a diet.)

4. To what extent is it true that an employee owes a duty of loyalty to a firm?

5. In what ways might women managers adopt a different style of management from men? To what extent would this be an improvement?

NOTES

1. M. Friedman, *Free to Choose*, Penguin, Harmondsworth, 1980, p. 40.
2. P. F. Drucker, *Managing in Turbulent Times*, Harper Row, New York, 1980, p. 181.
3. D. Clutterbuck *et al.*, *Actions Speak Louder*, Kogan Page, 1992, pp. 77–83.
4. J. Straw, *Equal Opportunities: The Way Ahead*, Institute of Personnel Management, London, 1989, p. 107.
5. Ibid., p. 70.
6. R. Duska, 'Whistleblowing and loyalty', in J. R. DesJardins and J. J. McCall (eds), *Contemporary Business Ethics*, Wadsworth, Belmont, 1990, pp. 142–147.
7. Ibid., p. 146.
8. J. L. Cotton, *Employee Involvement*, Sage, Newbury Park, 1993, p. 14.
9. *Financial Times*, 28 March, 1995, p. 12.
10. Cotton, *Employee Involvement*; S. Fernie, and D. Metcalf, *Participation, Contingent Pay, Representation and Workplace Performance: Evidence from Great Britain*, London School of Economics, London, 1995, pp. 14–17.
11. See, e.g., J. J. McCall, 'Participation in Employment', in DesJardins and McCall, *Contemporary Business Ethics*, Wadsworth, Belmont, pp. 165–173.

6 *Finance and Investment*

In the words of the well-known musical, 'money makes the world go around'. This is no mere cliché. We might like to think that there are other things which help to shape our world—such as human kindness, voluntary work, political involvement—but most humanitarian activities involve at least some financial backing. Political parties are always seeking for funding, volunteer organizations usually need some full-time paid organizer, and human kindness itself often requires finanical support. Far from being an arid area of ethical indifference, where we place our money enables us to cast a vote of approval or disapproval, not only in terms of whether we want the goods or services which firms offer, but whether or not we wish to give a company our personal ethical seal of approval. Even those with limited means have to decide whether to give the odd coin to the Oxfam or Christian Aid collector, and whether to buy bibles or pornography. When the Church of England decided to support the boycott of Nestlé, called by a number of consumer groups on account of its Third World marketing of powdered baby milk, Nestlé was sufficiently worried to write letters to clergy and prominent laypeople, in an attempt to persuade the General Synod to reverse its decision—an attempt that proved successful. Although it is not possible to determine the full effects of particular boycotts, it is widely believed that the boycott of South African goods which was implemented by consumers (as well as the sporting world) between the 1950s and 1993 helped to influence the emancipation of black South Africans—a view which was reflected in Nelson Mandela's announcement in 1993 that sanctions could now be lifted, and that Western consumers should now encourage the economic development of the country.

Increasingly the view has arisen in the United States and in Europe, however, that one not only ought to be monitoring one's purchases in order to act ethically. Investment, it is argued, is as much a matter of ethical concern as purchasing. The concern for ethical investment first took its rise in the United States in the 1970s. In 1983, the Church of England and the Society of Friends (the Quakers) were troubled by the question of whether they might inadvertently be giving financial support, through their investment portfolios, to companies whose strategies they would not support, if these were known. In particular, both religious organizations were concerned about financial interests in South Africa. Accordingly, these two bodies, together with certain other interested organizations and charitable trusts, formed the Ethical Investment Research and Information Service—better known as EIRIS.

EIRIS now effectively monitors all the largest 700 'good' UK companies, and screens them on a variety of issues, many of which are ethical. EIRIS's categories include: advertising complaints, sale and production of alcohol, treatment of animals, environmental record, financial involvements, gambling, military involvement, mining, plantations, political donations, pornography, size by market value, tobacco production and sale, and transnational and overseas interests. EIRIS has now become a self-financing company; it charges individual investors and financial advisers for its services, which are principally in the form of supplying fact sheets and 'screening' services. EIRIS's aim is to inform, rather than to persuade or campaign, and members of the public can state what their areas of ethical concern are and request details of companies or unit trusts which are consistent with these concerns.

COURSES OF ACTION

Once would-be ethical investors have decided which firms are morally acceptable and which are dubious, the question then arises as to what one should do about the matter. In her book *Socially Responsible Investment*, Sue Ward suggests three possible courses of action: avoidance, positive choice and shareholder action.

AVOIDANCE

EIRIS's information, at least initially, was geared towards the first of these, and a number of accountants and financial advisers became interested in providing ethical investment services for clients, enabling them to avoid having financial interests in activities of which they morally disapproved. Special unit trusts were devised to offer ethical portfolios to ethically conscious clients. The first company to do this was Friends Provident, originally set up by Quakers—hence the name. The Friends Provident Stewardship Fund was launched around Christmas in 1984, and, although the Christmas season is reckoned to be a notoriously bad time for financial launches, it was substantially oversubscribed, thus indicating a significant public interest in 'stewardship' (Friends Provident's term to describe ethical investment).

Friends Provident was of the opinion, which is now shared by the majority of ethical investment companies, that an ethical fund should not simply offer a portfolio which had been screened by EIRIS. In the financial world the situation can change: companies can reinvest their capital, for example, and hence a company which was once deemed to be 'clean' can become tarnished, and vice versa. Accordingly, Friends Provident pioneered the basic structure for an ethical fund: a specific manager responsible for the fund, a set of definite 'green' and ethical criteria to drive its activities, and independent external research which would determine which shares might acceptably be purchased. Internally, Friends Provident established an 'ethical committee' which would monitor the changing situation and initiate investigations into any criticisms of companies which came from various sources.

Following the inception of Friends Provident, various other ethical investment trusts arose. At the time of writing, Friends Provident remains by far the largest in terms of funds, and perhaps the best known. Other funds which have been rated highly, both in terms of ethics and financial return, include the Abbey Life Ethical Trust, the Scottish Equitable Ethical Unit Trust and the Clerical Medical Evergreen Fund. Different funds use slightly different ethical criteria, thus enabling the would-be investor to select the fund best fitted to his or her ethical stance. Alternatively, financial advisers who offer ethical services can tailor a portfolio to the client's wishes.

The use of a set of 15 or so criteria for avoiding investing in a company has been criticized for being negative. Should not an investor take into account positive company policies, such as improving the environment, and positively select those firms to entrust one's capital? According to one line of thinking, the negative tactic of avoiding companies with a dubious ethical track record is useless in any case. To those who are unfamiliar with the world of investment, it may seem as if disinvesting is tantamount to recalling a loan, and that if all shareholders were to disinvest this might starve the ethically failing company of funds and prevent further business operations. Sadly, this is not the case. Most investments are not loans. Unlike, say, a building society, where house purchases are actually curtailed when investors withdraw monies, a company that is financed by shares is actually owned by its investors. Once a firm has raised money by its initial flotation on the stock market, it has acquired the money it needs to initiate its business activities.[1] That initial money is not taken away by disinvestment, even if share prices drop as a result of the behaviour of ethical investors. Although dwindling share prices can make a firm more vulnerable to takeovers, or limit its ability to make further acquisitions, such effects are rare. When the then Prime Minister Edward Heath described Lonrho as 'the unacceptable face of capitalism' in the 1970s, many business companies engaged in *avoidance*, thus impeding Lonrho in engaging in further take-overs. However, such examples are rare, and indeed it can be argued that selling shares in a morally dubious firm only has the effect of encouraging some other, less scrupulous investor to make immoral gains.

It could be argued that disinvestment is a way of drawing attention to malpractices of business organizations, and that by drawing attention in this way to such practices one might embarrass a company into mending its ways. When the General Synod of the Church of England debated whether to divest itself of its Nestlé shares, this received considerable publicity. The General Synod, however, decided in the end to make no change in its investment portfolio; had it done otherwise, perhaps it would have generated more public disapproval of Nestlé's business practices. In any case, the argument about drawing attention to mal-practices is really one which applies to larger organizations who have investments; a private individual disinvesting is, of course, not so likely to influence the thinking of the wider public.

The companies who offer ethical portfolios or unit trusts to investors tend to provide information to their clients (usually through EIRIS's information service) rather than engage in active campaigning against offending companies. Their continuous monitoring of companies' track records results in their switching of clients' investments on occasions, although, as Ward argues, this presents little by way of undesirable consequences to the companies concerned. One or two com-panies are rather more proactive, however. When an alleged malpractice comes to light, Scottish Provident engages in 'constructive dialogue' with companies with which it has dealt, and it claims to have had favourable results. Scottish Provident in fact positively invites its clients to write to them regarding criticisms of the companies they use, and undertakes to investigate them.

So far our analysis of disinvestment has focused on the consequences of shareholder activity. A non-consequentialist, however, might suggest that there is a different reason for disinvestment in ethically suspect companies: it is immoral to benefit from something that we consider to be wrong. Even if disinvestment could not dissuade a firm from malpractices, it might be contended that financial gain from such investments is 'simply wrong'. Just as one might argue that, if stealing is wrong, then receiving stolen goods is also wrong, similarly one might argue that if selling arms, tobacco or animal-tested cosmetics is wrong, then so is financially benefiting from those companies that market them.

The problem of 'being an accessory' to the ethical shortcomings of business has proved a particular problem for campaigning groups and charities, and in fact contributed to the rise in concern about ethical investments. As ethical investment increasingly became an issue in the 1980s, some trade unions discovered that they had investment portfolios which included firms with a poor employee relations record; at least one charity for cancer research discovered that it was inadvertently benefiting financially from the tobacco industry. On the principle that if one does not approve of something one should not benefit from it, there was clearly a need to disinvest.

POSITIVE ACTION
Ward's second strategy—positive action—enables positive consequences to emerge from ethical investment. Positive action, as the term implies, aims at giving positive

encouragement to firms who engage in positively commendable activities. This tactic therefore involves selecting those firms which have a good track record—perhaps for exemplary employee relations, or for improving the environment—and rewarding them for their good conduct by selecting them for investment. Examples may include that paragon of virtue The Body Shop, water companies, companies that manufacture air purifiers or water filters, and companies that research and market alternative sources of energy such as solar or wind power.

At first appearance, positive choice may seem to be subject to the same criticisms as avoidance tactics. After all, it may be argued, companies like The Body Shop have already raised the monies needed for their business operations, and their activities are neither helped nor hindered if share prices rise as a result of increased demand. Although positive choice has little effect on already established companies, Ward points out that this strategy can significantly help smaller companies at their inception, when they desperately need funding in order to make a start on their business activities. Such firms are therefore likely to be private rather than public limited companies, and hence cannot be quoted on the stock market or dealt with by financial advisers. It is usually necessary for individuals to find these privately (e.g. in the small ads column of 'green' or ethical consumerist journals) and make their own arrangements.

The problem about investing in new companies is that the risk is higher. Because of the risk, financial advisers would not normally recommend them for purposes such as pension contributions, for example. Unit trusts are obliged by law to avoid small, unlisted companies, so investors will normally approach the small ethical company direct. In this area of the business world at least, good business ethics is not necessarily good business! Those who have money to spare and who can afford to be philosophical about losing a few hundred pounds might well consider supporting a good cause. (Minimum investments are often as small as £100.) Returns from some of these smaller firms have been surprisingly good, however—the Ethical Consumer Research Association, for example, was recently able to boast a 10 per cent dividend from shares at a time when inflation was running at around 2.5 per cent.

'Green' businesses in particular are often promoted as potential investments on the grounds that 'greenness' entails 'being ethical'. However, it is important to recognize a distinction between (i) firms that are ethically 'clean'; (ii) firms that have 'green' policies; and (iii) firms that actively seek to improve the environment. Of course there is some overlap, but would-be investors should recognize that the so-called 'ethical and green' investment funds that are offered by financial advisers can offer very different packages, based on differing criteria.

For example, at the time of writing, the Scottish Equitable Ethical Unit Trust, described as 'almost perfect' in its avoidance of animal testing, political donations and banks,[2] uses no environmental criteria at all. By contrast, the TSB Environmental Fund does not purport to avoid companies which are deemed to fall short of EIRIS's criteria, but rather seeks to invest positively in companies that 'demonstrate a positive commitment to the protection and preservation of the natural environment'. TSB has attracted considerable controversy by including ICI, Shell UK and Unilever in its portfolio. (Unilever has been criticized for testing cosmetics on animals.) Even on its pro-environmental choices it has only achieved a 14 per cent avoidance rate on companies which are responsible for water pollution.[3] (TSB does not in fact claim to avoid companies which pollute water; however, would-be ethical investors might reasonably suppose that this was a criterion for selecting appropriate investments for such a fund.)

SHAREHOLDER ACTION

Ward's third approach is shareholder action. Avoidance of a firm means that one disposes of one's right to have a say in its policies. By contrast, staying in means that one can attempt to change a firm's policies. For example, shareholders have the right to attend the annual general meeting of a company, and some ethically concerned shareholders have used this right to table questions that highlight ethical issues and draw attention to malpractices. Those who engage in shareholder action generally only purchase the minimum number of shares required to give them this privilege, and hence they will benefit financially from morally suspect operations in the minimum possible way.

Shareholder action has rarely involved a major change in company policy, although it was instrumental in the case of Barclay's Bank in the early 1970s, when some students bought token shares and attended AGMs, where they drew shareholders' attention to the bank's South African involvements during the apartheid regime. This attracted publicity, and undoubtedly had some influence on Barclay's eventual decision to pull out of South Africa. Shareholders' questioning can at least embarrass the directors, and on occasions gain negative publicity for the company.

Of course, Ward's three tactics are not mutually exclusive. When making a decision about where to place one's investments, an individual can decide simultaneously to avoid certain types of firm, to offer positive encouragement to others and, if he or she feels sufficiently militant, to buy a token number of shares in 'dubious' companies, and attend shareholders' meetings to voice their complaints. Our discussion has shown just how complicated is the question of where to invest our personal fortune, if we are lucky enough to have one!

SOME OBJECTIONS TO ETHICAL INVESTMENT

Few members of the public have the time or the financial means to trek round shareholder's meetings to protest at malpractices, or the knowledge about how to raise their concerns. Faced with the prospect, too, that positive action is likely to have limited success, one might be forgiven for thinking that ethical investments make little difference to the behaviour of firms. Faced with the complexity of the issues surrounding ethical investment, and the degree of interdependence of firms, a would-be investor might be forgiven for despairing of finding some firm that was entirely clean.

In the light of the preceding discussion, one of two extreme positions seem to be warranted. One response might be to claim that where one's money goes makes little ultimate difference and that one should simply use conventional criteria of acceptable risk and good profitability to determine one's portfolio. A more radical approach might be total avoidance: keeping one's money under the mattress, although unprofitable, might at least keep its owner ethically untarnished!

In the final section of this chapter we shall consider some of the objections which are made to the notion of ethical investment, and indicate the possible responses.

'NO ONE IS PERFECT'

In the light of the numerous analyses which have been undertaken of ethical investment portfolios, there are none that we know of which come out as absolutely and uncontroversially 'clean'. The Abbey Life Ethical Trust, for example, excludes from its portfolio companies which have more than a 10 per cent interest in other firms which do not satisfy Abbey's ethical criteria. However, investors might well consider that 10 per cent is 10 per cent too much, and that a portfolio should not include any company whatsoever that has the slightest financial interest in the sale of arms, tobacco, alcohol or animal-tested products. Even the 'almost perfect' Scottish Equitable Ethical Unit Trust does not use pornography as one of its criteria, and indeed includes shares in W. H. Smith as part of its portfolio. W. H. Smith has been the target of campaigning for selling 'soft porn', and also, jointly with Boots, owns Do-It-All, which has attracted recent criticism for the sale of tropical hardwood.[4]

In reply to this criticism we can argue that, even though no ethical trust may be 'perfect', this does not entail that all are equally deficient and that none are better than others. If none are white, at least we can choose the lightest shade of grey.

'WHAT'S WRONG WITH IT, ANYWAY?'

Allied to this criticism is the view that ethics admits of different points of view, and that many of the assessment criteria which are typically listed by ethical investment firms and ethical consumer groups include components that are at best debatable. After all, someone might claim, is there really anything wrong with the sale of armaments? Surely all countries need a defence system and should be free to choose how much they spend on arms? If politicians think it undesirable that certain countries, such as Iraq or North Korea, should develop certain types of weapon, then international action can be taken to ensure that they comply with international agreements. It is only a minority of citizens who totally avoid the consumption of alcohol, so why should one be prepared to consume a product but not invest in it? Regarding tobacco, organizations like FOREST have campaigned for the right of the individual to decide whether or not to smoke, and, notwithstanding its pro-smoking stance, FOREST seeks to encourage responsibility on the part of smokers. It has been pointed out, too, that it is hypocritical for any investor to disapprove of gambling—after all, is not stock market speculation itself a game of chance? The scientific case against pornography remains unproven, as far as the present writers are aware. Although many may find it distasteful, there is no uncontroversial firm evidence that it renders readers more likely to commit sexual offences. If some citizens find it distasteful, this may present a case for displaying it more discretely, or even for requiring customers specifically to ask for it; but, it may be argued, this is not a case for not selling it at all, or for disinvesting in companies with a financial interest in it.

We have already dealt in Chapter 2 with the view that ethics is merely 'a matter of opinion', and we need not repeat here our criticisms of this view. Suffice it to say that there is a difference between holding that there simply are no right and wrong answers to ethical questions ('relativism') and the observation that it is not possible to secure universal agreement on controversial ethical matters. This latter observation need not imply relativism at all; it simply shows that, much of the time, ethical questions (like some non-ethical questions) are difficult to answer. Bearing in mind that many questions in ethics are controversial, we would certainly endorse the view that no financial adviser has the right to impose his or her ethics on clients, who, at the end of the day, must decide which ethical concerns (if any) are relevant to their investment decisions. The fact that different unit trusts offer slightly different emphases enables investors to do this, and most financial advisers are happy to offer a tailor-made portfolio which takes into account investors' concerns and interests. Ethical investment firms typically regard themselves as advisers rather than moral arbiters.

In a chapter specifically aimed at finance and investment, it would be inappropriate and unrealistic to launch into a discussion of the morality of war, animal rights, or the pros and cons of smoking and alcohol consumption. Nevertheless, the fact that such issues have arisen from a discussion of finance is a strong indication that finance is not an activity confined to an accountant's desk or a stock exchange television monitor! Those who wish to pursue the moral debate on these matters can be referred to the plethora of books which those subjects have recently generated. It may be appropriate, however, to comment briefly on three issues—political donations, Third World debt and currency speculation—which are often raised in connection with finance, and which raise the question, 'What's wrong with it?'

Political donations

It may seem as if companies that make political donations incur Friedman's criticism that they are imposing a form of 'taxation without representation'. If customers know that a company makes political donations (and the majority of shoppers do not), there is no way in which they can buy the goods and opt out; they must either donate, switch brands (which is not always possible) or go without. Shareholders are affected, arguably, to an even greater extent: once a donation has been made they cannot recoup any of their depleted profit. On the other side of the argument, those who favour political donations may contend that certain types of company thrive better under particular forms of government, and hence, since the Conservatives are often reckoned to be the champions of the business culture, it is reasonable for any firm, by way of maximizing its profits, to help to secure the appropriate political climate.

There are other dimensions to the controversy. Those who object to political donations appear principally to object to companies donating to the Conservative Party. This is no doubt due to two principal reasons. First, critics of business probably tend to have leanings towards the political left wing, and, second, it is the Conservative Party that benefits most from political donations. In 1992–1993 there were 342 company donations to the Conservative Party, amounting to £5 333 552, compared with three to the Liberal Democrats, totalling £14 400, and only one to Labour of a mere £2200. Additionally, some companies donate to the BUI (British United Industrialists) which has been described as 'a money laundering agency for the Conservative Party'.[5]

In law, a company's annual report and accounts must declare political donations of £200 and above, but it is under no legal obligation to consult its shareholders. In 1989 the Labour Party sought to introduce legislation requiring shareholder approval to sanction political donations, but the motion was defeated. Labour supporters have felt that the government operated a double standard, in view of the fact that in 1984 their Trades Union Act required unions to seek members' approval concerning political funds, most of which go to Labour. Trade union members can opt out of the special political levies, while shareholders cannot recoup any proportion of a firm's political donations if they object to them.

Finally, the fact that political parties—especially the Conservatives—rely so heavily on political donations from companies gives considerable power to business. Many would argue that such power is excessive, interfering with the democratic process. Should not political campaigning and the outcomes of elections be determined by the policies of the various parties and the quality of political debate, rather than by the amounts of money they are able to spend on their publicity? As things stand, companies are in a position to exert influence on a government by indicating that they might withdraw financial support if certain policies are not implemented.

Third World debt

The involvement of the 'Big Four' UK banks in collecting interest on Third World debt is a subject which continues to attract attention. Aid agencies are often quick to point out that the cancellation of all Third World debt to the West would achieve more for developing countries annually than the total annual donations for all the relief organizations put together. According to one statistic, for every £2 in aid given to developing countries, £9 is demanded back in interest.

To sceptics, this will appear to be only one side of the argument. Might it not be contended that paying one's debts is itself an ethical principle, and that those who owe money—whether in the West or in the Third World—should not expect magnanimous cancellations? A poor citizen who owes money to a large firm (perhaps for a much-needed cooker or heater) cannot expect the firm simply to cancel the debt on the grounds that he or she is poor.

Those who champion the cause of the Third World will contend that the situation is rather more complex. Those who owe the debts have in fact inherited those debts from previous generations, through no fault of their own. (One might note here a disanalogy with the personal debt example: we are not responsible for our parents' debts if they die insolvent.) The debts were frequently incurred through disreputable and incompetent political regimes, often by dictators who sought no public mandate for their misspending. A substantial amount of that spending has been on armaments which were used for crippling military conflicts.

Third World debt, it is argued, has the effect of placing developing countries at a disadvantage when negotiating financial deals, and hence lays them open to disadvantageous—many would say unfair—trading conditions. In many cases, physical resources have been diverted from the production of basic food-stuffs to cash crops. A country such as Ghana, for example, produces cocoa for export, instead of cereal crops to feed its own population. Furthermore, in order to repay debt, some developing countries have resorted to selling off precious resources such as timber from tropical rainforests—a practice that is surely to no one's long-term advantage. The Third World's debt problems are further compounded by high interest rates imposed by the West, over which they have no influence. The problem of Third World debt, then, is more than a problem about what figures should appear on bank balance sheets.

Currency speculation

Currency speculation is a further area within the financial world which arouses comment, and of which brief mention should be made. The practice itself is straightforward enough. The speculator makes a profit by buying a foreign currency when exchange rates are favourable, and sells it either when it has appreciated significantly and he or she wishes to realize the proceeds, or when rates are about to fall and it is prudent to pull out.

At first appearance it may seem that to invest in this way is simply a mark of financial astuteness, and it might be asked whether such a practice is any different from, say, buying a precious antique at a good price and selling it later for a profit. Critics of currency speculation will argue that there are important differences: in particular, currency speculation involves no product or service. One can at least admire the antique piece of furniture while it appreciates in value, but in the case of currency speculation one is only trading in symbols of value, and those who make their livelihood by speculation are offering no product service that is of benefit to anyone except themselves. Unlike the investment, which is needed to float a company, there is no benefit to trade and industry in buying and selling foreign currency, and such speculations often tend to do harm rather than good. For example, if a country's currency is doing badly, speculators' pulling out can only exacerbate that country's monetary crisis, causing its exchange rates to spiral downwards.

The Co-operative Bank is one organization which has taken a definite stance on the issue of currency speculation. It resolutely rejects the practice and will not invest customers' monies by speculation in foreign exchange rates.

'FINANCIAL ADVISERS HAVE DOUBLE STANDARDS'

We have noted that the lack of agreed answers to these questions about investment make it inappropriate for financial advisers to impose their own judgements on their clients. However, their consistent and understandable refusal to adopt the role of moral arbiters to their clients also entails that they do not require their clients to select their portfolios on ethical grounds at all. Not only will most advisers assist a client who sees no reason to avoid the armaments industry, equally those same financial advisers are happy to suggest portfolios which are devised simply on the grounds of profitability.

It has been argued that this policy entails a double standard. Surely those financial advisers who claim to specialize in 'ethical investment' should not be prepared to profit from investments which might generally be considered to be unethical. If they are prepared to deal with ethical and non-ethical portfolios alike, then have they done anything more than locate a gap in the market (ethical portofolios) from which they are happy to benefit?

Most financial advisers point to their responsibility to advise clients of the width of choice which lies open to them, and indeed it is a requirement of the Personal Investment Authority (their regulatory body) that they do so. To confine one's recommendations to a few 'ethical' firms would be to offer too narrow a selection to clients.

There is one British financial adviser who claims to have the courage of his convictions and advises on ethical and green investments only. This adviser accepts the conclusion that one cannot consistently champion the cause of ethical investments and at the same time enable clients to gain (and bring profit to himself) from firms which he judges to be blatantly unethical. This firm also has a policy of donating 50 per cent of all profits to charities named by clients.

Although such policies may seem attractive, these practices have not gone uncriticized by other ethical investment consultants. In particular, these critics point out that any financial adviser has an obligation, as a trustee, to secure maximum returns for clients, or at least to point out where these can be found. Such policies also entail that clients' full situations cannot always be accommodated. For example, an adviser with such policies could not consistently offer full life cover, since there are no wholly ethical policies which can achieve this. One critic describes the charity donations as a 'gimmick', pointing out that they are tax deductible, and hence not as generous as they seem; this rival firm prefers to charge clients considerably less for services, thus enabling them to decide the destination of any extra monies.

IS ETHICAL INVESTMENT PROFITABLE?

One argument often used in favour of ethical and green investments is that one need not have to choose between ethics and profits, since ethical investments can hold their own against, if not perform better than conventional stock. The evidence for this is conflicting. Ethical investment reduces considerably the number of companies which can be potentially included in one's portfolio, and those companies tend to be the smaller ones. (According to one specialist, 80 per cent of the top 100 FTSE-listed companies would be considered unsuitable for an ethical fund.[6]) On the other hand, it has been suggested that, as consumers become increasingly concerned about ethical issues and about the survival of the planet, a gravitation towards ethical and green funds may itself cause an increase in share price through increased demand. As demand for green goods and services increases, so the performance of companies involved in their supply is likely to rise. Future government legislation on pollution and other environmental matters—assuming this will happen—is likely to have a twofold effect on the ethical and green sector. First, those companies that are already environmentally responsible will have little, if any, need for sizeable expenditure in order to comply with future legislation, and hence are likely to be significantly ahead of their currently less environmentally concerned competitors. Second, any new legislation is likely to require existing companies to purchase green goods and services in order to comply—which would be good news for green companies and their investors.

These arguments are theoretical, however. In actual practice, there is little to choose from a purely financial standpoint between ethical/environmental and conventional investments. One broker, James Capel, has produced a 'green index' with which to compare the two types of company. Its base date was 30 December

Case study

Feminism and finance

At first appearance the world of accounting and finance may seem to have radically different concerns from those who debate about feminist ideology. However, it has recently been noted that, when it comes to ethical investment, there are significantly more women than men who look to 'ethical' funds to manage their capital.

One can only speculate about the reasons for this. Accountancy and investment have typically been male dominated. It was only in the early 1980s that women were allowed to work in the stock market. The world of finance still remains largely male dominated, and even more 'enlightened' firms who offer ethical investments do not use inclusive language in their literature.

The management of money has traditionally been the man's prerogative, the husband in most domestic partnerships being the breadwinner and the woman the housekeeper. At one time a woman's property automatically became her husband's on marriage, with the consequence that the husband had the task of managing the couple's savings. If the female partner had a separate bank account at all, it was usually for housekeeping or for 'pin money', since substantial purchases such as cars were made by men.

The idea of a married couple being a single entity has been reinforced by religious traditions. St Paul, for example, asserts that 'the two shall be one flesh'.[7] With increasing secularization, however, the 'liberated woman' has become increasingly common, and as higher proportions of women have independent employment, the idea of 'running separate economies' has become more widespread. Hence greater numbers of women than before seek financial advice on how best to invest their money.

Why, then, should significantly more women than men turn to 'ethical funds'? It might be suggested that the reasons relate to women's presumed characteristics—compassion, caring, concern—in contrast with men, who are encouraged to assume a more 'macho' image which might be more compatible with investing in armaments or with oppressive regimes.

Whether or not the explanation is to be found in the different genders' typical characteristics, it is likely to be the case that women who run their finances independently are more likely to be aware of social and ethical issues than the traditional housewife who looks after the children and commutes between the kitchen sink and the local shops. Independent women are at least likely to have considered some feminist issues, and such deliberations may well be part of a wider concern about society in general. Hence such women are aware too of the ways in which organizing their finances connects up with wider ethical issues.

Other explanations for women's disproportionate ethical investment are more pragmatic. Since women on average still own less money than men, ethical funds are more suited to them, since a number are more geared up to the small investor. Furthermore, many men have already made arrangements to organize their finances, and may now be discovering that they are 'locked into' investment schemes from which it is hard to pull out. If one has invested, say, in a managed bond fund which has run for over half its term, it is a poor financial decision to cash it in. (If it is linked to a mortgage, the building society may not even allow this.)

There is no single reason to explain every investor's decision. However, as attitudes to gender become increasingly reappraised, and as new generations of young men consider where to invest their monies, we may well see new patterns of investment emerging. At least we can conclude that finance *is* a feminist issue!

1988, and the Financial Times Share Index was rebased (to 100) to the same date. On 17 May 1991 the green index stood at 118.55, with the FTSE at 136.55; the following year the green index was at 136.06, with the FTSE at 145.52. Thus for the two-year period 1990–1992, the conventional shares had the advntage, although in the 1991–1992 period the green shares had the edge (1.15 per cent growth, as compared with FTSE's 1.07 per cent).

Other statistical data are more encouraging for the ethical investor. In the United States, for the five-year period ending at 31 December 1992, the cumulative return for ethical investments was 95 per cent, compared with a cumulative return of only 80 per cent for conventional investments. The magazine *Pensions Management* (an FT independent publication) analysed the performance of four ethical pension funds which had been in operation over the five-year period from 1988 to 1993. The average growth of the four funds stood at 14.2 per cent, compared with a growth rate of 13.4 for the average equity pension.

By contrast, however, Clerical Medical's Evergreen Trust showed an 8.1 per cent decline in 1991–1992, compared with a 4.2 per cent decline in the FT-A World Index for the same period. Jupiter Tyndall Merline's Ecology Unit Trusts plummeted from £10 million to £8.6 million in 1991—mainly due to a large institutional investor pulling out, combined with the weakening of the dollar. Indeed, most of the available data relate to the period around 1991, which is generally agreed to be non-typical for share performance in general.

'ALL INVESTMENT IS UNETHICAL ANYWAY'

There is a more radical criticism that can be offered of the world of investment. It may be suggested that there is little point in distinguishing between ethical and unethical investment, since there is something morally objectionable to the whole idea of investment in any case.

This type of criticism comes from two quite different sources. The first stems from the type of critique of capitalism given by the political left wing, especially the Marxist. The second type of critique of capitalist ownership comes from Islam, which has a consistent total prohibition on 'usury'. According to the Muslim, one must earn one's money as a result of one's labour, by means of inheritance or as a gift, not through means which involve risk or chance, such as gambling or stock market speculation.

The Muslim way of thinking about economics has often attracted Western curiosity about how banking and entrepreneurial activities are possible in Islamic countries. More pertinent here, however, are the grounds on which Islam is critical of Western capitalist methods of running an economy. Within a capitalist economy, if we have insufficient capital to start a business we take out a loan from a bank or lending company. The rate of interest will probably be fixed, with the obvious result that, if our profits exceed the amount of interest payable we can pay ourselves salaries or make drawings from the excess; the lender will not demand any additional interest if our newly established firm has become particularly successful.

Obviously this is good news if the new firm is doing well. However, if we make a loss, not only have we failed to earn ourselves a living, but we are still in the position of owing the lender who has put up the initial capital the original sum plus accrued interest. To Muslim economists and business people this consequence has always seemed unjust. According to Islam, the lender must always have an active interest in the business, and, if this does not amount to contributing labour to the day-to-day running of the firm, at least it must entail the willingness to bear the appropriate proportion of loss as well as to accept any proportion of profit. Thus, in an Islamic-style business, if we, the proprietors, put up £10 000 capital and borrow £10 000 from a lender, then, in event of the business failing, proprietor and lender alike have lost money. A business failure does not entail, as it does under capitalism, a continued debt to the lender, or the relatively unpalatable alternative of declaring oneself bankrupt.

CONCLUSION

We hope we have shown that there is much more to investment than simply calculating figures. Financial transactions route monies in definite directions, with substantial implications. While we have offered no definite advice to readers on how to invest their personal fortunes—if they have any—at least we have highlighted some of the difficulties involved in attempting to invest monies 'ethically'.

There can be no simple and uncontentious division between 'clean' and 'unclean' investments, although there is a difference between those who are concerned with earning profits in an ethically acceptable way and those who are not. Some investors will feel more strongly about certain ethical issues than others, and in this light determine the degree to which they practice avoidance, positive choice or shareholder action.

Finally, on the wider question of whether it is ethical to make money through investment—a form of unearned income—it might be worth commenting on the famous saying that 'the love of money is the root of all evil.' The saying is often misquoted to read, 'Money is the root of all evil,' but our discussion has shown how money can do good as well as harm. However, if love for money takes precedence over concern for ethics, then, as we have shown, there is much scope for sanctioning many evils which exist in contemporary society.

DISCUSSION TOPICS

1. Is the search for an ethically clean investment portfolio a quest for the impossible? If so, why bother?
2. You are a financial adviser who has recently been approached by a client who has inherited a legacy, and wants to invest the money 'ethically'. What would you advise, and what information would you want to have?
3. Consider the merits and deficiencies of (a) avoidance; (b) positive choice; (c) shareholder action—discussed earlier in this chapter.
4. Most Westerners drink and gamble, although not to excess. Is it not therefore hypocritical of them to object to investing in the alcohol and gambling industries? Examine the problems of reconciling one's personal behaviour with one's investment patterns.

NOTES

1. This does not exclude a firm engaging in borrowing or seeking additional funding through new share issues, however.
2. *Ethical Consumer*, October/November 1990, p. 23.
3. *Independent*, 3 July 1993; *Financial Times*, 30 May 1992.
4. *The Ethical Consumer Guide to Everyday Shopping*, p. 153.
5. Ibid., p. 213.
6. Holden Meehan, *An Independent Guide to Ethical and Green Investment Funds*, 5th edn, 1994, p. 6.
7. 1 Corinthians 6.16

7 *The Ethics of Advertising*

Advertising is an issue in business ethics which affects everyone. British advertising currently accounts for 1.2 per cent of the national GDP, a total of approximately £6500 million per annum. This accounts for an annual total of 26 million printed advertisements, 7000 television commercials, thousands of hoardings and posters, and hundreds of cinema advertisements. According to one estimate, the average member of the British public sees 1700 advertisements each day. If it were not for advertising it is doubtful whether many of today's news media would survive: well over half the revenue of quality newspapers comes from advertising, with the tabloids netting between one-quarter and one-third of their sales revenue from this source.

Advertising certainly arouses the strongest emotions among the general public. Its critics allege that it encourages excessive spending, even debt; that it extols materialist values such as greed and acquisitiveness; that it misleads and deceives; that it treats the public like morons; and that it degrades women. Not surprisingly, advertisers themselves do not agree. A survey in Britain by the Advertising Association concluded that, on the whole, the public were reasonably satisfied with the industry: only a small percentage of the population wanted change and no one at all wanted to see the abolition of advertising altogether.[1]

The word 'advertising' comes from the Latin word *advertere*, meaning 'to make known', and clearly anyone who seeks to provide goods and services in a market economy cannot do so unless he or she makes them known to potential purchasers. Advertising is therefore an essential part of business activity, and it is unfortunate that much of the debate surrounding advertising has seemingly polarized into 'pro-advertising' and 'anti-advertising' camps. The real ethical issue is not whether business men and women should advertise, since the end of advertising would make a market economy in its mass consumer form virtually impossible. Assuming people in the industrialized West want to preserve such an economy, what ought to be in question is where the morally acceptable limits of advertising lie.

Until the second half of the twentieth century there were relatively few controls on the advertising industry or on the sale of goods generally. In Britain, the Indecent Advertisements Act (1889) ensured that certain minimal standards of decency were observed by advertisers, and misdescription of beer and spirits in advertisements became an offence. The Sale of Goods Act (1893) required goods to be of 'merchantable quantity', which meant that they must be 'fit for the purpose for which they were intended'. Consequently, consumers had some redress against manufactures who promoted goods that failed to serve their specified purpose. In somewhat more recent times, the Trades Descriptions Act (1968) served to ensure that descriptions of goods and services which appear on advertisements and labels are accurate and not misleading.

Until after the Second World War, advertising tended to confine itself to projecting a brand name, perhaps with a slogan highlighting some supposed merit pertaining to the goods. During the 1920s some attempts had been made to professionalize advertising, principally in the form of a number of 'primers' which offered advice to vendors. The most famous of these was a work by Daniel Starch (1927) entitled *Principles of Advertising*. Starch's advice was that for an advertisement to be successful, a total of five criteria had to be satisfied. An advertisement (i) must be seen, (ii) must be read, (iii) must be believed, (iv) must be remembered, and (v) must be acted upon.

In the 1920s newspaper and journal advertising usually existed in black and white column mode, often with some pictorial illustration, but usually with a considerable amount of text—much more than would be deemed acceptable by today's standards. Posters were often in colour, usually bearing a fairly brief and straightforward message. This was the state of the art when Starch wrote, and consequently his advice seemed plausible at that time. Even today, a private individual who wanted to sell a second-hand bicycle or refrigerator could do worse than to follow Starch's recommendations. It is unlikely, however, that any of today's major advertisers would follow Starch. If one considers, say, the 'abstract' advertising of the cigarette industry (Silk Cut is a prime example) there is ostensibly nothing to read, believe or remember (apart from the health warning); indeed much of the time the brand name is even omitted from the advertisement. Yet, this type of advertising, with only a few exceptions, has proved to be singularly successful.

The trouble with Starch and his contemporary 'primer' authors was that their writings were derived from somewhat ingenuous market research in which members of the public were questioned straightforwardly about their likes and dislikes. Although Freud had by that time made his mark on the academic world, in-depth examination of people's minds was confined to the psychiatrist's couch rather than the market researcher. At best, advertising theorists might offer 'home truths' which seemed intuitively obvious to contemporaries, but which have now been consigned to the museum of advertising history in the wake of more sophisticated methods for determining the effectiveness of advertising strategies. Modern advertisers now engage in much more in-depth psychological testing of consumers. One strategy is to monitor the eye-movements of experimental subjects when they read a newspaper, to determine the type of copy on which the human eye is more likely to rest. Market research, based on very detailed questionnaire analysis, is commonplace, and advertisers will not simply offer a manufacturer's wares to the public generally, but will single out sectors of the potential market that are more likely to be persuaded to buy the product.

It was greater sophistication of the marketing industry which prompted the best-selling writer Vance Packard to write his famous book *The Hidden Persuaders*.[2] Although it was written and first published in the United States, Penguin Books brought out a British edition, which sold widely and became a landmark in the debate about advertising.

Packard's attack on the advertising industry is targeted at those companies that use psychological 'in depth' research on human motivation and behaviour. According to Packard, these constituted roughly two-thirds of US advertisers in the 1950s. Packard contrasts the new motivational research (MR) with those older techniques of market research, in which participants are simply asked what their purchasing preferences are. This older technique assumes that people know what they want, are prepared to divulge their likes and dislikes, and that they essentially behave rationally. MR calls such assumptions into question. When asked what magazines one reads, for example, consumers will tend to admit reading the more prestigious ones, not mentioning their less cultured tastes; they may think they buy products which serve their purpose best, when in fact they are buying a self-image, or relieving a hidden anxiety.

The advent of MR was heralded by a questioning of rationalistic views of human behaviour, and MR sought to penetrate deeper levels of consciousness on the part of consumers. There were positive reasons to encourage consumers to act on irrational motives. At a time of increasing mass production, underconsumption was a distinct danger, since—rationally speaking—consumers had already suffi-cient cause to be satisfied with what they possessed. Free market competition often meant that there were no good logical reasons for choosing one brand rather than another—brands of petrol, to take one example, have few, if any, comparative merits or deficiencies. What was needed, then, was to exploit the non-logical causes which underlie consumer decisions. For instance, since petrol companies could not truthfully claim that their petrol gave greater economy, made a car more powerful or was less harmful to the engine, an advertising consultant could probe beneath the conscious rational levels of human awareness to one's unconscious desires. A certain brand could thus create an image of power, masculinity, thrift or whatever, by its presentation of the product and its advertising message. If car manufacturers could not rationally persuade consumers that they really needed new cars, perhaps they could instil the psychological impression that a car was 'out of date'.

Packard highlights a number of methods used by motivational researchers. In order to ascertain what factors underlie human behaviour, 'depth interviews' may be conducted by psychologists, in which painstaking attempts are made to ascertain the deep-down desires, pleasures, fears and frustrations which a product connotes. Indirect psychological tests may be used, such as the Rorschach ink-blot test, or requesting subjects to fill in speech balloons in cartoon pictures. Galvanometers (lie detectors) can be used to probe subjects' reaction to suggestions, and eye movements can be monitored to determine the degree to which advertisements and product labels are alighted on. Hypnotism affords a further means for psychologists to probe the inner workings of the human mind.

The results of such tests, Packard discloses, can enable psychologists, and hence the advertisers who hire them for such purposes, to build up profiles of likely customers, and to determine what kinds of features will psychologically induce consumers to make the relevant purchases. Thus, for example, many women have been shown to prefer skin cream to soap, not because it makes them any cleaner, but because skin cream appears to offer a promise of beauty. Various types of car are designed, not for different kinds of use, but to enable owners to acquire, according to taste, self-images of aggression, affluence, pride, stability or youth. Brands of cigarettes are not predominantly chosen for their flavour (Packard reckons that, by and large, there is little brand differentiation), but because of what they symbolize—virile maturity, reward for hard work, relief of tension, glamour.

Roughly four decades on from 1957, when Packard first wrote, much of this may seem old hat. We have become accustomed to fairly sophisticated methods of researching markets, and are familiar with the concepts of a self-image, and the exploitation of our deepest desires. Even Packard was prepared to see some advantages in a sophisticated persuasion industry. He recognized that people are likely to be more contented if their psychological needs are met as well as their more rational ones, and that increasing consumption is good for the economy, in so far as it increases the gross domestic product and employment. Packard believes too that many consumers have already acquired a healthy scepticism about advertisers' claims and can exercise the choice not to buy needless or unaffordable commodities.

Nevertheless, Packard finds the new-style persuasion industry reprehensible. It encourages non-rational, impulsive spending; it plays on the weaknesses of the public; it manipulates people—including children—and encourages waste by instigating needless consumption. Worse still, Packard argues, manipulative advertising subordinates truth to desire, preying on hidden psychological motivation, which is obtained by means that intrude on the depths of the human psyche and which are largely unrecognized even by those who are subject to them.

INFORM OR PERSUADE? SOME THEORETICAL ISSUES

The Hidden Persuaders was a polemical piece of work. It unmasked some of the worrying aspects of the marketing industry and attacked them vigorously. What is less clear, however, is what Packard would have wished to see in place of such strategies. Would he have preferred the old-fashioned, unresearched 'home truths', or Starch's simple surveys? Would he have wished all advertising simply to 'inform' rather than 'persuade'? Or would he have wished to see the total abolition of advertising altogether? Packard raises plenty of problems, but, unfortunately, few solutions. However, Packard was certainly instrumental in raising consciousness about the persuasion industry, and a number of subsequently landmark events are no doubt due, at least in part, to Packard's contribution to the debate.

Packard's analysis of the advertising industry raises the question of whether any form of irrational persuasion is ethically wrong, and whether advertisers should feel a moral duty to confine themselves to *information* rather than *persuasion*. The different moral theories which we consider in Chapter 2 may seem to lead to different conclusions on this subject. Consequentialists will point to the undesirable outcomes of certain types of persuasion, while non-conseqentialists might insist that there is something inherently objectionable about the methods of certain types of persuasion themselves.

Let us take as an example an area of advertising which has attracted much criticism for some considerable time—the promotion of 'timeshare' schemes. (In a 'timeshare' scheme purchasers buy a proportion of a property, normally in a holiday location, which gives them the right to occupy it for a period of time each year.) Consumers' introduction to such schemes has often been heralded by a mailing which invites them to an event at which they will receive a generous free gift (perhaps a microwave, a camcorder or an expensive gold watch). There appear to be no strings attached, except that they will hear a sales presentation—it is not always mentioned that a timeshare scheme is being sold. Attendees have often claimed that they were subjected to 'hard sell' tactics, making it difficult, if not impossible, to leave the event until they had agreed to buy a timeshare.

From a rights-based perspective, the presumed 'right to know' is paramount here: consumers at least have a right to know what product is being promoted. They have a right to fuller disclosure about the sales tactics which are likely to be used. They have a right to disclosure of full information about the cons as well as the pros of timeshare, in order to reach a balanced decision. If the sales tactics of timeshare promoters result from 'motivational research', then Packard and his supporters would question whether the advertisers have a right to information about individuals that goes deeper than their own awareness of themselves.

For Kant and his supporters, the principle of 'respect for persons' may be construed as demanding that the rationality of the individual, one's characteristic endowment as a human being, must be respected absolutely. It may be suggested that any form of persuasion which is less than rational could therefore be construed as an assault on the integrity of the individual and hence unacceptable. For many critics of timeshare sales methods, a significant part of the problem lies in the fact that they feel that such promotions are insulting—the absurd wording on some of the envelopes, the suggested urgency of response, or their presumed credulity insult their intelligence. (One of the authors once received an apparently personal mailing which read, 'Please check that your address is correct, since we do not want to send your prize to the wrong Chryssides family!') But perhaps most of all, the Kantian would object that, even more than most sales techniques, such promotions treat consumers as a means to an end: the promoters do not seem to value their satisfaction at all, but only the profits that can be obtained through their purchases.

The utilitarian, by contrast, would appeal to the consequences of the sales promotion. Although timeshare schemes have been heavily criticized, they can provide positive benefits to the owner: a regularly available venue for one's annual holiday, a means of investing one's capital, and of course the major prize—if it exists! Such benefits might well be considered to outweigh any negative feelings about advertising hype. On the other hand, the utilitarian would wish us to consider the disadvantages of timeshare as well. Timeshare properties have not always been completed on time; timeshare companies have been known to go into liquidation, sometimes leaving purchasers with no means of communication with each other, and hence no easy means of selling their share. At the time of writing, property is not a good investment, and does one really want to be tied to the same holiday venue year after year? Depending on the result of weighing up these conflicting factors, utilitarians will reach an appropriate conclusion regarding the desirability of timeshares, and their decision may go either way.

The example of timeshare promotions is a good illustration of the way different theoretical perspectives can complement each other. What they would all have in common is that they agree on the necessity for disclosure of information. The rights-based approach stresses the right to know; respect for persons entails not duping them into decisions which bypass their rational processes; and the utilitarian needs full information on which to assess the consequences of acceptance and rejection. Such a unanimous insistence on honest disclosure is obviously very challenging to advertising. Does it mean that advertisers should only offer us bald facts about products? Against this, Packard himself acknowledges with approval that some advertisements can be colourful, diverting and even artistic.[3] People have emotions, desires, imagination, and we are often happy to make decisions that are not always governed by logic. This being so, it is perhaps legitimate to appeal to aspects other than reason. To demand that advertising only stated facts would arguably make life much more boring.

Should advertising, then, persuade or simply inform? If the latter, then the proper model for the advertiser–consumer relationship is to see consumers as having predetermined wants, and the ideal advertisers as those who give them the relevant information to satisfy these wants in the best possible way. Thus, if a family needs a new car, what they then need to decide is how to satisfy this predetermined desire in a specific way. The relevant factors which will contribute to a rational decision might be the car's cost, its reliability, its comfort, its petrol consumption, its luggage-carrying capacity, likely maintenance costs and the after-sales service. (According to taste, one might specify other factors such as appearance, accessories, speed and so on.) If the various car manufactures provide honest information on all the relevant features of their cars, then the family can make an informed and rational decision.

If, however, persuasion is legitimate, then a very different model of the consumer–advertiser relationship comes into play. On the 'persuasion' model, the advertiser does not merely enable the consumer to satisfy existing desires: the advertiser can create new wants. A car advertiser might therefore not only target those drivers who really need to change their car (presumably a very small proportion of car buyers), but encourage existing owners to change their car more often, or entice them to upgrade their vehicle by offering greater performance, or an array of new features such as power steering, tinted glass, electric windows or even enhanced sex-appeal!

The first model is not necessarily superior to the second in all respects. After all, buoyant consumption is good for the economy: it means increased production and more job opportunities. Nor is it always the case that persuasion is harmful. How many of us have been cajoled by friends into going to a party or seeing a film and been glad we were? There are often positive benefits, too, in being persuaded to go beyond satisfying our immediate desires: we sometimes only appreciate fully the benefits of a new product once the purchase has been made. (Consider microwave ovens, for example: the benefits may not altogether be apparent before purchase, but many owners now wonder how they ever lived without one!)

The question of whether advertisers should simply inform consumers, and so only enable them to satisfy existing wants, or whether they may also persuade and thereby create new and arguably artificial wants, is an issue that has been debated by two leading economists: the Keynsian John Kenneth Galbraith (author of *The Affluent Society* among other influential works), and the late F. A. von Hayek, a notable exponent of the free market approach.[4]

GALBRAITH VERSUS VON HAYEK

According to Galbraith, in an impoverished society a high importance would be attached to the production of basic goods. There would still be unsatisfied demand for the basic necessities of life such as food, clothing and shelter. Production would be undertaken to meet this already existing demand, and there would be no need for promotion of such basic products. One might, presumably, need to make people aware of the outlets for these necessities, but there would be no need to persuade them that they needed them.

In an affluent society, by contrast, Galbraith argues, there is no 'urgency of wants' and hence no 'urgency of production'. Faced with the situation where men and women already have all that they strictly need for survival, the manufacturing industry can only market more by creating new higher-level desires. Thus the affluent society creates a new breed of consumers who no longer simply desire a crust of bread to keep them alive, but a new car, a home computer or a camcorder.

But these latter desires are not 'innate' within ourselves, like desires for basic necessities. We have learned to desire them as a result of two causes. First, there is the pressure which society exerts whereby we feel an overwhelming urge to 'keep up with the Joneses' and to feel envy at the Jones's new car when our own is five or six years old. Second, Galbraith contends, there is the influence of modern advertising and marketing, whose prime function is to create new desires, so that manufacturers can increase their production and hence their profit. Consequently, advertising reinforces the social pressures, fuelling consumption.

This gives advertising a very necessary role within the affluent society. In the impoverished economy, demand already exists and the task of producers is to endeavour to satisfy it. In the affluent society, production greatly exceeds demand; hence advertising has to create extra demand, giving rise to artificial wants, which can even masquerade as needs. It is wrong, Galbraith insists, to think that supply (production) rises to meet demand; in truth, he claims, the situation is a spiralling one: producers lead consumers to demand more, and, as demand for these newly created desires becomes satiated, producers lead consumers into desiring newer and ever less necessary products. Galbraith calls this the 'dependence effect'.

Galbraith does not wish to argue that the society is made less happy as a consequence of this process—he modestly assumes that it is not for him to say. What he does argue, however, is that products which satisfy merely artificial wants carry no utility. In being neither needed nor truly wanted, they bring no intrinsic benefits to society. Worse than this, an economy that is driven by these artificially created demands comes to have a somewhat lop-sided emphasis. The emphasis is on the production of consumer products, leaving the provision of public services, such as health, education and welfare, lagging behind. No advertiser or salesperson will try to create demands in these areas: they will not be paid to do so! Yet, increased provision of such services may well carry very great utility. Advertising is therefore directing resources away from area of possible benefit to areas of no intrinsic benefit whatsoever.

Galbraith's argument faces a formidable battery of criticism from Hayek. Hayek claims that, even if our wants would not have come into existence if we had not been influenced by advertising, it does not follow that these wants are non-urgent or unimportant. Indeed, civilized society, Hayek maintains, demands that rather more than just spontaneously arising wants are satisfied. He insists, for example, that aesthetic feelings are 'acquired tastes'; we do not have basic desires for music, art or literature. An author does not wait until a demand arises for his or her latest idea for a novel and then write it: the novel is written first, and then the demand arises. Indeed, it is difficult to see how things could be otherwise. Nevertheless, we would accept that this artificially created demand is something of very real benefit to society.

Hayek also argues that there is an ambiguity in Galbraith's contention that advertising makes consumption dependent on production. 'Dependent on' can simply mean 'arising from' or 'the result of'. If this is what Galbraith means, then Hayek concedes that this is indeed often the case, since people often do make purchases to keep up with their neighbours or because a sales promotion has made a particular product look attractive.

However, 'dependent on' can also mean something like 'at the mercy of' or 'deliberately determined by'—as if producers had preselected what consumers must buy and, through skilful manipulation, placed them in a situation whereby consumers had no choice but to comply. Consumers have choice, Hayek insists. Indeed it is the function of advertisements, catalogues and store displays to present to consumers the wide range of choices available to them. Admittedly, they may spend their money in ways which others would consider unwise, but this does not imply that they do not have needs—over and above the basic survival needs—which are important to satisfy.

Hayek is a defender of free markets because he wishes to see the minimum intrusion on individual freedom. The state should not impose judgement on which choices are sound and which are not: individual consumers must have the freedom to decide this for themselves, and there must be overwhelming reasons for state interference which reduces freedom of choice. (An example might be the free availability of certain prescribed drugs which might cause undue harm.) So if, Hayek has argued, advertising enhances individual choice, it follows that restrictions on advertising would be an intrusion on that individual freedom which Hayek sees as paramount.

ADVERTISING AND SELF-REGULATION

However much disagreement may be generated about whether modern advertising is harmful, whether it assists or impedes consumer choice, or whether it creates wants or helps to satisfy needs, it can certainly be agreed that there are at least certain minimal ethical standards which advertisers can be expected to observe. In the post-war period a number of important events have occurred in the battle to ensure that consumers did not fall victim to the wiles of the truly unscrupulous advertiser.

One important landmark was the formation of the Consumers' Association in the 1950s and the publication of the journal *Which?*, famed for its detailed testing of consumer products and for its recommended 'best buys'. *Which?* sought to make consumers aware of impartial research on products, as opposed to advertisers' 'hype', and it made consumers aware of their legal rights, how to assert them and how to complain about faulty goods and poor services. (It should be mentioned that *Which?* is no longer a strictly independent journal, since it is now owned by the *Readers' Digest.)*

Close on the heels of the Consumers' Association came the Advertising Standards Authority (ASA), which produced the first British Code of Advertising Practice (BCAP) in 1962. The code applied to press advertisements in UK publications, to hoardings and to cinema commercials. Television commercials were later covered by a separate code of practice, The IBA Code of Advertising Standards and Practice (1981). [The IBA (Independent Broadcasting Authority) together with the Cable Authority were jointly replaced in 1991 by the Independent Television Commission (ITC).] Advertisements with more restricted circulation came under different guidelines: for example, the Code of Practice of the Association of the British Pharmaceutical Industry was later devised to cover advertisements aimed at medical and paramedical staff; mail order traders produced their own code of practice; and telephone advertising is now governed by a set of guidelines which are bound into every telephone directory. All of the codes of practice mentioned above are voluntary codes (that is to say, they are self-regulated) and do not have legal status, with the exception of ITC code, which is enforceable by law (as was the former IBA code).

The ASA soon became known by its famous slogan, 'Are you legal, decent, honest, truthful? Advertisers have to be.' In terms of the approaches to business ethics which we outlined in the first chapter, advertisers in effect were no longer saying that 'business is business' but rather that standards of ethics within the advertising industry were to be no less stringent than those of one's own personal life.

As well as enjoining advertisers to observe the basic principles of legality, decency, honesty and truth, BCAP spelt out numerous basic ethical requirements which were expected of advertisers. For example, advertising copy must be clearly distinguishable from editorial material; advertisers must not mislead the public about their identity; advertised products must be available, and not advertised as a means of testing potential demand, or for the purposes of 'switch selling'. BCAP enumerates specific regulations for named categories of advertising, notably medicinal and related products, cosmetics, mail order products, financial services, employment opportunities, products aimed at children, alcoholic beverages and cigarettes.

The ASA is financed by advertisers, via the advertising media, who pay the ASA a surcharge from advertising expenditure. The ASA does not normally scrutinize advertisements in advance of publication—apart from cigarette advertising and adverts for pregnancy testing and counselling services—but has a Copy Panel which is willing to offer advice to any advertiser prior to publication. In the main, the monitoring of advertisements is undertaken in response to public complaints, dealt with by the Committee of Advertising Practice (CAP). Where there is a case for an advertiser, the CAP's findings are published in the *ASA Monthly Reports*, which are sent to anyone on request. Where complaints are upheld, the ASA normally requests the advertiser to withdraw an advertisement; if the advertiser refuses to co-operate, the CAP can instruct participating media to refuse to publish further advertising copy. The ASA does not impose fines on offending advertisers, as is done in Eire, and it does not require them to buy further advertising space to disclaim an offending advertisement—a sanction which is imposed in the United States.

Codes of practice, such as BCAP, fulfil a twofold function. First, they indicate to those within the profession the rules by which they must abide. Second, they indicate to the wider public the standards which they have a right to expect. Of course, this can work in both a positive and a negative way. Positively, it can encourage members of the profession to clean up their act, where this is needed, and live up to the regulating body's expectations. Negatively, however, a code of practice can signal areas in which there is license. For example, although the ASA has acted in numerous instances where advertisers have portrayed scantily clad or naked women (a portrayal which is considered 'indecent' within BCAP's terms, unless it is relevant to the product), there are no prohibitions on sex-role stereotyping of women. Although many feminists deplore this, they have no redress under the present terms of BCAP, and advertisers will no doubt continue to portray women in this way when they wish to do so.

STATUS QUO OR SOCIAL CHANGE? WOMEN AND ADVERTISING

The topic of women in advertising is one which has attracted considerable attention in recent times, and there is now a considerable body of literature on the subject. For this reason it may be useful to explore this particular issue at greater length. Perhaps one of the main reasons why many advertisers have been slow to change their portrayal of women is that the issue is an ideological one. Unlike issues of misleading claims or the exploitation of children, where most people would agree about what constituted acceptable practice, the portrayal of women is—in the words of BCAP—one of 'attitudes or opinions about which society is divided'.[5] For every campaigning feminist, one can no doubt find at least one anti-feminist. As far as advertising is concerned, all the ASA can recommend is that

Particular care should be taken to avoid causing offence on the grounds of race, religion, sex, sexual orientation or disability.[6]

Various feminist campaigning groups have complained about the role of women in advertising on various grounds. Firstly, and most obviously, they have objected to gratuitous nudity and semi-nudity in certain advertisements. Secondly, the portrayal of women is alleged to stereotype them—usually as mothers in a traditional nuclear family where the woman is white, young and in a traditional 'housewife' role, while the man is cast as the bread-winner. The highlight of her day, it appears, is seeing the children off to school, while her pinnacle of achievement is either the cooking or washing clothes, when she goes into ecstasies about the latest 'new improved' washing powder which washes them whiter than white!

A classic critique of advertising comes from Ervin Goffman, who produced a copiously illustrated book entitled *Gender Advertisements*. Goffman considered a wide number of advertisements, drawn principally from television and hoardings in the United States, and concluded that women are portrayed in advertisements as having radically different behaviour patterns from men. The most obvious difference lies in the way in which women have often been depicted lying on a bed, half clad, while engaging in conversation on the telephone—how often do advertisers ever portray a man clad only in Y-fronts making a telephone call? Women are often depicted as less intelligent, less independent and more frivolous than men. Legs are raised in the air to advertise shoes, for example, or a woman might simply be used as a little more than a prop to add 'glamour' to a car advertisement. Goffman found that there appeared to be only one area in which men were allowed by advertisers to appear less competent than women—and that was in the kitchen. In one advertisement on which Goffman comments, a somewhat comic looking man displays total incompetence at cooking a bolognese, the message being that he is much better off with a manufacturer's ready-made bolognese sauce!

In car advertising, gender differences seem particularly apparent. Although, as Hayek has claimed, we live in a free society where consumers can examine the range of goods and make whatever purchases we think best, nevertheless car manufacturers have seemingly predetermined which models of car are suitable for women and which are for men. Indeed Volvo recently advertised in the national press that 'Your wife drives on the most dangerous roads', as if wives were not even capable of reading the advertisement, let alone making their own decision! In general, 'women's' cars are smaller, designed to do the shopping and ferry children to and from school, and are sometimes promoted on the grounds that they are 'easy to park', or—perhaps somewhat more commendably—that they are 'ecological'. By contrast, size, speed and performance are deemed to win male approbation.

Case Study

Benetton—united colours or divisive marketing?

'United Colors of Benetton' is the slogan used to advertise Benetton clothing—a theme that has been reflected in the company's recent advertising campaigns. Initially, the company used hoardings depicting children from different countries wearing Benetton clothes, but subsequently Benetton advertising took a more controversial tack.

In 1991 an advertisement appeared depicting two children, one white and one black, the former depicted as an angel with blonde curls and the latter as a devil with black horns protruding from her hair. Over 60 complaints were sent to the ASA, some via the Commission for Racial Equality, and the ASA upheld the complaint on the grounds that it was likely to cause widespread offence.

In the same year, Benetton commissioned hoardings depicting a blood-smeared, newly born baby, complete with its umbilical cord. At other times, Benetton displayed a terrorist fleeing from a burning building, a dying AIDS victim and—following a disastrous oil spillage at sea near the Shetlands—a bird covered in oil, In its defence, Benetton claimed that it was acting in the public interest by drawing attention to areas of serious public concern. The ASA disagreed on all these occasions, with the exception of the oil spillage advertisement.

Because of the controversy that was sparked off by these advertisements, Benetton gained publicity in the media, and no doubt the public discussion of the controversial advertisements encouraged Benetton's name to be mentioned considerably more times than a gentler advertising campaign would have generated. German franchisees, however, did not share the view that the controversial advertisements generated useful free publicity. They claimed that they had lost sales through Benetton's strategy, and they sought redress—albeit unsuccessfully—through legal action.

As a well-established firm with considerable experience of promoting its wares, it is unlikely that Benetton did not realize that the ASA might be called upon to adjudicate on their advertising and might ask, as they did, for the offending material to be taken down. No doubt Benetton considered the likely outcome: complaints upheld by the ASA certainly do not have disastrous implications for offenders, as Benetton and a few other regular offenders have shown.

The Benetton phenomenon provides further fuel to the ASA's critics who claim that it is a 'toothless tiger'. Although the majority of firms endeavour to comply with BCAP, a few companies will take the view that any publicity is good publicity, and either flout the ASA's authority or sail as the near the wind as they safely can.

Those who are less sympathetic to the cause of sexual equality may well ask why all this matters. After all, it may be argued, can we not treat men and women equally, however advertisers portray them? Further, the advertiser's role is surely to sell a product, and if advertisers find that these supposedly 'sexist' strategies deliver the goods, then surely they must do this, rather than support feminist ideology? An advertiser, in short, is there to sell, not to reform society.

Ideology apart, there is some evidence that firms are indeed losing potential custom rather than gaining it as a result of advertisements which women consider to be demeaning. In most areas, it is customary for the advertiser to compliment his or her target audience by appearing to raise its status, rather than to lower it. This is seen, for example, in the way in which the average home portrayed in a television commercial often seems quite improbably affluent: depicting the actors in more modest surroundings would fail to enhance the status of the product—something which the advertiser naturally wants to do. Similarly, to depict women as non-serious, as housewives, or as sex objects is to downgrade them and potentially alienate them from the product.

Second, feminist critics have pointed out that, notwithstanding the recent Sex Discrimination Acts (1975 and 1986), women are unlikely to be treated with genuine equality in the workplace if people are subjected to a diet of television commercials which trivialize their contribution to society. One of the aims of sexual equality is encouraging qualified and experienced women to apply for those key jobs which have typically been bastions of male supremacy. Constant exposure to stereotyping and constant inculcation of the view that men are higher achievers than women—a conclusion which could certainly still be drawn from a significant amount of contemporary advertising—could no doubt have the effect of discouraging some women from aiming to have equal status with men.

As things stand, there is still no provision in the BCAP to ensure that advertising is non-sexist. The ASA has tended to view feminism as a campaigning movement, and has claimed that advertising should reflect the status quo and not seek to change it. The ASA has commissioned two major studies of the role of women in advertising, *Herself Appraised* (1986) and *Herself Reappraised* (1990). The first study tended to confine itself to the portrayal of the naked or semi-nude female body—something which constitutes a part of the complaint against some contemporary advertising, but is by no means the whole of the grievance. The second report did little more than reinforce the findings of the first, and again failed to address other issues such as sex-role stereotyping. In the meantime, the CAP has become fairly conscientious in outlawing gratuitous portrayals of nudity and semi-nudity, but continues to take the view that it should not actively campaign to improve the perceived status of women in contemporary society.

DISCUSSION TOPICS

1. How effective are bodies such as the ASA in ensuring that the advertising industry behaves responsibly?
2. Do you think that advertising should give consumers more information and less persuasion?
3. Identify a recent advertising campaign which particularly appeals to you. To what extent have the advertisers been aware of any ethical issues, and how have they dealt with them?
4. Consider the role of women in advertising. Are changes in advertising regulations still desirable?

NOTES

1. M. J. Waterson, *Speaking Up for Advertising*, The Advertising Association, London, 1982.
2. Vance Packard, *The Hidden Persuaders*, Penguin, Harmondsworth, 1957.
3. Ibid., p. 15.
4. Reprinted in George D. Chryssides and John H. Kaler, *An Introduction to Business Ethics*, Chapman and Hall, London, 1993, pp. 423–435.
5. BCAP, 9 edn, 3.1.
6. Advertising Standards Authority, *The British Codes of Advertising and Sales Promotion*, The Committe of Advertising Practice, London, 1995, 5.1.

8 Green Issues in Business

No book on business ethics would be complete without some reference to the 'greening' of business, which has attracted considerable attention in recent times. The general public, as well as business people and students of business studies, have no shortage of material in the area. Much of the available material is essentially 'campaigning' in nature—no doubt with justification. In addition, there is material occasionally written by companies, designed to demonstrate that their environmental record is acceptable, even commendable. (Most information packs which firms send to students on request contain positive comment on the firm's environmental record.)

A critical survey of business ethics—such as this one—must do more than simply tell business students and managers to 'be green'. Although it is 'politically correct' to be 'pro-green' and to manifest this in business policies and in one's personal lifestyle, the notion of 'greenness' is actually fraught with difficulties, and no competent authors can afford to ignore these, even if at times they may appear to be going against the trend.

It is impossible to be a business man or woman in today's world without being aware of the 'green lobby' and the changes which its supporters would wish to see within society. The recent interest in 'green' affairs was brought to the fore in the early 1970s, when a report entitled *The Limits to Growth* was published. This report was published by a group who came to be known as 'The Club of Rome', so called because they met in April 1968 at the Accademia dei Lincei in Italy's capital city, to discuss the 'economic, political, natural and social' future of humankind. The contributors included scientists, industrialists, civil servants and educationalists, and the first phase of the study—on the 'Predicament of Mankind'—emanated from a computerized global model, devised by Professor Jay Forrester of the Massachusetts Institute of Technology. The model incorporated factors which contributed to humankind's future. Professor Dennis Meadows directed the first phase of the subsequent study, in which the Club of Rome team examined the five basic factors which imposed limits to economic growth on the planet. These

138

five factors were: population, agricultural production, natural resources, industrial production and pollution.

The authors of *The Limits to Growth* drew three conclusions. First, present trends of growth in all these five areas cannot continue indefinitely. Food production, for example, is being outstripped by exponential growth in population. The limits to the earth's capacity to increase the standards of living enjoyed by its inhabitants would reach its limit within the next century. After the year 2050, or thereabouts, there would be a decline in both population and industrial capacity, which would be both sudden and uncontrollable.

That was the bad news. On the more optimistic side, the Club of Rome expressed the belief (its second conclusion) that future trends were not inevitable if something were done soon to prevent this imminent catastrophe. Birth rates can be controlled; polluting waste can be reduced; industrial capacity can be improved—although obviously not infinitely. Third, the Club stated that individuals and governments are obliged to decide which of these two options they wish to pursue—the imminent 'doomsday', or 'no growth' policies which involve population and pollution control and less prodigal demands on the earth's natural resources.

The computerization of the Club of Rome's model enabled the researchers to examine a number of possible scenarios. The earth's citizens might try to increase the land yield; they might try to reduce population; they might try to increase industrial production; and so on. The findings of the researchers were that controls on all the factors must be carried out simultaneously; paying regard to one or two would be insufficient. Further, all controls must be implemented by 1975 (stabilization of population, pollution, industrial output, food per capita and available natural resources), otherwise the final 'doomsday' could not be avoided under any possible scenario. Those who accept the Club of Rome's model will note that, of course, the year 1975 is now well and truly past, with no dramatic changes in the five factors that the Club identified: the end, therefore, is well and truly nigh!

Previous to *The Limits to Growth* it had often been thought within the business world that population growth was good for business. Increased population ensured continued demand for goods and services and the assurance of future and indeed expanded markets. This seemed good news for employment, expansion and increased profits. The 1960s had, further, seen a trend towards 'planned obsolescence' of consumer goods. In the 1940s and 1950s, post-war technology had enabled many consumers to purchase their first cars, washing machines and refrigerators. This was good news for the manufacturers and retailers in the short term, but, after saturating this new market, how could they then persuade these consumers to make subsequent purchases? One answer was to persuade them that they needed superior models of such goods; indeed there are many consumers today who see it as a personal affront not to own the latest model of car. Another answer was to ensure that consumer 'durables' had a limited lifespan, for example by reducing the thickness of the metal (a strategy apparently used by Volkswagen, among others), or by whatever means ensuring that key parts failed within a certain length of time. Obviously that length of time had to be sufficiently long for consumers to feel that they had received sufficient value for money to consider buying from the same manufacturer, but not so long as to deprive that manufacturer of sufficient future custom

CRITICISMS OF THE 'DOOMSDAY' APPROACH

While there were those who were impressed with the computerized model of humankind's future, there were others—particularly scientists, who were thoroughly acquainted with the new generation of technology—who were scathing about the findings, pointing out that a computer could only produce reliable findings if it were fed the right sets of data. 'Rubbish in, rubbish out', they commented.

One vociferous set of criticisms was levelled by the economist Robert M. Solow. Solow argues that one vital ingredient missing from the Club of Rome's analysis is any kind of price mechanism. As natural resources and supplies of food dwindle, their costs will inevitably increase, thus reducing demand. Demand for commodities will not run relentlessly on simply because population is growing. Further, Solow points out, the doomsday model views the earth as a totality, and tends to make general predictions about the fate of humankind. However, as we all know, some nations fare better economically than others: on 1988 statistics, the United States came top with $19 815 GDP per head, with countries like Zaïre, Ethiopia and Rwanda near the bottom with a mere $193, $114 and $60 per head, respectively. (The situation is not markedly improved by taking into account the differences in purchasing power within these countries.) For some underdeveloped countries, there is a sense in which doomsday has already occurred.

Further, Solow points out, if a model purports to predict future scenarios accurately, it ought to be able to 'retrodict' with similar precision. Solow believes that the doomsday model fails to do this. If we extrapolate the rate of labour productivity backwards, we find a statistic for labour productivity in 1492 which is markedly lower than must have been the case. If Solow is right, this shows that the recent exponential growth in population, demand for food and natural resources, and levels of pollution may be a temporary phenomenon which will either level off, increase only arithmetically or even fall at some future point in time.

Solow argues against the 'no growth' lobby. 'Green' supporters often see the environmental crisis as emanating from economic growth, suggesting that, if all the countries of the world had a 'no growth', or even a dis-growth policy, then somehow the tide of environmental pollution and excess use of the world's resources would be turned. The alternative to 'no growth' and dis-growth is, of course, *sustainable growth*.

As Solow concedes, the Club of Rome's failure to include the price mechanism in their deliberations does not mean that the price mechanism will automatically solve the environment's problems. On the contrary, the price mechanism may operate too slowly to conserve the earth's resources acceptably; or may fail to operate perfectly because firms are failing to pay the proper costs of the environmental damage they are inflicting. More often than not, the firms that damage the environment, or consumers who use environmentally harmful products, do not pick up the costs of their actions. A firm whose factory chimney belches out smoke does not normally pay for stone-cleaning adjacent buildings. A vehicle owner pays a fixed amount of road tax, there are tolls on a few important bridges and of course there is a tax on petrol. But, overall, the cost of road use is not directly proportional to the mileage driven. RailTrack, which is fully responsible for the maintenance of its railway system, is thus forced to compete with coach companies who are not necessarily picking up the full price of their activities.

OTHER CONTRIBUTIONS TO 'GREENISM'

Whatever criticisms may be levelled against the Club of Rome's model, the authors succeeded in drawing attention to the plight of the planet, and *The Limits to Growth* was an important piece of consciousness raising on behalf of the 'greens'. It was much discussed in academic circles and given momentum by influential bodies such as the World Council of Churches. Even the critics of the Club of Rome had to concede the existence of an environmental problem. Solow himself acknowledges that a problem about depleting resources and pollution exists and that it is necessary to tackle this.

A number of further important contributions to green awareness followed in the wake of *The Limits to Growth*. The year 1973 saw the publication of E. F. Schumacher's classic *Small is Beautiful*. Writing at a time when the multinational company was in the ascendant, Schumacher's main line of attack was on the firm which had grown so large and impersonal that its overall profitability had taken priority over the individual employees who made up the firm, and indeed without whom no firm could survive. Schumacher was no armchair theorist who nostalgically hankered after a supposed bygone golden age: he had himself worked for 20 years (1950–1970) for the National Coal Board in Britain.

Notwithstanding Schumacher's main focus, *Small is Beautiful* was also pioneering in drawing attention to important environmental problems. Two essays in particular, 'The Proper Use of Land' and 'Buddhist Economics', highlight some of the issues. Schumacher argued that businesses were too concerned with profits, and insufficiently concerned with people, with the environment and with making a contribution to the world as a whole. In 'Buddhist Economics', Schumacher advocates company policies based on *dana*, the Buddhist term for 'giving', rather than *tanha*, the Buddhist concept of selfish desire, which is the essential contributor to the world's unsatisfactory condition.

The idea that firms should be doing something for the wellbeing of the world, not merely extracting profits from it, was taken up by the environmental organizations which were starting up at this time. Friends of the Earth and Greenpeace were established in 1971, and close on their heels came the formation of the Green Party in 1973. (It was then known as 'People' and later as The Ecology Party.) Although the Green Party has never been particularly successful in gaining votes in Britain (unlike its counterpart in Germany), it has achieved much by way of consciousness raising, particularly by putting environmental issues on the political agenda. Faced with mounting concern about a global environmental crisis, the major political parties could no longer afford simply to ignore green issues. Indeed David Gee, Director of Friends of the Earth, has given an evaluation of Margaret Thatcher as having

> done more to push environmentalism to the top of the political, business and economic agendas both here and abroad than any other politician, although Mikhail Gorbachev has not been far behind.[1]

(Needless to say, Gee goes on seriously to question whether the Thatcher governments have done anything like enough for the environment.) In addition to a number of speeches in the late 1980s, the Thatcher government commissioned the White Paper, 'This Common Inheritance', which appeared in 1990.[2] Although the paper said little, if anything, that was new about the need for conservation, it put on record the government's awareness that there is a serious environmental problem, and officially stated its commitment to do something about it.

At a more global level, the 1980s saw a number of international top-level conferences on the environmental crisis, culminating in the famous Earth Summit of 1992, held at Rio de Janeiro, and attended by major world leaders, including Britain's Prime Minister John Major, and US President George Bush.

FINDING A DEFINITION OF 'GREENNESS'

The first and most basic problem about 'being green' is pinning down the concept to a reasonably clear and manageable definition. As the phrase tends to be used by green proponents it is at worst merely a slogan, and at best a multifaceted concept. The first and most obvious aspect of the concept is the preservation of the environment: felling more trees than are being replaced; the destruction of tropical rainforests, with resulting climactic changes; soil erosion and the depletion of water

no CFCs'. In fact, no comparable packaging that we know of has ever contained CFCs; the real issue, which this claim disguised, is that styrofoam itself is an environmentally harmful substance, since it is totally non-recyclable and non-degradable.

Until 1994 one of the main problems facing consumers was the lack of consistent definitions of environmental claims. As a consequence of the Trade Descriptions Act (1968), specific claims were required to be true: for example that lead-free petrol contains no lead, or that McDonald's styrofoam contains no CFCs (even if the latter is irrelevant or even misleading). What was not controlled were the more nebulous concepts such as 'ecological', 'environmentally friendly' and the like.

In order to achieve some degree of standardization of product labelling, the EC inaugurated an Ecolabelling Scheme in May 1992. It is a voluntary scheme, whereby manufacturers may apply to use the official ecolabel (a symbolic plant with starred petals and a letter 'e' in the centre) as an award for a product's appropriate environmental qualities. In Britain the scheme is administered by the UK Ecolabelling Board (UKEB); manufacturers pay £500 for a three-year licence to use the ecolabel, and, if successful, a further fee of 0.15 per cent of EC sales. So far the public have seen little of the ecolabel, apart from only the Hoover New Wave washing machine.

The assessment of a product is carried out by UKEB's 16 board members, who have expertise in commerce, retailing, consumer affairs, trading standards and environmental matters. A product is assessed in a 'cradle to grave' audit, spanning five stages of a product's lifespan: (i) the extraction of raw material; (ii) the production process; (iii) packaging and transportation; (iv) the product's use; (v) disposal of the product when its lifespan has finished. Environmental impact is considered for each stage, against the following criteria: contribution to waste, earth pollution, water pollution, air pollution, noise, energy consumption, consumption of natural resources and effects on the planet's ecosystems.

The scheme is no doubt a step in the right direction, but it has not gone uncriticized. In a recent edition of the *Ethical Consumer*, the ECRA offered four major criticisms of the scheme. Their first objection related to the composition of UKEB: at the time of writing only two members were selected from environmental non-governmental organizations, compared with four from the manufacturing world and a further two from retailing. A third environmental member resigned in 1993, claiming that the industrial representatives had out-voted the environmentalists on the matter of toilet paper and kitchen rolls, as a result of which chlorine-bleached paper could still qualify for an ecolabel, despite the serious impact of bleach on the environment. More generally, ECRA believes that industrialists inevitably have a vested interest in diluting the criteria which products must match.

Secondly, avoidance of animal testing does not feature at all as a criterion for awarding the EC ecolabel. A recent campaign sponspored by the British Union for the Abolition of Vivisection (BUAV) carried the slogan 'Don't give animal testing the green light', and was supported by Jonathon Porritt and Anita Roddick. In a recent poll commissioned by the BUAV through The Body Shop, 78 per cent of respondents stated that they believed that animal testing was a significant environmental issue. Amazingly, UKEB's Chair, Dr Elizabeth Nelson, responded, 'We sympathise with what is being said but they are talking ethics!'[7]

ECRA has drawn attention to other missing criteria. The EC ecolabelling scheme does not include human toxicity, for example. It also does not consider a company's environmental record as a whole, thus allowing an otherwise irresponsible company to carve out a niche market with a single environmentally friendly product, thus enhancing its environmental prestige. In The Netherlands an ecolabelling scheme also includes a product's repairability, requiring the availability of spare parts for a minimum of five years, thus reducing waste.

The Women's Environmental Network (WEN) has proposed the following six criteria which, it believes, should disallow a product from earning an ecolabel:

- Disposable products
- Products tested on animals
- Products using virgin wood fibres and unsustainable forest sources
- Products using excess or unnecessary packaging
- Products using unnecessary toxic chemicals, including organo-chlorines and pesticides[8]

Finally, ECRA has criticized the scheme for merely defining two categories of 'pass' and 'fail' respectively. This, they claim, fails to reward those companies who have gone significantly beyond the minimum standards of environmental acceptability, and gives no further incentive for merely passable firms to improve their record further.

DIFFICULTIES FOR GREEN CONSUMERISM

Many would-be 'politically correct' consumers have chosen products on the basis of 'environmentally friendly' labels, however inexact these may be. For many, a description like '100 per cent recycled' carries the suggestion that their consumption has made no inroads into the earth's resources, since the product is merely a previous one in a new incarnation. Such consumers might confess to feeling guilty if recycled plastic bags or toilet rolls made from recycled paper are not available and they are forced to buy a more traditional alternative. For many consumers, the logic appears to be that if commodities such as wood, metal and plastic are being reintroduced in the manufacturing process, no further plundering of the earth's resources is required.

This way of thinking is seriously flawed, however, as a little reflection will readily demonstrate. For a start, recyling involves an industrial process: to recycle paper one requires water and electricity among other commodities; transport is also required to take the paper from paper banks (if that is where it came from) to the processing plant and to the retail outlets. Also, if recycled goods have to travel a long distance to reach the stores, then it may actually be more environmentally friendly to buy a non-recycled product which has travelled a much shorter distance.

Sometimes the difficulties in the way of green conumserism are put there by businesses. Thus, it has been alleged that, in some cases, so-called 'recycled paper' has been derived from unused paper material; hence, although it has technically been 'recycled', it has not been reused, since it was never used in the first instance. Where firms have claimed that a new tree has been planted to replace each old tree used as raw material, it is not necessarily the case that the new tree is of comparable type or quality. Some manufacturers have labelled a product 'recyclable', possibly encouraging consumers mistakenly to conflate 'recyclable' with 'recycled', and often providing no obvious means of enabling consumers actually to recycle such a product. One credit card company recently introduced a 'green' credit card: for each amount spent a small proportion is donated to an environmental organization. However, there was no restriction on what one might purchase with this supposedly 'green' card; presumably purchases of bleach, animal-tested products, diesel fuel and all sorts of environmentally harmful products could be bought while enabling consumers to suppose that they had done their bit for the environment. In any case, to consume at all is, arguably, to harm the environment, and any sector of the business world which encourages consumption (as credit cards undoubtedly do) is environmentally damaging.

This last point takes us on to a further difficulty with green consumerism. Even if one sells 'environmentally friendly' products, even to 'buy green' is still to consume and hence to use the earth's resources. Some green proponents therefore insist that what is more important than 'buying green' is simply consuming less. It is only by consuming less that one is reducing demand on the earth's dwindling bank of resources. Such a solution, of course, is likely to be unpopular in the business world, where the general aim is to maximize sales. Policies such as making one's purchases last longer, mending goods, buying replacement parts rather than a new product altogether, sharing consumer durables such as washing machines, organizing car pools, and simply doing without unnecessary products are likely to be unpopular with maunfacturers and retailers.

The topic of doing without unneccessary products has called into question the green credentials of The Body Shop:

one of the greenest businesses of them all, on the surface—The Body Shop—is, after all, in the cosmetics business, and who needs cosmetics anyway when much of the world's population is hungry and the future of the planet is at stake?[9]

Against this must be counted the fact that The Body Shop has, of course, declared a policy of purchasing raw material and products from developing countries. To avoid Body Shop cosmetics might therefore involve depriving parts of the Third World of important trade, and push them further towards having to rely on charity. Oxfam's slogan, 'Trade not aid', reminds us of developing countries' need of a secure niche in the marketplace, rather than having to rely on aid from the West.

However, even trade brings problems. For example, it has been alleged that developing countries have used agricultural land for supplying developing countries with produce, leaving themselves short of home-grown food. This is the case, for example, with Ghana and its dependence on cocoa as a cash crop. (Cocoa was not an indigenous plant, but was imported from the West Indies to supply Western markets.) Also, because of Third World debt, developing countries are in a poor bargaining position, and, it has been argued, are forced to sell to the West at ludicrously low prices. However, the alternative is to forgo trade altogether— probably an even worse option.

GROWTH OR NO GROWTH?

What ought surely to be the most important consideration in the green debate is not 'growth versus no growth' or 'limits to growth', but rather sustainable growth. There is an important difference between *using* resources and *using them up*—a distinction that is not always acknowledged by green supporters. When an economy is growing in such a way as to allow future generations to enjoy comparable standards of living, natural resources and quality of environment, there can surely be no objection to growth. By contrast, where levels of growth are achieved at the expense of depleting resources and environmental quality in such a way that posterity will suffer, this cannot readily be justified.

It is also worth mentioning that since the calculation of GDP is done by summing the totality of all domestic purchases and transactions, implementing policies which enhance the environment will themselves add to the total GDP and thus contribute to economic growth. Fitting a catalytic convertor on one's car, for instance, enhances the country's GDP; employing people to clean up the litter left by fast-food consumers also contributes to economic activity.

As economists generally agree, using GDP as a measure of a nation's wellbeing only gives a rough indication of how well off it is, and there are numerous anomalies. A country whose citizens have to replace their cars frequently

Case study

McDonald's—green company or green customers?

Western fast-food companies have attracted considerable criticism, not least McDonald's, the world's biggest. The commonest criticism of the burger companies has been that they market 'junk food' which has little nutritional value. The packaging, it is claimed, is wasteful and pollutive, at best causing litter, and at worst causing waste which is harmful to the environment. The packages were rumoured to contain CFCs.

At first McDonald's was accused of using meat which had been ranched on ground cleared of precious tropical rainforests. When McDonald's refuted this allegation, its critics then argued that, wherever McDonald's meat came from, McDonald's were increasing demand for cattle ranching, causing increased competition for scarce land resources. Other farmers, it was claimed, were left with little alternative but to deforestate in order to ranch their cattle.

McDonald's employment policy came up for criticism too. Allegedly the company paid low wages, and most of its staff were young and supposedly exploited. In 1991, 75 per cent of staff were under 21, and there was a high staff turnover—60 per cent on average, with an 80 per cent turnover amongst part-time staff, and a staggering 159 per cent among hourly paid staff. McDonald's refused to recognize trade unions, claiming that unions had no place in modern business.

McDonald's has taken pains to produce publicity material which purports to rebut such criticisms. As well as providing nutritional information that is designed to correct its 'junk food' image, McDonald's *Fact Book* claims that the company does the public a substantial service, providing food for one million people a day in the United Kingdom alone. McDonald's has 'democratized' eating out, since its meals are affordable by the masses. McDonald's supports several charitable projects, invariably featuring its Ronald McDonald clown.

As for treatment of staff, crew rates at January 1994 were stated to be £3.68 in London (the highest) and £3.38 in the north (the lowest), with various fringe benefits. McDonald's is committed to equal opportunities and is a member of the Opportunity 2000 project which began in 1992. It is true that McDonald's does not recognize unions; however, it has initiated a system of 'rap' sessions, where crew members can air any grievances anonymously to a more senior staff member from another region. McDonald's states that it is currently setting up an employee participation scheme.

The company states that it does not use cattle that have been subjected to hormonal treatment, or purchase beef whose rearing threatens tropical rainforests. Not only does McDonald's claim to have discontinued using packaging containing CFCs in 1988, but it affirms a commitment to introducing CFC-free refrigerators and other kitchen equipment. Critics point out, however, that McDonald's continues to use styrofoam containers, which do not decompose.

Faced with mounting criticisms, which McDonald's rejected, the company decided that enough was enough when a pamphlet appeared detailing them. McDonald's initiated libel proceedings against Helen Steel and Dave Morris, both supporters of Greenpeace in London. At the time of writing, the trial is still progressing, and may well turn out to be the longest libel trial in British history. McDonald's are unlikely to gain financial compensation, since the two defendants, being ordinary private citizens, lack the wealth to pay huge compensatory sums. However, the outcome should enable McDonald's customers and critics to ascertain whether McDonald's are justly nicknamed McGarbage, McProfits and McCancer!

because they are unreliable, for example, is theoretically better off than a country where fewer but more durable cars are typically bought. A country where a large police force, burglar alarms, expensive locks and security equipment are all necessary will, all other things being equal, have a higher GDP than a country that does not need these. GDP is thus a measure of quantity, not of the benefit to society of the goods and services bought. Whether one buys bibles or pornography, a purchase is a purchase, and it is the monetary transaction which is measured.

Some economists have recently considered the possibility of counting the cost of environmentally harmful policies and purchases. A factory that belches out smoke may make substantial profits and pay wages to local workers. However, by its environmentally harmful policies the firm gives rise to 'externalities'—that is to say, costs which are external to the firm, and which are not picked up in its accounting system. Although the firm has avoided paying for these, someone else has to bear the costs of stone cleaning, fitting double glazing to nearby houses, hospital treatment for those who incur lung infections and so on. These, it is argued, might be costed and subtracted from the firm's contribution to the GDP, thereby being defined as factors contributing to 'dis-growth'. It might also be suggested that one should add a notional figure for the unpleasantness and inconvenience which such activities cause. What would be the just compensation to the local population? (This is usually done by asking those peole how much they would accept as compensation.)

This notion of external costs has given rise to the 'polluter pays' principle.

There is a cluster of issues surrounding this. First, there is the sheer complexity of measuring pollution and attributing it to specific polluters with any degree of exactitude. Second, there are certain types of pollution which cannot be paid for, no matter how affluent we become: one cannot put back the ozone layer, for instance, however much one spends. Accordingly, this last point makes a case for prohibition and not merely the payment of compensation which the 'polluter pays' principle demands.

In conclusion, if we acknowledge that there is a very serious environmental crisis facing the planet which is exacerbated by consumption, then for both firms and consumers alike there are some very difficult questions to be faced about avoiding irreparable damage to the earth and to the quality of life enjoyed by many (although, of course, not all) of its inhabitants. Given that acknowledgement, the important question is not *whether* producers and consumers need to be green, but *how* they can best achieve greenness; in particular, how they can distinguish between policies that will genuinely contribute to the earth's sustainability and those which are merely window dressing.

DISCUSSION TOPICS

1. Imagine you are the manager of a large supermarket. To what extent is it your company's duty to ensure that 'environmentally friendly' products are available to customers? If 'environmentally products' are more desirable than their conventional counterparts, should you remove the latter from the shelves altogether?
2. McDonald's and their critics are both very ready to present their case. Examine the available literature on both sides of the controversy, and draw your own conclusions.
3. Consider the arguments for and against animal testing.
4. What advice would you give to consumers who wanted to be 'greener' in their shopping? Consider *how* and *where* to buy, as well as *what*.
5. To what extent should a firm be made to pay for its 'externalities'—the costs which do not appear on their accounts books?

NOTES

1. J. Elkington and J. Hailes, *The Green Consumer's Supermarket Shopping Guide*, Gollancz, London, 1989.
2. *This Common Inheritance: Britain's Environmental Strategy*, Cmnd 1200, HMSO, London, 1990.
3. G. D. Chryssides and J. H. Kaler, *An Introduction to Business Ethics*, Chapman and Hall, London, 1993, p. 457.

4. J. Elkington and J. Hailes, *The Green Consumer's Supermarket Shopping Guide*, Gollancz, London, 1989.
5. Genesis 1
6. G. D. Chryssides, 'Britain's Changing Faiths: Adaptation in a New Environment', in G. Parsons (ed.), *The Growth of Religious Diversity: Britain from 1945, Vol. II: Issues*, Routledge, London, 1994, pp. 68–70.
7. *Ethical Consumer*, issue 32, November 1994, p. 6.
8. Ibid., p. 7.
9. C. Plant and J. Plant, *Green Business: Hope or Hoax?*, Green Books, Bideford, 1991, p. 3.

9 Ethics and International Business

The poet John Donne wrote, 'No man is an island unto himself.' The same may be said of countries, even—paradoxically enough—of an island like Britain. It is commonplace to say that no economy can be self-contained and self-sufficient: we all know how trends in the Dow Jones index will affect overnight (quite literally) the prices on the FT Index or the Nikkei Share Index, and vice versa. The government of a single country cannot always be held wholly responsible for a boom or a recession, or for high or low rates of inflation—phenomena which are to some extent determined by world trends rather than the actions of individual nations.

With increased and improved communication and moves towards greater free trade, world markets have opened up as never before. The year 1992 was heralded as having great significance for British business people because it marked the setting up of a 'single market' within the European Community (now the European Union), though many companies had, of course, been operating on a much wider front long before then. In particular, multinational companies have a long-established and ever-growing role within the world economy—something which has also given rise to a particular type of ethical problem.

To those who are unfamiliar with the international character of business operations, and accept a non-relativist view of ethics, it may seem as if there ought to be no moral dilemmas which specifically stem from international operations. After all, it may be suggested, if something is right in Europe, then surely it is right in Japan, India and the United States? If an activity is wrong in Europe, then surely the same goes for those other countries also? Can the fact that one has travelled a few thousand miles make a moral difference to what seems to be the same state of affairs?

There are several reasons why travelling those few thousand miles may

[handwritten margin note: 'NON RELATIVIST']

155

[handwritten margin note: FACTORS CAUSING DIFFERENT ETHICAL VALUES IN DIFF COUNTRIES]

establish very different conditions and with that a very different basis for moral evaluation. First, different countries have different standards of <u>wealth</u>. At the time of writing, British politicians are debating the desirability of a minimum wage of £4.15 per hour, while the hourly rate for manual workers in India is on average 12 rupees (approximately 25 pence). If a multinational company can locate its labour-intensive operations in a country where wages are low, this makes good economic sense. But is it exploitation? Some will argue that it is, while others will contend that the work which multinationals bring is preferable to unemployment and, even worse, poverty.

Second, different societies have different <u>laws</u>, which enable business transactions to take place in one country which could not happen in another. For example, it is possible to market electrical goods in India which would not meet safety requirements in the West; drug companies have the opportunity to 'dump' medicines which have passed their 'sell by' date on countries in the Third World. Those who deplore such practices should at least acknowledge that they are not totally indefensible. It may be argued that poorer countries would prefer to have inferior electrical goods to none at all, or somewhat inferior drugs than continuing disease. In very different economic conditions different standards have to apply—different not in underlying principle, but different in the respective conditions which are judged to be acceptable?

Third, different cultures have different religions and ideologies. True, drinking alcohol does not suddenly become wrong when one enters an Islamic country while remaining right—in moderation, of course—in the West. Nor is it simply the case that international variations in behaviour are due to differences in human beings' biological or psychological make-up. It would be implausible to believe that different standards of female modesty in dress could be attributed to different degrees of male arousal in the Middle East and the West, respectively. For the Muslim, expectations about the way men and women behave were received by Muhammad from God himself, and hence it is highly unlikely that a practising Muslim will be readily persuaded to abandon his or her practice for the sake of making business transactions easier. *Shari'ah* law does not vary in accordance with time or place.

Fourth, there are differences in management style between different cultures. Europe and the West have traditionally favoured theoretical training for management, with fierce competition and high rewards for top jobs. Japan stresses *sempai-kohai*—imitation of the practice of the more senior employee by junior staff—and a heavy emphasis on company loyalty, with lifelong contracts. (It is unusual in Japan for workers to leave one company to go to another, unlike the West, where personal ambition dictates where one works.) Once again, we are operating with two very different sets of expectations, which have to be given due consideration if disrespect and dysfunction are to be avoided.

IS THERE AN INTERNATIONAL 'COMMON CORE' IN BUSINESS ETHICS?

There is reason to think that on certain fundamental aspects of business practice there will be near unanimity between business people in many different cultures. During the period 1984–1993, HRH Prince Philip and HRH Crown Prince El Hassan Bin Talal of Jordan convened a series of consultations on international business ethics between Christians, Jews and Muslims. Various interest groups contributed, including academics, business managers and government officials, and the result was 'An Interfaith Declaration: A Code of Ethics on International Business for Christians, Muslims and Jews', which appeared in 1994.

The Declaration recognizes that these three 'Abrahamic' faiths, although different, have certain key principles in common. [The term 'Abrahamic' signifies that their followers are said to be descendants of the patriarch Abraham (early second millennium BCE).] These principles are: 'justice (fairness), mutual respect (love and consideration), stewardship (trusteeship) and honesty (truthfulness)'.[1]

These principles, the Declaration affirms, must manifest themselves in three broad areas of business activity. First, there is the socio-political and economic system in which businesses operate. Second, there are the policies which companies formulate for their operations, and which affect their principal stakeholders. Third, there are the firms' employees who must implement those policies.

The compilers of the Declaration require justice (or fairness) to function within a particular socio-economic order—specifically, one involving competition, which they regard as the most efficient way of utilizing resources and keeping down costs and prices. They accept that this entails regulation to prevent monopolies, price fixing and other anti-competitive practices. The authors recognize that businesses operate in different countries under different legal frameworks, and that this can create variations in business practice, for example in relation to employment. Justice demands that laws 'be scrupulously followed', but in countries where laws are less rigorous, the company's most stringent standards should be followed, not its most lax.[2]

The duty of mutual respect applies to all stakeholders. These include employees, owners and those who provide finance, as well as customers, suppliers and the wider local and national communities who are affected by businesses' operations. With regard to employees, health and safety considerations are to be implemented fully, and fair levels of remuneration must be awarded. A company should not discriminate against individuals 'on grounds of race, colour, creed, or gender'.[3] The authors recommend that company boards should issue written statements of their obligations towards stakeholders and how these are to be observed.

The notion of stewardship entails the efficient use of the earth's limited resources. The Declaration sees future generations as stakeholders in businesses' operations: businesses have a responsibility to ensure that short-term profitability does not militate against their own longer-term viability or against the quality of life that posterity might enjoy. The scriptures of the three traditions insist on the term 'stewardship' and not 'ownership': human beings are therefore God's trustees, and must use the earth's resources efficiently and sustainably. The community must be protected from harmful emissions, unnecessary noise and endangerment of human, animal or plant life.

The concept of honesty spans truthfulness, reliability and accuracy in 'thought, word and action'—in short, 'integrity'. Among other things, this entails maintaining agreed standards of quality, appropriate after-sales service, un-ambiguous written contracts where appropriate, and clear, accurate information, especially where matters of safety are involved. Suppliers should be paid promptly, and firms should not use their buying power unscrupulously. Bribes are intolerable, and buyers should report offers of generous gifts or favours. In the words of the Qur'an, 'true scales, true weights, true measures' should be every-one's expectation.

The Declaration is certainly to be commended for setting out principles and implications which, if put into practice, would undoubtedly result in higher standards of business ethics and a better deal for most business stakeholders. The Declaration has the obvious limit of being confined to the three Semitic ('Abrahamic') traditions; in addition, traditional socialists might well find difficulty with its endorsement of competition, and secular humanists would no doubt have problems with the way in which ethical concepts are given anchorage in religious terminology. However, if one aims to find common ground between different faiths and cultures, the Declaration provides a start, and there is certainly much that other non-Abrahamic traditions might agree to. For example, many Hindus and Buddhists could find close links between their fundamental tenets and the Declaration's endorsement of non-violence to human, animal and plant life.

Having said this, however, there are, inevitably, ideas with which other faiths and cultures might find difficulty. The Hindu caste system, to take one obvious example, fits uneasily into a code of ethics which affirms equal opportunities, although even in India there is legislation guaranteeing job and educational opportunities to 'scheduled castes', to ensure that the lower castes do not continue to have the poor deal which has historically been their lot. Conversely, Western culture might wish to add to the 'equal opportunities' list. As we have seen, sexual orientation and disability are now two key areas of concern in Europe and the United States, and in the latter there have been vociferous campaigns to secure equal opportunities for those who have an unfortunate physical appearance. Such areas are more controversial, and it is unlikely, for example, that the Muslim contributors to the debate would have welcomed greater tolerance for homosexuals. It is inevitable, therefore, that any such agreed declaration reflect a 'lowest common denominator' rather than the highest possible ideal.

It is always possible to be cynical about statements like the Interfaith Declaration. What good do they do in reality? Do they really make any significant difference to business companies' practices? As the authors acknowledge, the Declaration requires endorsement 'at the highest level of business management' as a first step, and awareness by employees at all levels as a second. The authors also suggest that it might be reproduced, used as induction material for new employees and featured in in-house training courses.

Dissemination of ideas is one thing, however; implementation is another. (The value of disseminating codes of practice will be discussed in Chapter 10.) Disseminating codes of practice can certainly raise stakeholders' consciousness, and provide individuals and interest groups with standards by which they can measure a firm's performance and protest where infringements occur. The real difficulty, however, in extracting agreed standards from such inevitably generalized statements of principle is that such codes of practice do little to resolve the burning issues around which debate centres. The authors of the Declaration refer to safe and healthy working conditions, but give no indication of what minimum standards are to be expected in this area. Are conditions in coal mines 'safe and healthy', for example? Should companies manufacture fireworks, knowing that at least some children will use them on Guy Fawkes' night and get injured? The Declaration refers to 'a partnership between the provider and the user' of financial investments,[4] but does this entail that a borrower may not receive unearned income? (In an Islamic economy, lending requires taking an interest in the borrower's business activities, and accepting a reduction or even cancellation of a debt if the borrower's business fails.) Although the Declaration rejects bribery and extortion, does this cover business operations in countries where (as we saw in Chapter 2) business operations would be exceedingly difficult to conduct without bribes?

In sum, we can say that, if it could be implemented, the Interfaith Declaration would no doubt do much to clean up business, but, as it sets out a 'lowest common denominator', this still leaves many controversial ethical issues unresolved.

THE 'GLOBAL ETHIC'

The next universal declaration is something of a contrast. It was compiled by two contemporary theologians, Hans Küng and Karl-Josef Kuschel, on behalf of the 'Parliament of the World's Religions'.[5] This 'Parliament' met in Chicago in 1993, to commemorate the centenary of a previous Parliament of World's Religions, also in Chicago, where an astonishing 7000 representatives of all the world's major religious traditions met and debated many of their points in common and points of difference.

In contrast with the Duke of Edinburgh's Interfaith Declaration, Küng and

Kushel focus on setting out ideals and goals for all humanity, rather than simply recognizing principles that a number of specific faiths have in common. The Declaration therefore begins by drawing attention to the 'agony' which the world experiences: violence, the destruction of the planet, fear, estrangement, poverty, injustice and death. The authors make the bold claim, however, that amidst humanity's plight,

> a common set of core values is found in the teachings of the religions, and that these form the basis of a global ethic.

Emphasizing the 'golden rule' principle, which appears in similar form in most of the world's major religions, the authors stress the importance of treating others as we would wish them to treat us. The authors believe that this entails respect for life and dignity, acknowledging the individuality and diversity of members of the human race. It entails forgiveness, kindness, generosity and, in particular, consideration for the more vulnerable members of the human race: 'the children, the aged, the poor, the suffering, the disabled, the refugees, and the lonely'. The Global Ethic continues by affirming the equality of human beings, explicitly mentioning the equality of the sexes, and condemning sexual immorality, domination and abuse.

The document concludes by holding up to all human beings the ideals of a non-violent (global) culture, in which justice, mutual respect and peace is to be found. Such a culture would have a just social and economic order, with equal opportunities for all, and an absence of prejudice and hatred. Greed would be a thing of the past, and theft and lust for power and prestige would be gone.

The authors recognize, of course, that this is an ideal, but they believe that it should not be dismissed simply because of its utopian character. On the contrary, they invite all men and women, be they religious or not, to hold such an ideal in mind, 'by disciplining our minds, by meditation, by prayer, or by positive thinking'.

The Global Ethic expresses fine ideals. However, it does little to resolve the pressing questions which concern those who have to make ethical decisions in an international business context. Although it highlights some broad principles of agreement, it gives no clear guidance for resolving ethical disputes in areas on which disagreement exists. It may be fine in theory to affirm the equality of the sexes, for example, but such an affirmation leaves unresolved the question of what such equality entails. For the Western feminist it means identity of treatment, except where obvious biological differences dictate otherwise; for many Muslims, by contrast, the woman is said to gain status by having a life free from paid employment and in which she can be the home maker. To take another example, we can all agree that exploitation is wrong, but a commitment to eschewing exploitation does not specify when a business exploits workers or customers. It is all very fine to commit oneself verbally to bland concepts of universal peace and justice, but the Global Ethic gives no recipe for achieving this. Opponents of the arms trade may well see anything which contributes to armed conflict as evil, whereas oppressed peoples may believe that a just war is the only means of attaining a just peace. (Those who assume that it is unequivocally 'ethical' to avoid investing in armaments manufacture should at least acknowledge that there are two sides to the issue.)

RECOGNIZING DIFFERENCES

The two works which we have discussed so far appear to conclude that there is something fundamentally the same among different cultures. Even if this is true, there undeniably remain quite extensive variations which need to be acknowledged. We therefore propose to consider two very significant studies which have been carried out on cross-cultural values.

The first of these comes from three researchers—Haire, Ghiselli and Porter—who have ably argued that not all differences in management culture can be equated with differences in economic development or technological advance, and are therefore rooted in different value systems. The second is by George W. England, who through extensive interviews explored specific differences in managers' values between different countries. Both studies focused on the values of managers, rather than the workforce at large, but notwithstanding this limitation, their work is immensely important in attempting to identify possible differences in values among different cultures, and perhaps in drawing conclusions about the possibility of defining some 'global ethic'.

HAIRE, GHISELLI AND PORTER

Haire, Ghiselli and Porter's study, *Managerial Thinking: An International Study*, appeared in 1966. Haire and his associates consider the degree to which managers in different countries have significantly different values. They present three different possible explanations of these variations:

1. Differences among managerial values at an international level are not significantly greater than the differences which might be found at a national level. Consequently there are no culture-specific managerial values. Haire *et al.* label this view *universalism*.
2. There are significant differences between managerial values at an international

level, but these are directly related to the degree of economic and technological development of the culture. This view is labelled the *'economic clusters' view.*

3. There are significant cultural variations regarding managerial values, and these cannot be closely correlated with factors such as language or economic/ technological development.

Which of the these three views is most likely to be correct? In order to ascertain this, Haire and his colleagues undertook a massive survey of 3641 managers in 14 different countries. They devised a questionnaire which covered three main areas: leadership; the role of the manager in his culture; and his motives—that is to say, what kind of objectives he had and how well he felt these had been satisfied.

In order to ensure that the questions were understood in the same way in these different countries, Haire's questionnaire was translated into the relevant foreign languages, and then translated back again by a different interpreter. Adjustments were then made to ensure greater accuracy, until identity of meaning had been achieved. (For a fuller discussion of Haire's methodology, the reader can be referred to our earlier book, *An Introduction to Business Ethics,* in which part of Haire's study is anthologized. Better still, there is the study itself! Some readers may note the lack of inclusive language above: this is the researchers' doing, not ours. Although Haire, Ghiselli and Porter attempted to find an appropriate cross-section of managers, we do not know of any female managers who took part in their survey.)

The questionnaire was split into three sections. The first probed the manager's perception of his leadership role: how important to him was the capacity of subordinates, their efficiency, openness of information and so on? The categories were to be rated on a five-point scale, from 'very important' through to 'not at all important'. In the second section, a number of cognitive descriptions were given of a manager's role in his culture, and managers were asked the degree to which they agreed with these statements. Maslow's hierarchy of needs formed the basis of the final section. (The sociologist Maslow devised a scheme whereby basic needs such as food, clothing and shelter had to be satisfied before other more sophisticated needs, such as education and personal fulfilment could be dealt with.) How much opportunity is there for such needs to be fulfilled? How much opportunity should there be? And how important are the various 'needs' identified by Maslow in any case?

Space does not permit an extended discussion of Haire's methods and of his findings in any great detail. To cut a long story short, Haire, Ghiselli and Porter found that, as one might have expected, there were indeed significant differences between the values of individual managers, and, on average, differences among individual managers were 2.5 times as great as the differences in the average scores among countries. Nevertheless the researchers concluded that, 'National differences make a consistent and substantial contribution to the differences in managers' attitudes.' More specifically, Haire and his associates found that between 25 and 30 per cent of the variation in values was associated with the national origin of the managers they interviewed.

Comparing one country with another, they found that there were certain groups of countries ('clusters') within which the agreement on values was significantly greater than correlations between groups. In sum, they detected four main managerial value 'clusters':

1. Nordic-European (Norway, Denmark, Germany and Sweden)
2. Latin-European (France, Spain, Italy and Belgium)
3. Anglo-American (United Kingdom, United States)
4. Developing countries (Argentina, Chile, India)

There are some significant points to observe about these 'clusters'. First, although the two English-speaking cultures (United Kingdom and United States) form one cluster, the other groups do not speak the same language, and India of course has no single language. Second, although the first two clusters are fairly close to each other geographically, India and Latin America could scarcely be further apart. What the fourth cluster has in common, Haire concluded, is its stage of economic and technological development. Thus, economic and technological development seem to bear some relation to managerial values, but they certainly do not tell the whole story.

GEORGE ENGLAND

England's study of over 2500 managers in a total of five countries (the United States, Japan, Korea, India and Australia) is indeed impressive. England's work, *The Manager and his Values*, contains some theoretical material on defining the concept of a 'value'. Values are not simply attitudes, which are less stable, varying even from one part of the day to another. Values, by contrast, are 'more deeply embedded' in one's personality, and form a rational basis from which one's decisions are made.

England devised a total of 66 concepts connected with values from literature which dealt with organizations, and which related to individual or group behaviour. He divided these into five categories:

1. Goals of the business organization

2. Personal goals of individuals
3. Evaluation of groups of people and institutions
4. Ideas associated with people
5. Ideas about general topics

England then devised a questionnaire which contained two modes of evaluation. The first was the *primary* or *power mode*. The interviewee was asked to rate a given concept on a scale of importance: 'high', 'average' or 'low'.

The secondary mode attempted to elicit the interviewee's reason for his or her primary rating, by means of three categories: (1) pragmatic; (2) ethical/moral; and (3) affections/feelings.

An example may best illustrate how England's survey was conducted. Interviewers might be asked to rate the concept of 'patriotism'. Suppose they gave it a 'low' rating in the primary mode. Asked to explain why patriotism was important, interviewers might say something like, 'I like the royal family'—an 'affective' response in England's terms, since they were only stating what appealed instinctively to themselves. If their reply was that 'the Union Jack helps to sell our products abroad', this would be interpreted as a 'pragmatic' response: an interviewee who gave an answer of this kind would reveal an interest in what was likely to achieve a given end in one's business operations. If interviewees suggested that 'we owe a duty of loyalty to our heritage', this would be much more of an 'ethical/moral' response, for obvious reasons: the interviewee would now be talking about obligations which one had, over and above personal preferences, and over and above the achievement of predetermined results.

England drew a number of important conclusions from his findings, the most important of which for the present discussion are as follows. First, England found that there were quite significant differences in the values of individual managers within the same culture: belonging to one single culture did not appear to impose a blueprint of values which all managers then copied. Some managers seemed to emphasize ambition, obedience, achievement, competition and risk (England labelled them 'hard managers'), while others stressed loyalty, trust, tolerance, employee and social welfare and religion (England's 'soft managers'). As far as international business is concerned England found the correlations shown in Table 9.1 between manager's value systems in the five countries he surveyed. What Table 9.1 means is that England found, for example, a 92 per cent coincidence between the measured values of Japanese and Korean managers, a 67 per cent coincidence between Indian and Japanese, and so on. Thus, the closest similarities occur between American and Australian managers, with the greatest differences being found between the Australians on the one hand and Japan and Korea on the other.

Table 9.1 Correlation between managerial value systems

	Korea	India	Australia	USA
Japan	0.92	0.67	0.64	0.76
Korea		0.71	0.64	0.72
India			0.85	0.72
Australia				0.95

CROSS-CULTURAL VALUES: SOME IMPLICATIONS

There are several implications of the work of Haire *et al.* and of George England. Haire explicitly mentions three. First, the study of international values affords managers and students of business the opportunity to recognize and understand the managerial attitudes and values of one's own country. Often one can be tempted to assume that 'we' are normal, and 'they' are 'different'. Both pieces of research articulate the values of European and American managers as well as those from other parts of the world.

Second, there is an obvious implication for the training of managers who are likely to be sent abroad. Ascertaining the differences in cultural attitudes to managerial values makes it possible to identify the areas in which training is needed in order to do business abroad. In the light of Haire's and England's researches there can be no excuse for a foreign manager to blunder into a business organization in total disregard of a markedly different set of attitudes and expectations from his or her own. This may seem obvious, but the number and scale of blunders committed on the international scene is sufficient to be the subject of at least one entire book, *International Business Blunders*, written by David Ricks *et al.*

The third implication which Haire identifies relates to cross-cultural executive training. As companies become increasingly internationalized, there is a tendency to move managers around internationally, with the consequence that training programmes increasingly involve participants of different nationalities, bringing with them their different cultural values. Not only does this entail that there will be problems of reaching agreed 'answers' on issues relating to ethics and values, but there can even be problems about how to organize training courses. One professional business trainer, who had worked for a Japanese firm in England, reported to us that he had found difficulty in persuading Japanese managers to take part in a role-play exercise he had devised. While role-playing is something with which most American and British business people are comfortable, the Japanese managers found themselves unable to assume roles which were inconsistent with their real status within the firm. For them, their senior manager was still the 'boss' even though the rules of the role-play had defined a role reversal between the manager and the subordinates. While it may be tempting for Westerners to try to persuade Japanese business partners to participate in Western forms of training, such a temptation is likely to be a form of Western cultural imperialism, based on the assumption that 'we' are right and others are wrong. What is surely needed, although it is by no means easy, is a reappraisal of the forms of training used by Western trainers.

TACKLING ETHICAL DILEMMAS ABROAD

This is all very well, one may reply, but how does this enable us to decide how to behave in a culture whose ethical norms differ from our own? In order to consider this, it is necessary to refer back to Chapter 2 on ethical theory, where we identified three prime moral concepts which seem to us to be fundamental to making ethical decisions. We shall now suggest how these might be applied within some of the international business situations where the values of different business partners appear to conflict.

First, duties. Kant's fundamental 'categorical imperative' was that of respect for persons, and we endorsed Kant's view that it is fundamental to ethical reasoning and decision making that one should show respect for the individual worth of any individual. In a multicultural setting, respect for persons importantly entails respect for their distinctive moral and religious values, even (indeed, perhaps especially) where these differ from our own.

Respecting someone's religion involves a number of factors. In countries such as Britain and The Netherlands, where allegiance to organized religion is relatively low, it is easy to forget that religion is valued so greatly in other countries, such as India, the Arab states and indeed even the United States. When one of the authors recently discussed business activity in India with a group of Dutch students, and mentioned the firm Hindu belief in reincarnation, a number of the Dutch students commented that this was 'mere superstition'. Any such view of another culture's religion needs radical reappraisal if one is to be a sensitive and successful business partner abroad. This is not to say that religions never have their superstitious elements, but rather that the business partner should try, however difficult it may sometimes be, to avoid voicing such judgements. To do so is both prudent and respectful.

In any case, there are many occasions too when one can act in conformity with a different ethical system without in any way compromising one's own. One of our colleagues told us that, when he was a student, he had once been on the Temple Mount in Jerusalem (one of the most sacred Jewish, Muslim and Christian sites) eating his lunch: a seemingly innocent deed, if it had not been for the fact that it was Friday noon—the time of Muslim prayer—and in the month of Ramadan. A number of angry Muslims soon attempted to remove him from the area, much to his surprise. Having learned his lesson, our colleague subsequently became a specialist in international business. Although not professing any of the three religions which venerate the city of Jerusalem, he realized that he would not have been comprising any of his own values by eating elsewhere, or indeed by observing Ramadan in common with Muslims, as non-Muslim business partners are expected to do in Islamic countries.

There is also the issue of *law*. Normally business executives abroad should act within the law of the land in which they find themselves. Although we fully acknowledge that there is a distinction between law and ethics (see Chapter 1), and that there can sometimes be bad laws, observing the bare demands of the law is normally regarded as the baseline for ethical behaviour among business organizations. Only the avoidance of a very much greater evil could justify deliberate law breaking. However, to suggest that one should normally act in accordance with the laws of the land would, of course, be as grossly inadequate as a recipe for being ethical in international business as in anything else. Firms that 'dump' inferior or defective products on Third World countries, or engage in aggressive marketing of cigarettes or baby milk are acting within the law.

In addition to *duty*, we need to bring in our second notion of *rights*. The three fundamental rights traditionally identified by natural law theorists are life, liberty and, arguably, property. By identifying rights we can identify the corresponding moral obligations on the part of businesses. For example, policies that disregard dangers to human life violate the right to life. These include companies cutting corners on safety requirements when there is inferior health and safety legislation in a particular country; it also includes the irresponsible marketing of products such as cigarettes or powdered baby milk, which manifestly increase the danger to human life and health. As far as the more controversial property rights are concerned, we have to recognize a right to a just return on labour, as well as on capital (see Chapter 3).

Rights and duties are inseparable from considerations relating to our third ethical principle—human welfare. A firm that exploits its workers, engages in irresponsible marketing, or fails to provide adequate standards of safety is failing to pay due regard for human welfare as well as failing in its duty to respect rights. Also, where rights and duties conflict, arguably it is the human welfare criterion that must decide the issue. For example, when it comes to wages it is not realistic to suggest, as the authors of an Interfaith Declaration do, that one should accept the highest international standards. In a country such as India (as we saw earlier) it is simply not feasible to suggest that workers should be paid the same level of wages as can be paid in Europe. However, considerations of human welfare would dictate that wages be as high as is feasible under these conditions.

Making moral decisions then involves a difficult equation, and there is no easy recipe for balancing the three principles of duty, rights and human welfare. Ethical theories can provide a framework within which the relevant factors must be weighed, but they cannot automatically provide clear answers in all situations. In our previous book, *An Introduction to Business Ethics*, we offered a checklist of points to consider when engaging in international business. It may be helpful to repeat some of these points here.

- *Find out about the country with which you are expected to do business.* This involves some fairly detailed study, not merely acquiring a few 'top tips' in books which one sometimes finds on sale at airports, or believing in media stereotypes of Sikhs or Muslims or whoever.
- *Respect your own values and those of others.* It is important not to act contrary to one's own conscience, but equally it is important to expect business partners not to act contrary to theirs. 'Respect' entails that we do not simply assume that 'we' are 'right' and others are wrong.
- *Remember that religion is important.* If it is unimportant in shaping your own life, it is certainly still important in most parts of the world.
- *Consider how well you are suited to doing business abroad.* Not everyone can do it, and few can do it really well. If you cannot respect a different value-system, or if you have unthinkingly graded your own as 'the best', then think again. If you cannot let go of Western social activities such as drinking, or if you cannot try to speak at least a few words of greeting in the language of your host culture, then suggest that someone else might go in your place!

APPENDIX: GUIDE TO MANAGEMENT AND BUSINESS CULTURES

ISLAM

In Arab countries, business ethics—like all ethics—is founded on the teachings enshrined in the sacred text, the Qur'an (Koran). The Qur'an is held to have existed in heaven eternally, and was revealed by God to Muhammad in the seventh century CE via the angel Gabriel.

The Qur'an teaches the five 'pillars' of Islam: There is no God but God (Allah) and Muhammad is his prophet; The duty of prayer, five times daily facing Makkah (Mecca); The duty to give a proportion of one's wealth to the poor; Fasting during daylight hours during the month of Ramadan; If means permit, the Muslim must make a pilgrimage to Makkah at least once in a lifetime.

Being a relatively short book, the Qur'an cannot explicitly cover every conceivable ethical dilemma. It is therefore to be interpreted by means of *shar'iah*—the system of Islamic law. This means using: (i) the *hadith*—the tradition concerning the life and teachings of Muhammad; (ii) the principle of analogy— situations which are similar to those mentioned in the Qur'an bear the same ethical verdict; and (iii) *ijma* (consensus). There is a firm belief that God would never allow his followers to converge on an error; hence if the whole Muslim community is agreed on a particular matter, such belief is binding.

Islam teaches honesty in one's business dealings, compassion for the needy and hospitality. The Qur'an prescribes dietary laws (such as the avoidance of pork) and prohibits alcohol. The observance of prayer on Friday at noon is particularly important for the devout Muslim, as is the observance of Ramadan. Since the Islamic calendar is lunar, the timing of Ramadan changes in comparison with the Gregorian calendar used by the West. (In 1995, Ramadan began at the beginning of February.)

As previously mentioned, the Islamic economic system operates without interest on loans, although it is legitimate for a lender to share the risk bearing (whether profit or loss) with the borrower. This entails a rather different banking system from those of Western banks, and many Muslims in the West will prefer their own Islamic ones.

JUDAISM

A good practising Jew will conduct his or her business affairs in accordance with the Torah—the five books of the law which form the beginning of the Judaeo-Christian scriptures. The Torah is interpreted in an encyclopaedic work entitled the Talmud, which is studied meticulously by the rabbis (teachers of the law). The Torah covers all areas of life: worship and religious festivals, dietary laws, business dealings, and food and hygiene regulations.

The faithful Jew will observe the sabbath (Friday evening until Saturday dusk) meticulously, and not do any work. In the Jewish parts of Israel, everything (including transport) grinds to a halt on a Friday afternoon—rather like Christmas Day in the West—and in some quarters those who are not Jewish are expected to conform.

Many Jews in the West observe the sabbath strictly, while others will simply do what they can, perhaps finding it necessary to keep their business running in line with their Gentile colleagues. It is best, however, not to conduct business meetings or transactions with Jews on a sabbath, during the Passover (Pesach) period or on the Day of Atonement. Jews will normally indicate when these days fall; alternatively various organizations publish multi-faith calendars which set out their festivals.

CHINA, JAPAN AND KOREA

To Westerners, the idea of following several religions simultaneously seems alien. Traditionally many citizens in China, Japan and Korea have embraced three religions at once—Confucianism, Taoism and Buddhism, with additionally Shinto in Japan and Shamanism in Korea. The idea has been that different religions can be used for different purposes, and hence are not mutually exclusive. In any case, it can be difficult to disentangle what is Shinto in Japan, for example, and what is Buddhist: religions tend to merge together.

From Confucianism comes the notion of 'just and harmonious relationships'—king and subject, father and son, husband and wife, elder brother and younger brother, friend and friend. It is important that these relationships are duly honoured, and hence due veneration is paid to one's seniors, whether they be family members or superiors in a business organization. The type of loyalty which is shown to the family is also shown to the company in Japan, where it is normal to be given a lifelong contract, and in return to look for career advancement only in that same organization.

Taoism teaches that the universe flows onwards in a natural way, balancing the 'harmonious opposites' of *yin* and *yang*. This idea results in a rather less hectic attitude to decision making. Some Japanese companies, faced with different viewpoints at business meetings, prefer to give the opposing parties 'time to reflect' rather than to move to divisive votes: there is a 'right time' to decide things, which need not be immediately.

In Japan, Shintoism has enjoyed a significant revival in recent times, bringing an emphasis on Japanese nationalism. In China, of course, the ancient religions partly gave way to Communism under Mao Zedong—an ideology which still survives him.

INDIA

Indian society is predominantly Hindu, although there are Muslim, Sikh, Christian, Buddhist, Jain and Parsee minorities. Hindu society gives great prominence to displays of religious activity, such as temples and shrines; however, the main factor affecting business is the prevalent caste system. Caste is particularly strong in village life, and relates to three important areas: occupation, endogamy (marrying within one's own group) and commensality (with whom one may eat).

Because of the caste system it may be inappropriate for a business manager to assign certain jobs to certain castes, or to ask a member of a particular caste to combine his or her job with other duties which are more appropriate to a different

Case study

Nestlé: 'Some firms leave a nasty taste in your mouth.'

As businesses seek to expand their markets, they often turn to developing countries for new consumers. One company that has incurred much criticism for expanding into the Third World with its sales of baby milk powder is Nestlé, the world's largest food company.

Because water supplies in developing countries are often contaminated, breast milk is much safer. It is also better suited to human babies than powdered milk products, since it contains valuable antibodies. Consequences of using milk substitutes are claimed to be malnutrition, diarrhoea and gastro-enteritis—all of which have been responsible for numerous infant deaths. However, Nestlé has promoted baby milk powder, not only by advertising campaigns, but by providing free supplies to hospitals and clinics. In common with other milk powder companies, it has claimed that these gifts are charitable donations, but, as the pressure group Baby Milk Action has pointed out, introducing babies to powdered milk makes them dependent upon it. Also, the clinical environment in which the free supplies are provided gives them an apparent 'seal of approval'.

It is not merely pressure groups that disapprove. The World Health Organization has formulated a code of practice—The International Code of Marketing of Breastmilk Substitutes (1981). Under this code, baby food companies must not provide hospitals with free supplies or promote their products either to the public or to health workers; free samples may not be distributed to either. Pictures of babies must not be used on labels, and the labels must be written in a language which the mother will understand, and be accompanied by a health warning.

Nestlé, who has been criticized for violating the code in all these aspects, claims that the WHO code is addressed to governments, not to companies, and that it is the task of the former to introduce appropriate legislation. The company claims that its gifts are for health workers, who are able to use their professional judgement about their appropriate use. Until other companies agree about their marketing practices, Nestlé is unwilling to take the lead.

Baby Milk Action has attempted to encourage an international boycott of Nestlé products. It suspended its boycott in 1984, when Nestlé promised to observe the WHO code, but after evidence of continued violations, the boycott was resumed in 1988. The Church of England added its weight to the boycott, only to find General Synod members being lobbied by Nestlé marketing representatives. In 1994, a further vote was taken by the General Synod, which reversed the boycott decision by a narrow minority, and decided not to disinvest itself of Nestlé shares.

Ironically, Nestlé has attempted to improve its image by giving financial support to Childline (a telephone counselling service for children). Baby Milk Action is unimpressed, and continues to advocate the targeting of Nescafé with the slogan, 'Some firms leave a nasty taste in your mouth!'

caste. The caste system is rigid and cannot be changed easily. In city life, however, there are signs that the caste system is breaking down, and some citizens no longer regard themselves as belonging to a caste at all.

Hindus are not necessarily vegetarian: this is a common misconception. One's dietary obligations are related to one's caste, and high castes (such as brahmins) are less likely to eat meat or fish.

Non-Hindus remain outside the caste system, and therefore have no caste obligations. (Sikhs, however, sometimes group themselves into castes, and practise endogamy.) Sikh men are recognizable by their turbans, and Sikhs normally wear the five *khalsa* symbols: uncut hair, a comb (both of which are kept in place by the turban), a wrist bracelet, a dagger and a special undergarment.

Jains tend to belong to the business and professional classes, and are usually well educated. They show a great respect for life: Jain monks cover their mouths with gauze to prevent them from inadvertently swallowing insects. Although Jain laypeople are not so strict, respect for life includes filtering water carefully, and strict vegetarianism. Even certain types of vegetable are prohibited— principally those with roots, since it is the root that contains the life of the plant.

Parsees (Zoroastrians) tend to be centred around Bombay, although a few can be found elsewhere in India. Their presence is evidenced by several fire temples, in which their religious ceremonies are conducted. Their religion has traditionally viewed the world as a battleground between the forces of good and evil, with the assurance that in the end the god of goodness (Ohrmazd, or Ahura Mazda) will prevail. The hope of the restoration of a renewed earth makes the Parsee world-affirming. There is no need to withdraw from the world, as (say) the Buddhist monk does. The Parsee will therefore enter fully into business life. There is no special ethic associated with his or her religion, no prescribed dietary rules and no prohibition on alcohol—although one should eat and drink in moderation. The Parsee ethic is often summed up simply as 'good thoughts, good words and good deeds'—simple enough to understand, but of course much more difficult to put into practice!

THE CHRISTIAN LEGACY IN THE UNITED STATES AND EUROPE

Christianity is very much on the decline in Britain, with around 4 per cent of the population attending church on any one Sunday. However, Protestantism has left the 'work ethic', and citizens of the United States and Europe set great store on *activity*. The key to success is believed to be doing things rather than waiting for things to come naturally into fruition, as certain forms of Eastern philosophy advocate.

Protestants have tended to emphasize individualism—a concept which stems from the Reformation idea of the 'priesthood of all believers'. (Each individual could approach God without having to secure the aid of an ordained priest or one of the saints.) Western countries typically affirm the right of an individual to enjoy freedom of thought and expression, unhampered by state interference. This is often identified with adherence to *laissez-faire* economic principles. With this comes competitiveness: individuals competing against each other for employment, career advancement and the resulting wealth that goes with it. Among Roman Catholics, this individualism is, in theory, restricted by the laws laid down by the Church, but, even so, many modern Catholics would not necessarily regard themselves as being bound by traditional papal pronouncements.

As certain areas of Europe (particularly Britain) and the United States are affected by immigration by non-Western peoples, it cannot be assumed that a firm's staff will invariably have a Christian legacy; rather, they will come from a variety of religious and cultural traditions.

DISCUSSION TOPICS

1. The term 'Coca-Cola culture' has become almost a term of abuse. What are the objections to companies like Coca-Cola spreading to the Third World and to Eastern Europe? Are such criticisms justified?
2. Do you think there is a 'global ethic' that underlies the ethical thinking of every culture?
3. You are hosting a large conference in Britain, to be attended by business partners from various nationalities and cultures. What special provisions should you make for them, in order to treat their values with respect?
4. On the international scene, a business person is likely to see many things that run counter to his or her personal beliefs and values. To what extent should one invariably refrain from criticism and non-co-operation?
5. Is there any specific advice that should be given to women who are contemplating international business?

NOTES

1. *An Interfaith Declaration: A Code of Ethics on International Business for Christians, Muslims and Jews*, London, 1995, p. 11.
2. Ibid., p. 15.
3. Ibid., p. 16.
4. Ibid., p. 16.
5. Hans Küng and Karl-Josef Kuschel (eds), *A Global Ethic: The Declaration of the Parliament of the World's Religions*, SCM, London, 1993.

10 *How to be Ethical*

To conclude with a chapter on 'how to do it' might seem rather like ending a general book on ethics with a chapter on how to put the world to rights! However, if, as a result of the preceding discussion, the reader wants to take business ethics seriously, then he or she needs some framework in which to operate. By way of conclusion to this book, therefore, we offer some practical suggestions about implementing one's ethical convictions.

We turn first to consumer attitudes to business ethics. We do this because it is important that firms should be aware of consumer expectations, and the ways in which consumers might act if such expectations are unfulfilled.

OBJECTIONS TO ETHICAL CONSUMERISM

Not all consumers by any means pay attention to business ethics. Some members of the public may simply ignore such issues altogether, but there are others who may offer defences of non-ethical consumerism. One typical defence can be found in the maxim, 'Am I my brother's keeper?' On this view, the consumer bears no responsibility for other people's unethical behaviour: it is up to manufacturers and retailers to search their own consciences about the kinds of ethical questions we have considered in this book.

A second ethical stance which one sometimes encounters is that 'firms are all shades of grey' and hence it really does not matter which one tries to support or discourage. For example, changing one's bank because of their refusal to waive Third World debt is like going from the frying pan into the fire, since none of the main clearing banks have done so.

A third, equally negative, approach to ethical consumerism is defeatism. According to this—sometimes voiced—view, it is just too difficult to keep track of what every company is doing, to judge which is best and to find ethical products at a price one can afford. One of the authors recently sent a specimen copy of the

Ethical Consumer to a friend, who thanked him gratefully, but said that the prospect of assimilating its information on a regular basis was too demanding a prospect.

THE ETHICAL CONSUMER

Not all consumers are apathetic, sceptical or defeatist. Indeed there is a growing public awareness of issues in business ethics and of firms that fall short of desired standards of business practice. One body which monitors the way in which firms deal (or fail to deal) with ethical issues is the Ethical Consumer Research Association (ECRA), which publishes a bi-monthly journal entitled the *Ethical Consumer*. Consumers and business managers alike would do well to consult the *Ethical Consumer*—even if they do not necessarily share all its views—since this serves as a guide to the issues about which pressure groups are initiating action.

The *Ethical Consumer* rates companies according to the following criteria:

- *Oppressive regimes.* Negative points are given to companies operating in countries that have been criticized by Amnesty International for torture, extra-juridical executions and prisoners of conscience. 'Frequent official violence against the public' is a further negative. Products which are marketed as 'fair trade' are exempt from such assessment.
- *Trade union relations.* Ethical consumers may wish to identify businesses that are heavy-handed with trade unions, or who refuse to recognize them.
- *Wages and conditions.* A firm may be criticized for paying workers unduly low wages, or for subjecting them to dangerous conditions of work.
- *Environment.* We have already devoted an entire chapter to some of the ways in which firms can harm the environment.
- *Irresponsible marketing.* The *Ethical Consumer* flags companies who market products in a way which is detrimental to health, or which causes serious physical harm. (Consumers may wish to go further than this, and, for example, identify firms whose advertising strategy is in breach of professional guidelines.)
- *Nuclear power.* Where there is involvement in uranium mining, or where a company has an interest in the research, production or distribution of nuclear energy, the *Ethical Consumer* will indicate this.
- *Armaments.* Many firms are involved in the manufacture and supply of weapons, or have a financial interest in this area.
- *Animal rights.* The *Ethical Consumer* identifies companies that

have a licence to vivisect, and who subscribe to the British Industrial Biological Research Association (BIBRA), an organization which conducts animal testing on behalf of companies who may not have their own licence. The *Ethical Consumer* also provides information on firms' track records on factory farming and on 'other animal rights', by which they refer principally to interests in meat, leather and fur production, and also to provision of essential materials for the meat industry.

- *Political donations.* Companies' contributions to political parties may be of interest to consumers, who may wish to avoid making inadvertent contributions to some—or any—of them.
- *Boycott calls.* Various pressure groups have attempted to organize boycotts of companies or of certain named products. The *Ethical Consumer* will provide information about this, although the editors stress that such information does not imply their endorsement of the group's criticisms of the company.

Until recently, South African involvement was a particular subject of ethical concern, but since Nelson Mandela's speech of December 1993, most ethical consumers now feel constrained to encourage the newly democratized South African regime to develop economically.

Another publishing body, the New Consumer, rates companies on some of these criteria, and also a few more, as follows:[1]

- *Rewards.* The New Consumer identifies the standard of remuneration and other employee benefits, including career advancement and quality of training. Special comment is also given to the advancement of women and ethnic minorities.
- *Community involvement.* Credit is given to businesses, according to the percentage of pre-tax profits donated, and other non-cash contributions to charities.

Involvements in the alcohol, tobacco and gambling industries are noted, as well as military sales. The New Consumer also notes the degree to which the companies which they have surveyed provide disclosure of information. As several researchers have noted, some businesses are more ready to answer questions and disclose their activities than others. No doubt some are more dilatory than others;

some do not have the requested information available; but no doubt others do not wish certain facts to come to light to readily.

In addition to these lists, ethical consumers might also profitably consider a firm's track record in customer satisfaction. It is, arguably, an ethical matter as well as an astute purchasing decision to reward firms that have a good record for making quality products, honouring guarantees, exchanging faulty goods readily, and providing a good after-sales service (e.g. with readily available replacement parts at reasonable prices) and to avoid the more notorious offenders.

Additionally there are various special interest and pressure groups that provide consumer information. The RSPCA and the BUAV publish information that enables consumers to ascertain firms' track records on animal testing. Conservation organizations such as Friends of the Earth and Greenpeace also publish information which is firm-specific and relevant to ethical consumerism. Additionally there are specific campaign groups that issue information (others might say propaganda) on causes for concern—as, for example, Baby Milk Action has been in relation to Nestlé. The names and addresses of such organizations can be found readily in the *Ethical Consumer*.

Of course, there may be other concerns which readers have, such as pornography, angling (some firms sponsor angling competitions) and blood sports generally. We have even read of some citizens whose interest is in responsible driving, and who avoid companies whose lorries are driven carelessly.

There are other, more independent bodies, that disseminate information. The ASA publishes monthly reports, which are available free of charge to the public as well as the advertising industry, and the ASA, like a number of professional bodies, publishes a code of practice which members of the profession agree to abide by. The aspiring ethical consumer would certainly benefit from ascertaining what standards of ethics might reasonably be expected at the present time.

One also needs some information about who owns whom—otherwise one can inadvertently patronize companies of whom one disapproves. For instance, many consumers may purchase Ecover, because it is a 'green', non-polluting detergent, but how many of them realize that 50 per cent of Ecover is in fact owned by the security company Group 4? (Group 4 has been criticized for its allegedly violent removal of protesters at Twyford Down, who were opposed to the M3 extension.) Do-It-All is owned equally by Boots and W. H. Smith, who have both been criticized on ethical grounds. (Boots has been criticized for animal testing, and W. H. Smith for selling 'soft' pornography.) Information of this kind is not always easy to obtain, although again the *Ethical Consumer* publishes some from time to time. Related to this issue is the question of 'own brands' of supermarket product, where there is almost total secrecy as to who manufactures the coffee, cereals, butter and so on, which bear supermarket labels. Morally fastidious ethical consumers advocate avoiding all 'own brands', whereas others may feel that it is sufficient to practice avoidance only where they can clearly identify the producer.

All the criteria of assessment listed above may make ethical consumerism seem a formidable business, and may appear to lend support to the view that it is an impossible task. However, it is important to bear in mind that there is no divine decree (at least that the authors know of) which sets out these criteria in tablets of stone. Readers must themselves decide which of these issues are of ethical concern and which are not. Although the *Ethical Consumer* recommends 'best buys', it acknowledges that these are only 'best buys' relative to the criteria which it employs, and that readers may have different views on these matters.

WHAT DO WE DO ABOUT IT?

AVOIDANCE

Once we have decided which of all these issues are of ethical significance, a number of courses of action lie open to the would-be ethical consumer. The most obvious course of action is to avoid goods and services which we consider to be ethically reprehensible. This, of course, is something we do all the time: most readers would wish to avoid spending their money on instruments of torture, the services of a prostitute, a 'hit-man', hard drugs or National Front membership! It is therefore logical that those who object to animal slaughter, war, animal cruelty and smoking will decline to purchase meat products, war toys, hunting equipment and tobacco.

However, it might be argued that avoiding unethical products is not enough. One should not merely 'keep oneself pure'; one has a positive obligation to encourage ethical businesses and penalize unethical ones. Although it might be argued that ethical purchasing encourages firms to produce ethical products and discontinue unethical ones, there are certain activities of firms which cannot be directly encouraged or discouraged by confining one's purchases to inherently ethical products. Take the case of Nestlé once again. Since most readers are not consumers of powdered baby milk in the Third World, avoidance of the product would leave Nestlé unharmed. Consequently, there is a case for avoiding not only offending products, but the offending companies.

To do this, of course, is to make ethical consumerism much more complicated. The Vegan Society, for example, produces a copious list in its *Animal Free Shopper* of goods that are free from animal products and which have not been tested on animals.[2] However, approved brand names include Rowntree-Mackintosh, Libby's and Crosse & Blackwell, all of whom, ironically, are owned by Nestlé. The same guide also includes most of the major supermarkets, which—equally ironically—are quite happy to sell meat. In fairness to the Vegan Society, it should be mentioned that the *Animal Free Shopper* only claims to list *products* which are free from animal ingredients and animal testing; the editors fully acknowledge that there are other ethical considerations which consumers may wish to take into account.

Avoiding all offending products and businesses is, of course, a tall order, and makes ethical consumerism once again seem an impossible task. If one were to agree with all the criticisms voiced in almost any edition of the *Ethical Consumer*. one would avoid all supermarkets, most large retail outlets, almost every well-known brand name, the produce from several entire countries, and many more. Even a firm called Vegetarian Shoes has come in for criticism on the grounds that some of its products are made from polyurethane, which cannot decompose.

TARGETING

One solution to the problem is targeting. In targeting, consumers select one particular firm, or one particular product for avoidance and possibly campaigning. The 'target' is generally the firm which is deemed to be the worst offender, or else the market leader of the reportedly offensive product. Thus Baby Milk Action has singled out Nestlé, although it is not the only firm that promotes breast milk substitutes in the Third World. Since Nestlé markets around 125 UK products, consumers may find it difficult to remember which products are in fact Nestlé's (although Baby Milk Action produces a card list to remind shoppers), or inconvenient to avoid Nestlé products in their entirety. Baby Milk Action therefore encourages supporters to target Nestlé's brand leader, Nescafé.

Another example is McDonald's. Although the critics of McDonald's generally concede that its policies are very similar to those of Wimpy and Burger King, among others, presumably the reason for selecting McDonald's is that it is the largest and fastest growing of any of the American fast-food chains.

The advantage of narrow targeting is that it is easy for the consumer. Although it only directly affects one offending company, it can arguably have the effect of keeping other companies on their toes—they may be next for targeting, particularly if the currently targeted company mends its ways. One important objection to targeting is that it is discriminatory: is it fair to single out one single firm and let the others off scot-free?

At the other extreme, consumer boycotts have sometimes been targeted at entire countries rather than at manufacturers and products. Recent changes in South African affairs are no doubt to a large degree due to consumer boycotts. Current national targets have included all Spanish goods, on account of bull fighting, and—at the time of writing—all French ones, on account of France's renewed nuclear testing. As in the case of product and firm targeting, considerations of consequences weigh against considerations of justice, in a manner which is by no means easy to resolve. Arguably, Spain and France may be encouraged to 'mend their ways' if their governments see that exports and tourism are seriously affected. However, is it just to impose a boycott which affects all of a country's business men and women, many of whom may not support what their present governments do?

Avoidance is something which can be done at a personal level. However, if one wishes to engage in targeting, this can only effectively be done as part of a group. If individuals merely select their own 'targets', then—since these will probably differ from each other—individual avoidances and substitutions will cancel each other out. A collective boycott which is focused on one particular business or product is more likely to have effect, and of course has much greater opportunity for being publicized.

Of the issues that the would-be ethical consumer has selected, there may be specific interest areas. For some people 'being green' is paramount, for others vegetarianism may be a particular concern, while some may feel a greater urge to focus on unfair trading conditions with the Third World. Having a limited number of specific areas on which to focus is not to imply that other areas are of lesser ethical concern. It is simply to take the realistic view that success is more likely with fewer attainable targets than larger unattainable ones. One can more effectively channel one's efforts into a more finite area, particularly in the knowledge that there are other people who will be championing other, equally worthwhile causes.

How effective is boycotting and targeting? Supporters argue that, although sales of Nescafé have dropped marginally (3 per cent from January to September 1992), Nestlé has been obliged to put significant resources into combating the negative publicity which the campaign has attracted. The *Ethical Consumer* has drawn attention to a number of apparently successful boycotts—examples which spring to mind are (as previously mentioned) Barclays Bank and South African goods.

To some consumers, all this may seem very negative. What about rewarding firms for their virtues as well as punishing them for their vices? Obviously this can be done too, and the *Ethical Consumer* supplies postcards for those consumers who wish to inform companies that they have decided to patronize them for good practice! However, not all positive action meets with approbation. In 1993 Greenpeace announced a 'Buy at Safeway this weekend' campaign because of its decision to boycott Norwegian seafoods (3–5 December 1993). For at least one correspondent to the *Ethical Consumer*, Allen Hardy of Kidderminster, this was not good enough. He accused Safeway of donating to the Conservative Party, having little environmental concern, forcing smaller stores out of business, encouraging car use, and selling environmentally suspect products (*Ethical Consumer*, no. 28). Ethical consumers, he concluded, should surely avoid supermarkets altogether.

We can only leave the reader to decide whether one should give positive encouragement for what might appear to be the least shade of grey, or whether one embarks on an arduous search for businesses that are ethically whiter than white.

Many ethical consumers, however, believe that simple avoidance is insufficient. At the very least, they argue, companies should be informed of the *reasons* for such avoidance, and hence they recommend writing to companies to express their concerns. Indeed, there have been some remarkable examples of companies initiating change simply by virtue of a few consumer comments. The *Ethical Consumer* sells postcards bearing a standard boycott message which subscribers can send to the companies they have identified. For the more militant consumer there remains the option of 'shareholder action'—buying a small number of shares in order to gain the right to attend a company's annual general meeting. This was a tactic favoured by Ralph Nader, the champion of consumer rights in the United States, and famed for his one-man battle against General Motors. (Shareholder action was discussed in more detail in Chapter 6.)

POLITICAL ACTION AND DIRECT ACTION

Ethical consumerism need not be expressed exclusively by purchasing power or by informing businesses of one's concerns. Some ethical consumers may wish to consider writing to politicians to effect changes in legislation. To give one example: at the time of writing, the National Trust still permits hunting on its land. Campaigners against cruel sports have not been content to persuade the National Trust about their convictions, but consider that a change in the law is needed so that blood sports are abolished totally. Writing to one's MP may therefore be seen as a further step in ethical consumerism.

From time to time other ethical consumers have felt more militant and engaged in various degrees of direct action. Picketing is a most obvious and legal tactic, and some ethical consumers may feel a desire to persuade others in this way. (However, as the recent legal battle between Greenpeace and McDonald's has demonstrated, due regard must be taken of libel law.)

Other campaigners have gone further. During the time of the boycott of South African goods, some anti-apartheid campaigners took South African goods off the shelves and abandoned them at checkouts. Some environmentally campaigning consumers have unwrapped over-packaged goods at counters and left them there as an act of protest.

Whether more violent forms of demonstrating opposition to unethical company behaviour can be justified is debatable. When Dingles of Plymouth was 'bombed' in 1988, it was believed that animal rights activists were protesting against the sale of furs. If this was so, they obtained the desired result, since, to the best of our knowledge, Dingles never sold animal furs after that incident—as well as receiving the 'punishment' of having to close their store for a lengthy period.

RESPONDING TO ETHICAL CONSUMERISM

We turn now to the question of what it means for professional business people to 'be ethical'. As with the consumer, there is no uncontroversial answer to the question of what 'sound ethics' entails. There are various steps which managers might take in order to ensure that they are practising 'good ethics'.

First, company managers would do well to acquaint themselves with the various issues which concern ethical consumers, as mentioned above. In the light of the abundance of material which exists on business ethics, ethical consumerism, and on the various specific issues such as environmentalism and animal rights, there is little excuse for the uninformed business manager. Some of the concerns of ethical consumers may be remediable, but it may be argued that many of these concerns are matters on which public opinion is divided. A firm, it might be said, has no right to act as a moral censor on behalf of its customers. If a company recognizes that there is no ethical consensus on such matters, and takes the view that consumers themselves should be left to decide what are ethical purchases and what are not, it would at least be wise to allow customers the opportunity for making the appropriate 'ethical' choice. For example, stocking one's supermarket to include at least one non-animal-tested brand of cosmetic as well as the traditional animal-tested varieties would at least allow customers the right to avoid animal-tested products. (Obviously the provision of choice would not satisfy the more ethically fastidious consumers who had a mind to boycott offending companies, and not just products; and, of course, no supermarket could ever accommodate those consumers—and there are a few—who are, almost on principle, opposed to supermarkets as such.)

One obvious step towards becoming an ethical business is ensuring legality. As an absolute baseline, customers and employees are entitled to their legal rights. The firm that insists that it can only give an exchange, not a refund, for defective goods is as much unethical as it is illegal. Consumers must always be granted their statutory rights. Similarly, employees are entitled to basic standards of health and safety. The firm that does not enable its employees the opportunity to work in smoking-free areas, or that subjects employees to undue stress is acting unethically by failing to grant them their basic legal rights.

As we have already argued, giving people their minimum legal rights is not enough, since ethical rights are usually wider than legal ones. The firm that does nothing more for the consumer than is strictly laid down in a warranty may keep out of court, but is probably selling customers short on their ethical rights. Some firms take the view that dissatisfied customers should not only have their problem resolved satisfactorily—e.g. by repairing or replacing defective goods—but that they should receive additional compensation, such as free samples of other goods, or a money voucher which can contribute to their next purchase from the firm. Obviously there must be limits to companies' willingness to compensate complainants beyond the boundaries strictly laid down in law, otherwise they could end up generating increasing numbers of complaints. However, many firms tend to treat the complainant as an annoyance and adopt an adversarial stance, on the assumption that many complainants are unreasonable. There is some evidence that the reverse is more likely to be the case. Most people that complain have high standards and are willing to take the trouble to point out ways in which a business might improve itself—unlike the apathetic or submissive consumer. Further, it has been said that the average aggrieved customer will tell a total of 10 other people about his or her experience, when the average satisfied customer only tells of his or her satisfaction to four others. Thus, if considerations of ethics do not persuade a company to rate customer satisfaction highly, considerations of good business should!

CODES OF PRACTICE

Numerous businesses and professions now make a point of enshrining in a written code of practice those ethical obligations (as well as professional standards) which go beyond their strict legal requirements. The Hippocratic oath of the medical profession may well have been the first example of a profession formally assuming responsibility for its own standards. Later codes of practice have been adopted by various trades and professions in the twentieth century, spanning the advertising industry, personnel managers, market researchers, laundry and dry-cleaning companies, and travel agents—to name but a few. Some organizations—e.g. British Gas, British Telecom and Royal Mail—publish institutional codes of practice. The practice of publishing such codes was encouraged by Prime Minister John Major in 1991, with the introduction of the Citizens' Charter. It was believed that the public were entitled to know what standards of service they had a right to expect from key bodies and professions, and hence the early 1990s heralded a rise in these codes or 'charters', e.g. The British Rail Passenger's Charter, The Patients' Charter, the Post Office charter ('Putting the Customer First') and charters relating to various levels within the educational system. The purpose of these charters went further than defining the standards the customer had a right to expect and levels of compensation where such standards were not met; the relevant bodies undertook to monitor their performance and to publish statistical information on how well they were meeting their targets.

Might a firm consider devising its own code of practice? Where there are no existing codes of practice that cover a firm's activities, this can be well worth considering. There are several factors to bear in mind if doing this, however. First—and most obviously—it is important to identify those operations that are already covered by legislation: a code of practice must not erode anyone's legal rights. Second, it needs to be considered whether there already exist codes of practice which may be appropriate—some undoubtedly will, such as those which apply to advertising and personnel management. Rather than reinvent the wheel by writing a new code of practice from scratch, it makes better sense to become a member of a trade or professional body which has already defined a code of practice for its members: footwear companies, the motor trade, central heating consultants, and suppliers of electrical goods and services are examples of businesses to which this applies.

If a firm makes the decision to define its own code of practice, some measure of consultation at all levels is desirable. Not only is this likely to avoid industrial relations problems, but a greater level of compliance can be achieved if the relevant parties have agreed. There is little to be gained, and much to be lost, by defining sets of standards which are largely unheeded or targets which are unmet. Although we have argued that business ethics does not necessarily coincide with self-interest, it is legitimate for employees to want to see some personal advantage in a code of practice. Some indication of what is gained for the average worker is helpful in securing a necessary measure of compliance; hence those who draft codes of practice must also give due weight to workers' rights and benefits, not merely their presumed obligations. A code of practice should set out rights and duties for both management and workforce.

One matter on which ethical consultants, as well as most business managers are agreed is that there is little point in defining a code of practice if it simply remains inside a cupboard in the general manager's office. If standards of good practice are not disclosed to employees, how can they know what they are to live up to? Managers and staff must clearly know what is expected of them.

The publication of codes of practice has clear advantages. Not only does it indicate to employees the standards which are expected of them, and what improvements (if any) are needed, but the fact that such codes are publicly available indicates to employees and customers what they have a right to expect. An agreed code also ensures a measure of consistency in dealing with problems: if forms of compensation are defined in a code, for example, then this can avoid a customer services department having to adjudicate afresh on each customer problem, as well as avoiding inconsistencies in how different customers are dealt with.

Codes of practice can also have a negative function. They can limit a firm's liability by defining limits to standards, beyond which employees and customers have no right to expect. A code might set a limit to compensation for inadequate service, for example, or leave out a topic which some interest groups might wish to be covered (such as the ASA omission of sex-role stereotyping). One of the authors recently made a rail journey from Birmingham to London in order to attend a meeting. The train was delayed by over two hours, and the meeting was ending just as he arrived at Euston Station. British Rail explained that the Passengers' Charter limited compensation to £15 worth of rail tokens, although the journey had cost £19, plus the cost of 20 miles of car travel and parking—although British Rail did allow him first-class travel back at no extra charge.

KNOWING ONE'S BUSINESS: ENVIRONMENTAL AND SOCIAL AUDITING

In a large business it can be difficult for managers to be aware of all that is happening within the organization. However, the fact that managers may be unaware of something that happens within their organization does not mean that they are not accountable (see Chapter 4). When the media reported that the (then) British Minister for Agriculture William Waldegrave owned a farm that had sold some cattle to France and Spain for veal, he pleaded in his defence that he had not known the destiny of these calves. This only served to show that, at best, he neglected to find out something about his business about which he should have known.

Obviously any manager's knowledge of what is happening in a firm will fall short of omniscience, but in lieu of superhuman powers some form of auditing can be undertaken to determine whether the various goals and objectives of a firm are carried out. Just as systems of financial accounting and auditing are put into place to cope with the fact that managers cannot personally know of every transaction which occurs within a firm, so other forms of auditing can help to keep track of non-financial company objectives, and make stakeholders aware of the non-monetary track record of a company. Two forms of auditing which are currently emerging in the non-financial sector are environmental auditing and social auditing.

Environmental auditing aims to track the environmental impact of a firm in all its aspects. Just as no financial audit would be complete if it produced, say, sales figures alone, so an environmental audit must go well beyond boasts of using recycled paper or avoiding CFCs in aerosol containers, and produce a full picture of the firm's environmental impact. A full environmental audit must be from 'cradle to grave', taking into account each stage of a product's development and use: its raw materials, production process, packaging, likely use by consumers, waste emissions and method of disposal when its active life has expired.

As this book has shown, environmental considerations form only one issue in business ethics. Social auditing is a method which seeks to pick up the wider ethical and social impacts of business organizations, and is currently being pioneered by the New Economics Foundation. At the time of writing, two companies have undergone social auditing—Traidcraft and Shared Earth, both of which sell products that are purchased by means of 'fair trade' from developing countries. (The Body Shop currently undertakes its own internal social audits.) Whereas environmental auditing starts off from one particular area of concern, social auditing recognizes the existence of multiple targets within businesses, and notes that different stakeholders may have different interests and different 'indicators' for determining whether specific targets have been achieved. (Social auditing very much presumes a stakeholder model of businesses.)

By taking into account the views of stakeholders, social auditing leaves no 'loose indicators'—that is to say, an issue like 'environment' is not considered in isolation from the interested parties who are affected by environmental consider-ations. It may be the case, of course, that different stakeholders have different views regarding environmental targets and indicators; where disagreement occurs, dialogue takes place between the various interest groups, rather than some method of numerical computation based on cost–benefit analysis. Social auditing is therefore an 'inexact science', and conclusions are likely to be discursive rather than numerical.

The New Economics Foundation recognizes the importance of publishing its results and making its findings open to the various interest groups. Thus, since customers have helped to define a firm's targets and indicators, the Foundation upholds their right to disclosure of the level of success that has been achieved. Both Traidcraft and Shared Earth make their annual social audit reports available to customers and employees alike.

ETHICS CONSULTANTS AND ETHICS COMMITTEES

A further way of resolving ethical issues is for a firm to employ an ethics consultant. Since ethics is a controversial matter, the consultant cannot be expected to supply 'right answers' to any issue. In matters of ethics, it is important that the consciences of those who implement policies should be satisfied, rather than that some presumed authority figure should be heeded. A good ethics consultant should, however, be conversant with the issues, have experience of business organizations, and hence be in a position to suggest a range of ways to resolve an ethical dilemma, from which the firm's managers must choose. The ethics consultant is thus more of a facilitator than an ethical legislator.

In some organizations, the resolution of ethical questions is done internally rather than externally, by an ethics committee. This is the normal practice within British universities and hospitals, mainly in connection with research proposals, which must satisfy the ethics committee before the research can gain approval. Ethics committees are likely to draw on ethical guidelines which are already produced by professional bodies. For example, the University of Wolverhampton's Educational Research Unit implements the Ethical Guidelines for Educational Research (1992), drawn up by the British Educational Research Association (BERA).

SOME FINAL COMMENTS

We conclude this chapter with a few brief comments on some of the issues involved in being an ethical business.

DISCLOSURE OF INFORMATION

The authors would endorse the importance that the New Consumer attaches to disclosure of information. When firms fail to disclose their activities, they cannot but add fuel to the suspicion that they have something to hide. In the early 1970s, when environmental concerns were beginning to surface, Plymouth students invited various retail outlets to complete a questionnaire on their use of paper.

When asked to estimate how many paper bags they supplied to customers, many firms specified a number, but one well-known retail outlet simply wrote 'lots and lots'. This firm quickly became the target for a student demonstration, as well as bad publicity, although there was no obvious evidence that it was any more prodigal in its use of trees than any of its competitors. Its crime was non-disclosure. Although firms may sometimes find it a chore to provide information to enquirers, it can often be worthwhile to do so.

As well as disclosing information, the disclosure of one's mistakes has sometimes been the best policy too. When contaminated bottles of Perrier water were discovered some years ago, Perrier did not attempt to deny or conceal the evidence. Their disclosure was costly, since it cost millions of pounds to withdraw all their existing stocks. However, the public were reassured, and Perrier's long term sales do not appear to have been affected. By contrast, Exxon, by not fully accepting its responsibility for the notorious oil spillage in 1989, only made matters worse in the public's perception.

EQUAL RIGHTS

The issue of equal opportunities is one in which a firm can gain official recognition for good practice. It is possible to apply to the Equal Opportunities Commission and the Commission for Racial Equality for accreditation as an Equal Opportunities Employer. In order to achieve this one must not only be strictly impartial in one's selection processes, on the grounds of ethnic origin and gender, but one must also engage in monitoring procedures to determine how effective one's policies are. For disability, firms must have in operation relevant facilities within the workplace (appropriate toilets, wheelchair ramps and the like).

Some British organizations have an equal opportunities policy which goes beyond ethnic origins, gender and disability, and extend equal opportunities to include age, sexual orientation and religion. For those who wish to be at the forefront of ethical pioneering, attention might profitably be paid to the forms of discrimination which are not so well recognized, such as discrimination against people on the grounds of their size, or because they are disadvantaged in their physical appearance.

EXPLOITATION

While on the subject of employee rights, the would-be ethical company might profitably consider the appropriateness of sending employees to seminars on topics such as time management and stress management, which are currently fashionable. While such events may be helpful, they can be construed as sanctioning overwork and stress, and a company that it is committed to securing employee wellbeing might do better to consider altering workloads and working conditions. It is surely better to minimize problems than resort to supposedly effective means of coping with them.

Case study

Currys–Dixons: ethical concern or window dressing?

The well-known high-street retailer of electrical goods and cameras, Currys–Dixons, is the sponsor of the Dixons Chair of Business Ethics and Social Responsibility at the London Business School. Clearly the company seeks a high ethical profile, but how ethical is it in practice?

Since Currys–Dixons is a retailer rather than a manufacturer (it has no 'own brands'), there are, arguably, fewer ethical pitfalls. Retailers are not faced with problems about methods of product development (such as animal testing), research ethics and developing environmentally friendly products.

However, retailers can decide which brands to promote, and whether any should be vetoed on ethical grounds. As far as we are aware, Dixons has no such policy, and is happy to sell products manufactured in China—a regime which Amnesty International has identified as oppressive.

Dixons' US subsidiary, Silo Inc., has been listed in the US magazine *International Boycott News* as the subject of a boycott, because of a labour dispute. This began in 1992, and still awaits satisfactory resolution.

Dixons has given financial support to the Conservative Party (a total of £50 000 between 1992 and 1994), although it now appears to have discontinued this support. (Political donations, as we noted, are one of ECRA's assessment criteria, although readers will judge this aspect of Currys–Dixons' track record in the light of their own political persuasion.)

One area in which Dixons appears to encounter problems is its pricing policies and claims. At the time of writing, Dixons has had three complaints upheld against it by the ASA. Two of these related to claims that the company's price claims: its brochure boasted 'Lowest Prices Guaranteed', when, as the ASA pointed out, Dixons did not in fact offer lower prices than any other competitor, but merely offered to match a lower price that any customer discovered locally, within a week of purchase. Dixons made its price claim notwithstanding a previous reprimand from the ASA about a similar practice.

Retailers of electrical goods often seek to boost their revenue by offering customers extended guarantees, which can be purchased at extra cost. In common with a number of electrical goods retailers, Dixons follows this practice, which has been criticized by the Office of Fair Trading (OFT). Most electrical goods now have very high standards of reliability, and the OFT has questioned whether such guarantees offer value for money. Although these guarantees promise that any repairs are carried out within a certain time period, one service firm used by Dixons writes, 'With regard to Dixons Supercover Plus policy and the undertakings it provides, I can only comment that we have no contractual agreement with Dixons but we do endeavour to attend to any of their calls for service within 48 hours.' (Dixons guarantees a call within that time.)

Is the sponsorship of the Business Ethics Chair mere window-dressing or a genuine concern for business integrity? No firm is perfect, and it may be argued that Currys–Dixons is no worse than its competitors, who also feature from time to time in ASA and OFT Reports.

The authors invited Dixons to comment on its ethical policies, and sent it a brief questionnaire. They received no acknowledgement. No marks for disclosure of information!

DOING GOOD

Ethics can often seem to highlight what one should not be doing, rather than what one positively should. It is therefore worth mentioning that a firm that is concerned with its ethics can find positive opportunities for doing good, and not merely for avoiding harm. Such opportunities can include charitable donations and sponsorship of community projects. Since local and national communities support local firms by their custom, and are sometimes inconvenienced by externalities such as noise and litter, a firm has the opportunity to put something back into the community, over and above the jobs it provides and the service it offers to its customers. A firm may well wish to sponsor something that is seen as somehow 'appropriate': fast-food outlets are renowned for their sponsorship of waste bins—although cynics might see this as simply their way of enhancing their reputation against those who accuse them of causing litter!

NEW ISSUES

Finally, the truly ethical company will always be attempting to become aware of new issues that can be incorporated into its policies. As ethical awareness grows, new issues come to light, new 'isms' are devised to describe them, and, one hopes, new and imaginative ways will be discovered for managers and employees to cope with them. By keeping their fingers on the pulse of business ethics, firms will be best placed to do so.

DISCUSSION TOPICS

1. Consider the criteria used by the Ethical Consumer Research Association for evaluating businesses. Would you wish to take *all* of these factors into account in evaluating their ethical worth? Are there other criteria you would wish to add?
2. Can 'direct action' ever be justified against a supposedly unethical firm?
3. Is being an ethical consumer an unattainable ideal? What implications does your answer have for (a) a firm's policies; (b) your own activities as a consumer?
4. Consider the pros and cons of having a company code of practice.
5. Examine the ethical arguments for and against 'targeting'. What might you do if your company was targeted?

NOTES

1. S. Hamil, *Britain's Best Employers? A Job Hunter's Guide*, Kogan Page, London, 1993.
2. R. Farhall, K. McCormack and A. Rofe (eds), *Animal Free Shopper*, The Vegan Society, St Leonard's-on-Sea, 1993.

Conclusion

'Reach a definite conclusion', is the advice the authors often give their students. In a controversial subject such as business ethics, this is no easy matter, particularly since we have endeavoured to present the issues, rather than campaign for definite causes. If we were asked to sum up our positive advice about conducting one's business affairs, we could probably go a little further than the presenter in the Monty Python film *The Meaning of Life*, who concludes:

> Well, it's nothing very special. Try and be nice to people, avoid eating fat, read a good book every now and then, get some walking in and try and live together in peace and harmony with people of all creeds and nations.

We would at least hope that we have highlighted some of the important issues in business ethics, and indicated the fundamental principles which underlie the different stances which can be taken. We have provided some of the 'tools of the trade' for business people and students of business, and we leave it for them to decide what to make with them. Whatever conclusions one reaches on ethical dilemmas in business, we hope that we have persuaded the reader that there is more to business decision making than SWOT and PEST analyses, or statements of accounts. Good business can be bad ethics.

We believe that interest in business ethics is on the increase. If we were to guess at what future discussions in the subject area might involve, we would suggest that three issues are likely to arouse greater interest in the future.

First, environmental economics raises questions about our use of the planet's resources which the human race cannot fail to address. 'Green' issues are here to stay for some considerable time.

Second, the electronics revolution raises questions not only about confidentiality of records which are stored on computers. As greater numbers of people use the Internet, questions have already arisen about whether certain materials—such as pornography—should be available, and what steps might reasonably be taken to police what has become a very complicated information storage system. If and when telephones become replaced by videophones, who knows what might be sent along videophone cables? Can such material be controlled without constant monitoring, which is arguably an invasion of privacy? Or ought one to take a libertarian view in favour of freedom of expression? Is there a mean between the two extremes?

A final area which we believe will generate increasing interest is *auditing* of firms' ethical and environmental records. We have mentioned in the text that three firms have chosen to go down this avenue. Since quality assurance systems have gained ground in Western organizations, it seems likely that at least some firms will consider it appropriate to use similar means of assuring their standards of ethics.

For those who are interested in studying business ethics, we suggest that these are three important issues which will be increasingly discussed in the future. For those who are interested in being ethical, however, we can do no better than the Buddha, who, when asked to sum up his teachings on how to live, responded, 'Do not what is evil. Do what is good. Keep your mind pure. That is the teaching of Buddha.'[1] That seems obvious, but of course it is easier said than done, and does not in itself answer the question of *what* one must do to achieve it. However, if we have prompted the reader to reach some conclusions of his or her own, then our work has been successful.

NOTE
1. Juan Mascaró (trans.), *The Dhammapada*, Penguin, Harmondsworth, 1973, p. 183.

Bibliography

ADVERTISING STANDARDS AUTHORITY, *Herself Appraised*, ASA, London, 1986.

ADVERTISING STANDARDS AUTHORITY, *Herself Reappraised*, ASA, London, 1990.

ADVERTISING STANDARDS AUTHORITY, *British Code of Advertising and Sales Promotion*, Committee of Advertising Practice, London, 1995.

AYER, A. J., *Language, Truth and Logic*, Gollancz, London, 1935.

BENTHAM, J., *Principles of Morals and Legislation*, in JOHN STUART MILL, *Utilitarianism*, ed. MARY WARNOCK, Fontana, London and Glasgow, 1965.

CHRYSSIDES, G. D., 'Britain's Changing Faiths: Adaptation in a New Environment', in PARSONS, G., (ed.) *The Growth of Religious Diversity: Britain from 1945, Vol. II: Issues*, Routledge, London, 1994.

CHRYSSIDES, G. D. and KALER, J. H., *An Introduction to Business Ethics*, Chapman and Hall, London, 1993.

COTTON, J. L., *Employee Involvement*, Sage, Newbury Park, 1993.

DESJARDINS, J. R. and McCALL, J. J., (eds), *Contemporary Business Ethics*, Wadsworth, Belmont, 1990.

DRUCKER, P. F., *Managing in Turbulent Times*, Harper Row, New York, 1980.

DUSKA, R., 'Whistleblowing and Loyalty', in DESJARDINS, J. R. and McCALL, J. J. (eds), *Contemporary Business Ethics*, pp. 142–47.

ELKINGTON, J. and HAILES, J., *The Green Consumer's Supermarket Shopping Guide*, Gollancz, London, 1989.

Ethical Consumer Guide to Everyday Shopping, ECRA, London, 1993.

'Fair Shares for Workers', *Financial Times*, 28 April 1995, p. 12.

FARHALL, R., McCORMACK, K. and ROFE, A. (eds), *Animal Free Shopper*, The Vegan Society, St Leonard's-on-Sea, 1993.

FERNIE, S. and METCALF, D., *Participation, Contingent Pay, Representation and Workplace Performance: Evidence from Great Britain*, LSE, London, 1995.

FRIEDMAN, M., *Free to Choose*, Penguin, Harmondsworth, 1980.

GALBRAITH, J. K., *The Affluent Society*, Penguin, Harmondsworth, 1987.

GOFFMAN, E., *Gender Advertisements*, Macmillan, London, 1979.

HAMIL, S., *Britain's Best Employers? A Job Hunter's Guide*, Kogan Page, London, 1993.

HARE, R. M., *The Language of Morals*, Oxford University Press, London, 1963.

An Interfaith Declaration: A Code of Ethics on International Business for Christians, Muslims and Jews, London, 1995.

JENNINGS, J., GEIS F. L. and BROWN, V., 'Influence of Television Commercials on Women's Self-confidence and Independent Judgment', *Journal of Personal Social Psychology*, vol. 33, no. 2, pp. 203–210, 1980.

KÜNG, H. and KUSCHEL, K.-J. (eds), *A Global Ethic: The Declaration of the Parliament of the World's Religions*, SCM, London, 1993.

LOCKE, J., *Second Treatise on Civil Government*, in Barker, E. (ed.), *Social Contract: Essays by Locke, Hume and Rousseau*, Oxford University Press, London.

MARX, K., *Manifesto of the Communist Party*, Penguin, Harmondsworth, 1967.

MEADOWS, D. H. *et al.*, *The Limits to Growth: A Report for The Club of Rome's Project on the Predicament of Mankind*, Pan Books, London and Sydney, 1974.

NEW CONSUMER, *Good Business? Case Studies in Corporate Social Responsibility*, School for Advanced Urban Studies, Bristol, 1993.

PACKARD, V., *The Hidden Persuaders*, Penguin, Harmondsworth, 1957 and 1962.

PARSONS, G. (ed.), *The Growth of Religious Diversity: Britain from 1945*, Vol. II: *Issues*, Routledge, London, 1994.

PLANT, C. and PLANT, J., *Green Business: Hope or Hoax?* Green Books, Bideford, 1991.

PLATO, *The Republic*, trans. H. D. P. Lee, Penguin, Harmondsworth, 1966.

RICHARDS, J. R., *The Sceptical Feminist*, Penguin, Harmondsworth, 1982.

RICKS, D., FU, M. Y. C. and ARPAN, J. S., *International Business Blunders*, Grid, Colombus, Ohio, 1974.

RUNCIMAN, W. G. (ed.), *Max Weber, Selections in Translation*, Cambridge University Press, Cambridge, 1978.

SCHUMACHER, E. F., *Small is Beautiful*, Abacus, London, 1974.

SHAW, W. H., *Business Ethics*, Wadsworth, Belmont, 1991.

STEVENSON, C. L., *Ethics and Language*, Yale University Press, New Haven and London, 1944.

STRAW, J., *Equal Opportunities: The Way Ahead*, Institute of Personnel Management, London, 1989.

This Common Inheritance: Britain's Environmental Strategy, Cmnd 1200, HMSO, London, 1990.

VON HAYEK, F. A., 'The Non Sequitur of the "Dependence Effect"', *Southern Economic Journal*, April, 1961.

WARD, S., *Socially Responsible Investment*, Directory of Social Change, London, 1991.

WATERSON, M. J., *Speaking up for Advertising*, The Advertising Association, London, 1982.

WHITE, T. I., *Business Ethics: A Philosophical Reader*, Macmillan, New York, 1993.

Index